Language Arts Handbook

SRA Open Court Reading

Grade 5

McGraw Hill Education

mheducation.com/prek–12

Copyright © 2018 McGraw-Hill Education

All rights reserved. No part of this publication may be reproduced or distributed in any form or by any means, or stored in a database or retrieval system, without the prior written consent of McGraw-Hill Education, including, but not limited to, network storage or transmission, or broadcast for distance learning.

Send all inquiries to:
McGraw-Hill Education
8787 Orion Place
Columbus, OH 43240

ISBN: 978-0-07-900176-4
MHID: 0-07-900176-9

Printed in the United States of America.

1 2 3 4 5 6 7 8 9 QTN 22 21 20 19 18 17

Table of Contents

You Are a Writer! 8

The Traits of Good Writing 10

SECTION 1: The Writing Process 16

The Writing Process 18
- **STEP 1** Prewriting 20
- **STEP 2** Drafting 32
- **STEP 3** Revising 38
- **STEP 4** Editing/Proofreading 46
- **STEP 5** Publishing 50

Following the Writing Process 56

SECTION 2: Forms of Writing 66

Personal Writing 68
- Friendly Letter 70
- Business Letter 74
- Journal 80
- Learning Log 83

Table of Contents

Informative Writing 86
- Summary 88
- Research Report 92
- Problem-and-Solution Essay 102
- Responding to Literature: Character Analysis 108
- Responding to Literature: Setting Analysis 116
- Responding to Literature: Plot Analysis 122
- Responding to Literature: Literary Criticism 128

Narrative Writing 134
- Fictional Narrative 136
- Biography 142
- Autobiography 148
- Tall Tale 154
- Historical Fiction 160
- Science Fiction 166
- Fantasy 172
- Play 178

Descriptive Writing 188
- Writing a Description 190
- Explaining a Scientific Process 196
- Magazine Article 200
- Describing an Event 206
- Comparing and Contrasting 212

Opinion Writing 224
- Opinion Paragraph 225
- Persuasive Letter 230
- Persuasive Essay 234

Table of Contents

Poetry 240
Rhyming and Nonrhyming Poetry 242
Pattern Poetry 250

Timed Writing 252

SECTION 3
Writing Strategies 266

Sentence Fluency 268
Writing, Combining, and Expanding Sentences 270
Sentence Problems 280
Paragraphs 282
Variety in Writing 290

Ideas 292
Developing Narrative and Informative Texts 294
Research and Organizational Text Features 304

Organization 306
Ordering Information 308
Using Outlines 312
Graphic Organizers 316
Effective Beginnings and Endings 322

Word Choice 326
Using a Thesaurus 328
Using Academic Language 329
Figurative Language 330

Table of Contents

Voice 334
- Audience and Purpose 336
- Developing Persuasive Writing 340
- Adding Sensory Details 344
- Creating the Sound of Language 345

Conventions 346

Presentation 356
- Using Multimedia Sources 358
- Creating Oral Presentations 360
- Evaluating Growth 364

SECTION 4: Vocabulary 366
- Compound Words 368
- Antonyms and Synonyms 370
- Analogies 372
- Connotation 374
- Homophones and Homographs 376
- Multiple-Meaning Words 380
- Greek and Latin Roots 382
- Prefixes and Suffixes 384
- Context Clues 388
- Academic Vocabulary 390
- Adjectives and Adverbs 392
- Precise Verbs 394

Table of Contents

SECTION 5: Grammar, Usage, and Mechanics 396

Grammar 398

- Nouns and Pronouns 400
- Verbs 404
- Adjectives and Adverbs 406
- Prepositions 408
- Conjunctions and Interjections 409
- Subjects and Predicates 410
- Direct Objects and Indirect Objects 412
- Phrases and Clauses 413
- Sentences 416

Usage 422

- Verb Tenses 424
- Subject-Verb Agreement 426
- Using Pronouns 428
- Contractions 432
- Double Negatives and Misused Words 437

Mechanics 440

- Abbreviations 442
- Commas, Colons, and Semicolons 444
- Quotation Marks, Underlining, and Apostrophes 449
- Parentheses, Hyphens, Dashes, and Ellipses 450
- Capitalization 451
- Using Electronic Technology 458

Glossary 462

Index 472

You Are a Writer!

Who are some writers you can name? When people think of writers, they most often think of novelists, journalists, or others who make a career of writing. In fact, we are all writers, and we can all be productive writers with the proper tools and practice. You have already started to hone your writing skills. Look at the following examples and think about the kinds of writing you already do.

Writing around the House

Dear Mom,

 I'm so sorry I broke your sugar bowl. I really need to stop reaching across the table during dinner. Muffin likes it when I knock over my milk glass, though. Please forgive me—I'll try to do better!

 Love,

 Cynthia

Shopping List
- eggs
- milk
- yogurt
- carrots
- cat food

Cynthia's refrigerator note is meant to apologize for her mistake, while the shopping list will help the family remember what to buy at the grocery store. Writing notes can also help family members stay in touch and communicate deep feelings.

Writing at School

> Dear Ms. Kaplan,
>
>   I would like to try out for the part of Peter Pan in the spring show. I have seen the movie lots of times, and I already know all of the songs. I even know some of Peter's lines, and everyone tells me I'd be great as Peter. After all "I'll never grow up, never grow up, never grow up, not me!"
>
>   Yours truly,
>   April Carr

   This *persuasive* note is an example of trying to influence someone to see your point of view, and it is just one of the many types of writing you might use during the school day. Other types of writing are meant to *entertain, describe, explain,* or *inform.*

   As you can see, writing is an important part of our lives. Imagine what it would be like if you couldn't write letters or send e-mail messages to your friends. What if you couldn't take notes in class and you just had to remember everything your teacher said? It would make learning much harder.

   This handbook will answer many of the questions you have about writing. You can use it to help you with your school assignments or when you want help with *any* kind of writing.

FUN fact

Inventor Thomas Edison kept a mini-pencil (about 3 inches long) in his vest pocket for jotting down notes. Where do you keep *your* note-taking pencil?

The Traits of Good Writing

We don't have to guess what features contribute to great writing. Through the years, language experts have discovered certain *traits*, or qualities, that are common in excellent writing. Let's take a look at these seven important characteristics of writing.

Ideas

Ideas are the basis of all great writing. When writing is clear and focused, ideas are communicated. When writing is dull and confusing, ideas remain locked away, never reaching the intended audience.

Keys to Unlocking Ideas

Brainstorming

Get ideas for your writing by observing people and your surroundings and by thinking back on some of your own experiences.

Clarity

Your ideas must make sense to be understood by the reader. Try to figure out what might confuse a reader and fix it.

Focus

A topic should be narrow enough not to be overwhelming for either the writer or the reader. Don't try to cover too much in a single piece of writing.

Originality

Present ideas in fresh and different ways.

Information

Have all the information you need and more. Use resources from books, magazines, encyclopedias, radio, TV, personal experience, personal interviews, and the Internet.

Details

Make your writing come alive with vivid and concrete details that help readers understand your ideas.

Organization

Have you ever seen the framework of a new building before the walls are put up? The organization of a piece of writing is like the framework of a building upon which everything else is hung or attached.

Keys to Unlocking Organization

Leads

Grab your reader's attention with a strong opening.

Direction

Provide your writing with a beginning, middle, and end section, or a solid introduction, body, and conclusion. Give it some place to start—and some place to go.

Ending

Make sure your writing doesn't just stop, as if you ran out of time. Your ending, or conclusion, needs to *sound* like an ending without saying "The End."

Coherence

Make sure your structure is logical by organizing your ideas or information using main ideas and details. Your paragraphs should have topic sentences and supporting sentences. If you are writing a narrative, your story should follow a basic plot structure.

Unity

Make sure your ideas fit together as a whole. Read your writing aloud to figure out where you stray from your main idea or lose your focus. Eliminate distracting or unnecessary ideas and information.

Voice

Voice is the trait that makes your writing your very own. It's what separates your writing from someone else's writing. A writing voice full of enthusiasm and purpose will energize your reader from the very first sentence.

The voice you will use will change depending on what you are writing. If you are writing a story, you may want to use a writing voice that appeals to readers' emotions. Your goal may be to make them laugh or cry or have some other emotional response. If you're writing a report, you may want to use a voice that gives just the facts and that appeals to a reader's sense of reason. You may want to convince the reader that you are presenting a reasonable point of view.

Keys to Unlocking Voice

Uniqueness

Make your writing sound like your very own. Let it reflect your unique personality.

Influence

Write to influence your readers, whether it's to make them laugh or cry or feel admiration, concern, or astonishment.

Liveliness

Bring your ideas to life by painting vivid pictures for your reader to imagine.

Enthusiasm

Express energy and enthusiasm for your subject through the careful and deliberate choices you make in all aspects of your writing.

Word Choice

Language is the core of communication, so choosing the right word for the situation is important. There may be nine synonyms for the word *happy,* but only one will be the perfect choice in a particular sentence. Be a wordsmith, and choose your words carefully for maximum effect on your reader.

Keys to Unlocking Word Choice

Precision

Choose the most *precise,* or exact, word to express your intended meaning. Experiment by using words you haven't used before in your writing.

Word Pictures

Choose words that paint strong, memorable images in the mind of the reader or that influence them to think a certain way about your subject.

Avoid Repetition

Except for connecting words, such as *and, because,* and *therefore,* try not to repeat the same words over and over in your writing. Use a thesaurus to help you create variety.

Notice Word Choice

While reading, take note of unique word choices. Ask yourself, "Why is this word used here?"

Sentence Fluency

This quality is achieved when sentences flow smoothly and with ease.

Keys to Unlocking Sentence Fluency

Read Aloud
Make sure your writing is easy to read aloud.

Variety
Vary the length of your sentences. Begin them in different ways and avoid repeating yourself.

Transition Words
Use transition words, such as *however, because,* and *for example,* to show how a sentence relates to the one before it.

Rhythm
Be aware of the rhythm, or flow of sounds, of your sentences.

Conventions

Conventions are the mechanics of writing. You will use conventions in the editing and proofreading phase.

Keys to Unlocking Conventions

Correct Errors
Correct errors in spelling, punctuation, grammar, usage, capitalization, and spacing.

Remove Distractions
Take out anything that may keep your reader from understanding what you have written. Make sure it's clear and easy to follow.

Presentation

Presentation refers to how your writing looks. It should appeal to the reader's eye.

Keys to Unlocking Presentation

Clean It Up

Make sure your final draft is free from eraser marks and words that have been crossed out. Also look for any errors you may have made if you typed your paper.

Jazz It Up

Use images, charts and other graphics, bullets, and subheadings where appropriate. Also try experimenting with **bold** and *italic* type for emphasis, but use these sparingly.

Reading Your Writing

The traits of good writing are keys to making your writing successful. Use them and you will keep your readers entertained and interested.

SECTION 1

The Writing Process

The Writing Process 18

Prewriting 20

Drafting 32

Revising 38

Editing/Proofreading 46

Publishing 50

Following the Writing Process 56

Writing is a process that is done in stages. Each stage is different and has its own characteristics. These stages are prewriting, drafting, revising, editing/proofreading, and publishing. You can go back and forth between the stages as often as necessary until you are satisfied with what you have written. Using the writing process in this way will help you improve your writing.

SECTION 1
The Writing Process

The Writing Process

Beautiful plants don't just pop up overnight—they require care and nurturing. The process that a gardener uses, from planting to weeding to fertilizing, helps the plant grow.

Successful writing doesn't just happen automatically, either. Like a plant, it requires care and nurturing. The stages in the **writing process** will help you produce better work. It's important to be patient and not expect your writing to be perfect from the very beginning. Keep in mind that each stage in the process will help you improve what you've first written, making it better and better, until you end up with a piece of writing that makes you proud!

STEP 1 Prewriting

What does the prefix *pre-* mean? Did you go to *pre*school? If so, you know that preschool is a school you go to **before** you begin kindergarten. Understanding this, can you figure out what *prewriting* means? If you came up with "**before** writing," you are correct!

Before you start writing about a topic, you'll need to perform three important tasks: *think, brainstorm,* and *make notes* on a list, web, note sheet, or other organizer to write down the thoughts you'll want to include.

STEP 2 Drafting

Also known as a *first draft,* or *rough draft,* this is where you'll begin to organize your ideas and start writing.

STEP 3 Revising

Revising is what makes good writing great. It's where you make your writing better by adding details, taking out irrelevant information, rearranging ideas, and substituting more interesting words, phrases, and sentences.

18   The Writing Process

STEP 4 Editing/Proofreading

This is your chance to correct all of your mistakes, including spelling, usage, capitalization, and punctuation errors.

STEP 5 Publishing

Now that your work is ready to be shared with an audience, you'll need to neatly recopy it or type it on a computer. Finally you'll decide how you wish to share your writing with an audience. This is your chance to show the effort you've put into your work while you are sharing ideas that are important to you.

Not *every* piece of writing needs to be composed using the entire writing process, especially those that are intended for *your* eyes only. For example, journal entries and poems and stories that you write for your own pleasure often will not require that you use every phase of the writing process. On the other hand, for some writing you do, you may need to use every phase. You may even need to move back and forth between some of the phases. For example, you could be writing a research report, and during the revising phase you discover that you need to add more information. That could require that you go back and do additional research and draft it into your original piece. Once you understand the purpose of each phase of the writing process, you'll be able to move from one to the next automatically.

Reading Your Writing

Use the writing process to transform your ideas into a finished piece of writing. Your writing will be clearer and more readable if you do.

STEP 1 Prewriting

Getting started can be the most challenging part of any project. Fortunately, the **prewriting,** or planning, phase of the writing process is also the most exciting portion in the life of a writing project—it's where *your* ideas come alive!

Decisions before Writing

Prewriting

Prewriting is the time when you create the ideas you'll be expressing in words, phrases, and sentences. It's also the time when you'll be making important decisions and setting goals. Following the steps below will help you during the decision making process.

Choose a Topic

What's the assigned topic, or what topics interest you? What do you already know about the topic? What will you need to find out? What's the *focus,* or idea, you wish to concentrate on within the topic? What's the main idea you want the audience to remember?

Identify Your Audience

Who is going to read, or hear you present, your writing? Is it classmates, your principal, your teacher, or your family? Knowing your audience will help you make decisions about the purpose, form, and length of your writing.

Define Your Purpose for Writing

What are you trying to accomplish? Do you wish to explain, inform, persuade, or entertain your audience? Which form might best suit the chosen topic and intended audience?

Select the Form of Writing

Should you create a realistic story, a classroom report, a persuasive letter, or some other form of writing? Check the following chart for some types of writing.

Research Reports	Essays	Literary Analyses
Notes	Recipes	Journal Writing
Speeches	Summaries	Persuasive Writing
Observations	Poetry	Realistic Stories
Fantasies	Folktales	Magazine Articles
Plays	Quick Writes	Weather Reports

Length of Writing

Is there a *minimum* (smallest amount) or *maximum* (largest amount) number of pages required? If not, what length do you think would be appropriate given your topic, purpose, and audience? For example, something you wish to share with adults should be longer than something intended for kindergarteners.

Deadline

A *deadline* is the final day or time that the completed project is due. What is your deadline? How much time do you have to complete your writing? How will you plan your time? What tasks will you perform, and on what schedule? Use a calendar to organize and keep records of your writing activities.

SECTION 1

The Writing Process

SECTION 1

The Writing Process

Targeting Your Topic

Now that you've made some decisions, it's finally time to decide on a topic. Where do you get topic ideas?

Topic Webs

Your teacher may assign a broad writing topic. Suppose your class is learning about cities, and you are asked to write about a city you have visited or would like to visit. Or you might choose to write about the history of a particular city. A *topic web* can help you decide what angle to use when beginning your writing.

When you are creating a web, start by drawing a small circle in the center of the page. Write the key word (in this example, *cities*) inside the circle. Think of words or phrases associated with the key word and write them around your center circle. Circle each word or phrase you come up with and connect them to the circles to which they relate. Look at the example below.

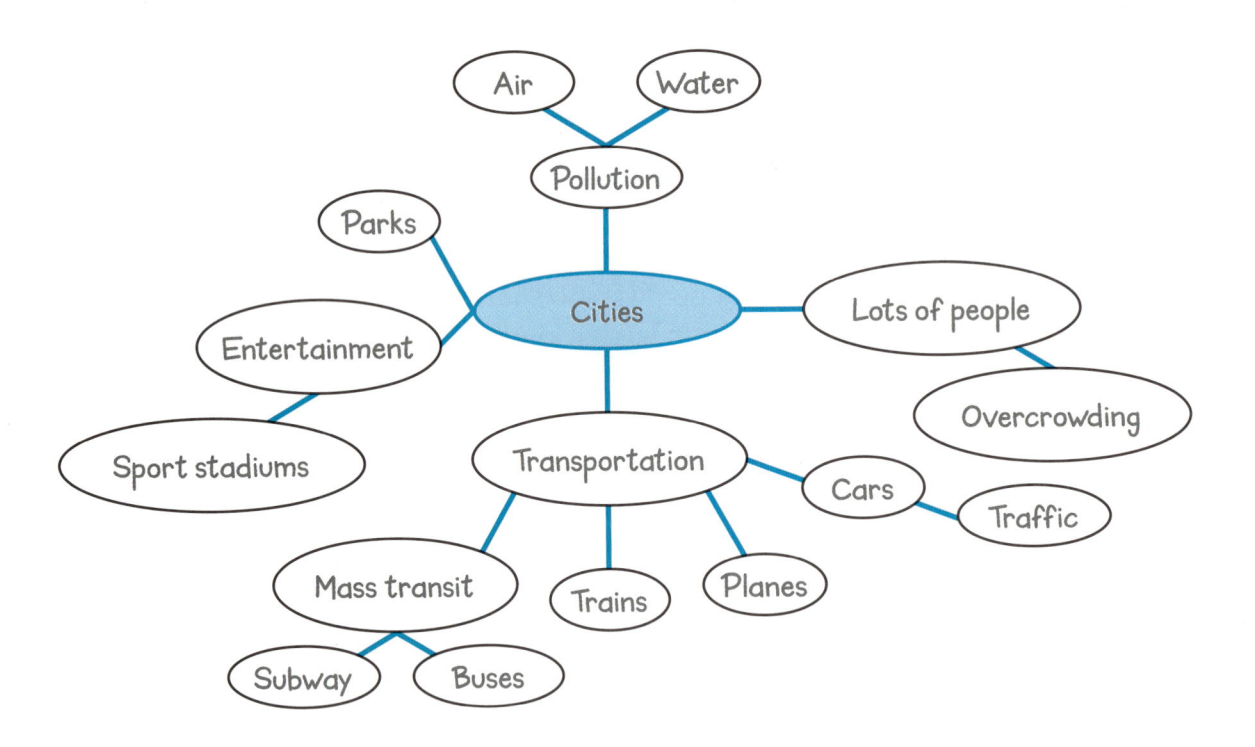

```
            Air     Water
              \    /
            Pollution
   Parks        |
       \        |          Lots of people
   Entertainment |         /
         \      |         Overcrowding
          \    Cities ———
   Sport stadiums  |   \
              \    |    Cars
           Transportation  \
           /    |    \    Traffic
    Mass transit  Trains  Planes
      /    \
   Subway  Buses
```

22 **The Writing Process** • Prewriting

At other times, you will be responsible for choosing a writing topic. Although finding your own topic is sometimes a difficult task, try making a list like this to spark your thoughts.

About Me
- My proudest moment
- How I overcame a doubt about myself
- My earliest memory
- One thing I can do now that I couldn't do before
- One thing I can't do that I could before

About the World
- My best friend
- My pet
- Someone who has influenced me
- The reason dogs have four legs
- The reason shirts button up and down instead of side to side

No matter what topic you choose, always keep your audience in mind when you write.

Try It!

Try adding some questions to the above list that may help you brainstorm possible writing topics.

Focusing Your Topic

Once you choose a topic, you need to narrow its *focus* so your writing is clear, concise, and specific. Sometimes, a writer chooses a topic that is too broad for the intended purpose and audience. When this happens, writing often lacks focus and direction, and this causes the audience to stop reading.

SECTION 1

The Writing Process

> **EXAMPLE** Here are some examples of topics that may be too broad to cover effectively. There's so much you could write about each one that it's hard to know where to start.
>
> - space
> - Washington, D.C.
> - music
> - my family
> - pets
> - the Civil War
> - electricity
> - computers
> - movies

Let's try to narrow some of these topics to focus on a specific portion of the topic.

Broad Topic	Focus Topic
Space	Black Holes
Washington, D.C.	The Day I (Almost) Met the President
Music	The Viola: The Glue of the Orchestra
My Family	My Twin Sister

Try It!

See if you can think of a focused topic for each of the broad topics remaining on the list: pets, the Civil War, electricity, computers, and movies.

Collecting Information

Your assignment is to write about *cities,* but you know you need to narrow your focus. You've decided to concentrate on *mass transit,* because you've always been fascinated by subway systems. Check your assignment requirements to make sure you know what features must be included in your writing. Because the topic of mass transit is continually growing, your research will have to explore sources other than the general summaries usually found in social studies texts or encyclopedias.

Your school media center or neighborhood public library would be a logical place to begin your search for information. If you have access to the Internet, numerous search engines will speed and narrow your search through *billions* of pages of current data. Make sure to take notes on your graphic organizer, noting the addresses of the websites you found helpful. This will speed up your return trips to the same addresses. Print the most useful information for later use.

Check with the mass transit authority in your city. Write a letter to its main office, explain your project, and request brochures, data, pictures, or printouts that can be sent to you.

Documentary videos are another good source of information. Don't forget to check the video collections in the media sections of your school media center or public library.

Once you've assembled and examined your research materials, it's time to organize your information according to your purpose and audience.

Important Note: When using information from sources for your writing, be sure to keep track of where you get your information. You will use it to document your sources in a bibliography. For more information on writing a bibliography, see pages 99–100.

SECTION 1

The Writing Process

Organizing Your Writing

All creators need plans. Builders need blueprints. Film animators need storyboards. Fashion designers need sketches. Teachers need lesson plans. Without a clear plan of action, any project can become a jumble of confusion, wasting valuable time and effort. The same is true for writing. Without a plan, writing will be disorganized and lack clarity, interest, and vitality. What might have been a thorough and thought-provoking project becomes unclear information without structure or purpose.

Because prewriting is one of the more important parts of the writing process, you should record your plans. One way you can do this is by taking notes on think sheets or note sheets and making an outline. Another way is to use charts called **graphic organizers.** These charts are often designed to help organize your writing project into smaller parts or to help you logically sequence your project's elements. For example, when you are planning a narrative, a plot line diagram can help you identify the conflict, climax, and resolution and record the key events of your plot. This will make it easier for you to draft your story events in an organized manner.

Graphic organizers also help you visualize the structure of the piece. Once you've filled in some parts of your organizer, it will be easy to make changes based on the purpose and audience you have selected.

Once your organizer is complete, you'll have a map of your writing journey. All you'll have to do is follow the map to your final draft destination.

Organizing Story Writing

Specific types of writing call for specific graphic organizers. Writing a short story would require a different type of organizer than the one you would use for a report. For a story, you could plan its narrative elements using the *story map* shown on the next page. You'd have to consider your characters (*who* is involved?); the setting (*where* and *when* does the story take place?); the *conflict*, or problem, to be overcome; the *key events* in your plot; and the story's *resolution* (how do things turn out?). Use a *working title* at the top of the story map. A *working title* is used to identify a piece of writing while the writer is working on the story. Don't write your final title until the story is completed. To grab the reader's attention, titles must be thoughtfully chosen and should not give away too much of the plot.

SECTION 1
The Writing Process

Try It!

Look at the story map shown on the next page and think about the words you would write in the boxes and ovals if you were planning a story based on cities or mass transit.

Prewriting • The Writing Process

SECTION 1

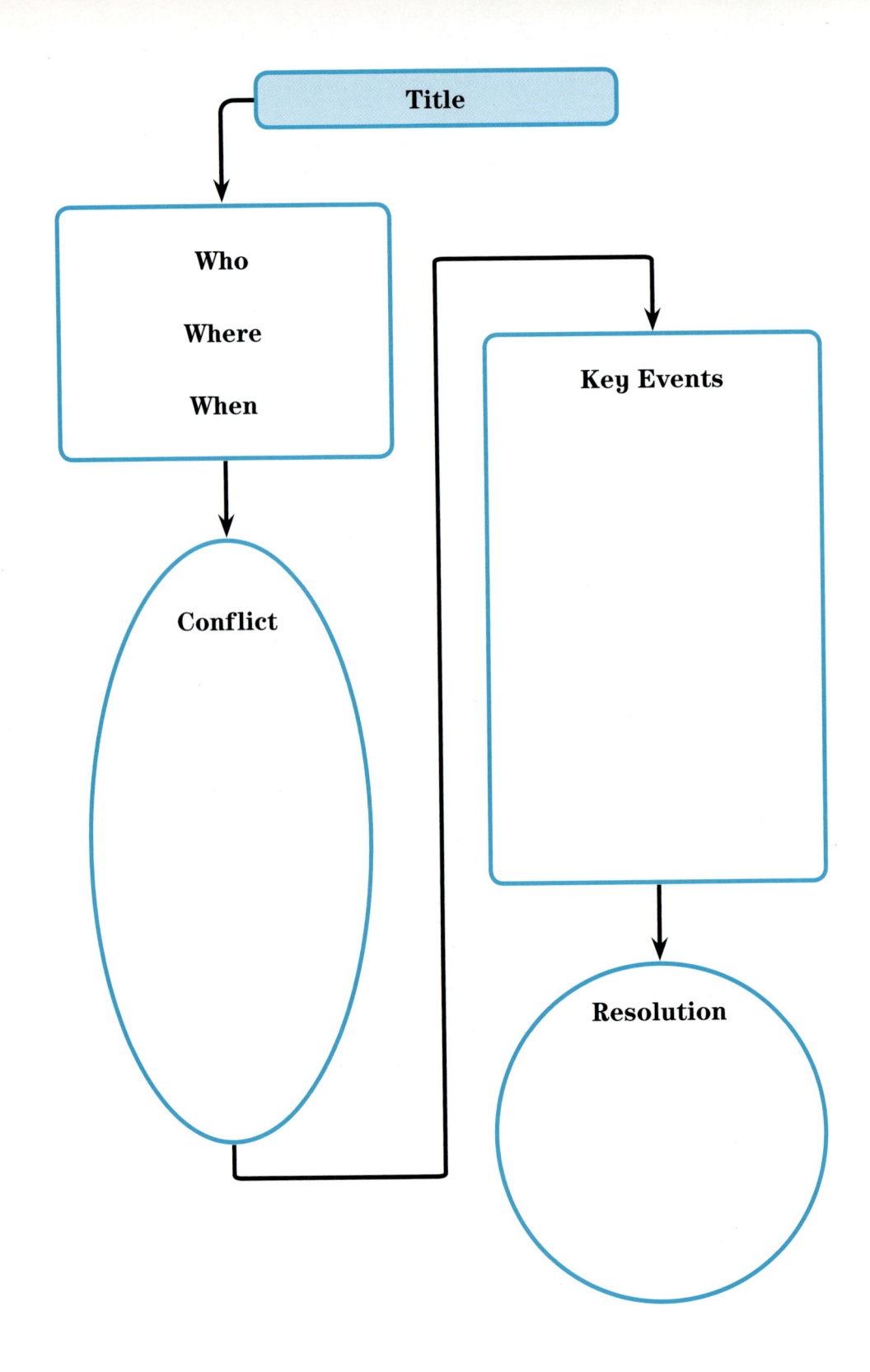

The Writing Process

Title

Who
Where
When

Conflict

Key Events

Resolution

28 The Writing Process • Prewriting

Organizing Informational Writing

SECTION 1
The Writing Process

The graphic organizer on the next page can be used to plan a piece of informational writing. Remember the example of a teacher-assigned writing project about *cities?* Under this broad topic, you chose the focused topic of *mass transit.* Once you began researching your topic, you found too much information and decided to narrow your topic even further. Now you have decided to concentrate on the New York City subway system, which is listed in the topic box at the head of the organizer. Beneath the topic box are three *subtopic* boxes, each with room below for three supporting details. Having read through your research, you've chosen several areas that you believe would interest your intended audience—your class.

SECTION 1

The Writing Process

Topic

New York Subway System

Subtopic

Ridership

1. _____
2. _____
3. _____

Subtopic

History of the System

1. _____
2. _____
3. _____

Subtopic

Air Pollution Relief

1. _____
2. _____
3. _____

Try It!

Your first subtopic is *ridership*. Below are some facts and ideas about ridership from your research and brainstorming. Which facts do you think would be the most interesting, fascinating, or eye-opening? Where would you place your selected details on the graphic organizer?

SECTION 1
The Writing Process

EXAMPLE

Subtopic: Ridership

- The New York City subway system officially opened on Thursday, October 27, 1904. One hundred fifty thousand people used the subway that first day.
- By 1946, daily ridership grew to eight million people.
- The number of people using public transit declined due to the car and highway boom of the 1950s and 1960s.
- How can the numbers be boosted to earlier levels?
- Who rides the subways?
- What is New York Transit currently doing about trying to increase ridership levels?
- Today, the subway serves 4.3 million customers on an average weekday and about 1.3 billion passengers a year.
- Ridership on the New York City subways is the fifth largest in the world, behind Moscow, Tokyo, Seoul, and Mexico City. Moscow's subway system serves almost three times the number of passengers served by the New York City subway system.

Reading Your Writing

Prewriting is the process of choosing a writing topic and planning the content of your writing. It will help you make your thoughts clear so your audience will not be confused when reading your writing.

Prewriting • The Writing Process

SECTION 1

The Writing Process

STEP 2 **Drafting**

Drafting is the second phase of the writing process. It's also called the *first draft* or *rough draft*. This is where you'll write your story or report in rough form, using the notes, research, and graphic organizers you've already completed in *prewriting*.

EXAMPLE Here's the first draft of an introductory paragraph from a student's essay about the New York City subway system.

> NY City Subways
> People often say that NYC has the biggest and best of everything. This is probably an exaggeration, but the "Big Apple" does shine in one respect: NYC's subway system is the fifth largest in the world!

Secrets of Successful Drafting

A **draft** is your first attempt at writing. The most important thing about a draft is to get your ideas down on paper. Here are some tips on how to get your first draft written.

Tips for Drafting

- Write on only the front of each page, and leave a blank line beneath each line of writing. Later, you'll have room to make revisions and corrections in the extra space.
- Write quickly. What matters most in this step is content, or information you include in the writing. Write in complete sentences with a capital letter at the beginning and a period or other punctuation mark at the end.
- If you want to change something you've already written, do *not* start over. Just draw a line through it and keep going.
- Abbreviations may help you write faster if you can remember what your abbreviations mean.
- If you are having a hard time figuring out the spelling of a tricky word, sound out the word and circle it so you'll remember to look it up during the *proofreading* step of writing.
- Keep your purpose and intended audience in mind as you write. Adjust your drafting as you visualize your audience reading what you've written.
- If you can't think of an exact word or phrase you wish to use, leave a blank space and come back to it later.

Remember, the purpose of a draft is to get your ideas down on paper quickly, not to write a perfect piece. Try not to think about any single concern for too long. Leave that for later.

SECTION 1

The Writing Process

SECTION 1

The Writing Process

Turning Notes into Paragraphs

Now it's time to shape the ideas and information you've gathered into paragraphs. A paragraph is a group of two or more sentences that tells about the same thing. A paragraph has a topic sentence, which states the main idea, and supporting sentences, which provide details. Here are some tips for writing informative paragraphs. Keep in mind that narrative paragraphs (like those in stories) don't always follow all of these guidelines.

Tips for Writing Paragraphs

- Each paragraph should feature only *one* main idea.
- The topic sentence should state the main idea of each paragraph.
- This sentence is usually, *but not always*, placed at the beginning of the paragraph.
- Supporting sentences should add to the topic sentence, providing details to develop and back up the main idea.
- Don't include unnecessary sentences that seem out of place with the other supporting details.
- When appropriate, you may add a final sentence that concludes or summarizes the main idea of the paragraph or that provides a good transition into the next paragraph.
- Be sure to *indent* the first line of each paragraph.

Reading Your Writing

Drafting will be easier if you remember to use your prewriting notes. Your notes or webs will help you put your ideas on paper. If you think of something new, always write that down, too.

Creating a Paragraph

Let's return to the informational writing piece on the New York City subway system. On the graphic organizer shown on page 30, we chose *ridership* as one of the first *subtopics*. Check out the list of facts and ideas related to *ridership* on page 31. Remember to rephrase the information in your own words. We're now going to turn some of the information chosen under the subtopic *ridership* into a paragraph about *ridership*. First, we'll need a topic sentence.

Topic Sentence: *The New York City subway system is the fifth largest in the world.*

Here are some details to support the topic sentence.

- The New York City subway system officially opened on Thursday, October 27, 1904. One hundred fifty thousand people used the subway that first day.
- By 1946, daily ridership grew to eight million.
- Today, the subway serves 4.3 million customers on an average weekday and about 1.3 billion passengers a year.
- Only Moscow, Tokyo, Seoul, and Mexico City have ridership greater than New York City's. Moscow's subway system serves almost three times the number of passengers served by the New York City subway system.

How do we form these separate details about *ridership* into a paragraph? Understanding how to use *transition words* can help.

Transition Words

Transition, or signal, words link sentences and paragraphs to each other. They help ideas flow smoothly. Transition words can be placed at the beginning of a sentence or paragraph and are used for different purposes, such as to show change, cause and effect, or the addition of more information and to signal order, time, or location. Below is a brief list of transition words.

Transition Words Showing Time and Order		
yesterday	before	then
tonight	after	when
last night	first	finally
today	last	by
tomorrow	the day after tomorrow	while
the next day		

Transition Words Showing Locations		
across	next to	in front of
under	as far as	into
over	behind	nearby
beside	above	

Transition Words Showing That There Is More Information to Come		
furthermore	first of all	the principal item
moreover	remember	it is important to note
also	a major event	
keep in mind	in addition	

Transition Words Showing Contrast		
although	on the other hand	different from
yet	but	rather
however	while	otherwise

Transition Words Showing Cause and Effect		
because	therefore	so

Using what we have learned about transition words, we can form a paragraph using the details we chose about ridership.

Only Moscow, Tokyo, Seoul, and Mexico City have more riders than New York City. When it opened on October 27, 1904, one hundred fifty thousand people rode New York City's subway. By 1946, this figure had grown to eight million daily riders. Today, only half that number rides the trains each day.

Try It!

Pick out the transition words in the paragraph about *ridership.* Which ones show time?

Next look at the *ridership* paragraph's *content* and ask yourself, "What question or questions will my audience have after reading these sentences?" You've introduced a bit of a mystery, telling readers that there were eight million riders in 1946 versus four million riders today. Why are fewer people riding the subway today than in 1946?

Your next paragraph should explore the reasons behind this dramatic drop in ridership. Present details that bring up thought provoking questions. This will keep your audience reading because they will want to find the answers to their questions.

Reading Your Writing

Drafting is the time to get your thoughts on paper. Remember to use transition words so your reader can easily follow your thinking.

SECTION 1

The Writing Process

STEP 3 Revising

Revising means changing. During this third phase of writing, your goal is to make your piece as clear, interesting, and well organized as possible. In *revising*, you are not *rewriting* your story, report, or letter; you are searching for ways to make your writing better by making changes directly on your rough draft.

You can also use the revising step to make certain your writing is appropriate for your audience. If you are writing a story for first graders, you should use easy words and simple sentences so they can understand and stay interested. If you are writing an essay about the New York City subway system for your teacher, you will need to use more complex words and sentences.

You may want to consider setting aside your writing for a while before you begin your revisions. This will clear your mind so when you come back to your writing you will be refreshed and ready to make changes.

Revising is concerned with presentation of *content*, not mistakes. Revising comes down to five major operations:

- ▶ Adding
- ▶ Deleting
- ▶ Consolidating
- ▶ Clarifying
- ▶ Rearranging

Continue reading this section of the Handbook to find out additional information about the five operations of revising.

Adding

You can add to your writing in several different ways. You can add ideas, characters, events, details, words, sentences, paragraphs, and sections. Adding material is probably the easiest of all the revising tasks. Additional details can make a sentence or paragraph more interesting.

> **EXAMPLE** Imagine you have written a personal narrative about your afternoon at the beach. The original sentence in your rough draft might look like this:
>
> *My grandma and I stood at the edge of the water.*
>
> After you revise your paper, your sentence might say,
>
> *My grandma and I stood close together at the edge of the water while the waves gently lapped at our feet.*

Try It!

Revise this sentence by adding details to make it more interesting.
My mom left work early so I wouldn't be late for the appointment.

SECTION 1

The Writing Process

Deleting

Sometimes, reading over your first draft will reveal material that needs to be **deleted,** or removed. This material might be a word, phrase, or sentence you've accidentally repeated. Perhaps you've decided that certain items or even entire paragraphs might be inappropriate or uninteresting to your audience. If you find something you want to delete, draw a line through it. Don't erase; you might want to use some of it later.

> **EXAMPLE** This paragraph contains some material that does not fit with the rest of the paragraph. Notice the deletions.
>
> *The African elephant is taller than the Asian elephant. A male African elephant is ~~is~~ about 13 feet tall, whereas a male Asian elephant is about 10 feet tall. ~~Both are shorter than a giraffe, which is 18-20 feet tall~~.*

Try It!

See if you can find some words, phrases, or sentences that should be deleted from the following paragraph.

Parakeets have always been my favorite kind of pet. Ever since I can remember, ever since I can remember, my mom has always had a happy, chirping little green or blue birdie in the dining room. I like dogs, too. Seymour was the first parakeet I can remember. With his green chest and little yellow head, his chatter brought more life into our house. My cousin Richie had a finch named Fluffy.

Consolidating

When you are revising your writing, you may notice some information that could be **consolidated,** or joined together. Consolidating usually involves taking two or more sentences that have similar purposes or structures and combining them into one sentence.

Consolidating information can make your writing more to the point. This helps readers more easily understand what you are trying to tell them.

SECTION 1

The Writing Process

> **EXAMPLE** Here are a few sentences from a rough draft.
>
> *Our class took a field trip. We went to the aquarium yesterday. We saw sharks while we were there. We also saw dolphins.*
>
> Here is the same information after being revised.
>
> *Our class took a field trip to the aquarium yesterday. We saw sharks and dolphins while we were there.*
>
> Compare the original and consolidated examples. Do you see where words were added and deleted?

Try It!

Try improving these sentences by consolidating them.

> The aquarium was filled with salt water. Salt water is the natural habitat of seals and dolphins. I thought we would see walruses. No walruses were there.

Revising • The Writing Process

SECTION 1

The Writing Process

Clarifying

Another way to make your writing better is to **clarify** it, or make it clearer to the reader. Perhaps your opening sentence is confusing or misleading. Maybe you've introduced a difficult idea or topic to the reader and you need to explain it more thoroughly. Clarifying requires that you look at your writing from the reader's point of view. Read your rough draft carefully and ask yourself, "Is the reader going to understand exactly what I am saying?"

> **EXAMPLE** Read this example sentence and ask yourself if there is a way to make the information clearer or more understandable.
>
> *We saw a killer whale and a calf in a separate tank.*
>
> Now read the revised information.
>
> *We saw a killer whale and a calf, or baby whale. The whales were not in the same tank as the sharks and dolphins.*

The revised information makes two pieces of information clearer. The first sentence provides the meaning of the word *calf*. The second sentence makes it clear that the two whales were in the same tank but not with the sharks and dolphins.

> **Try It!**
>
> Try improving this sentence by clarifying any confusing information.
>
> We ate lunch with the creatures in the aquarium.

Rearranging

Another way to revise your writing is through *rearranging*. When you rearrange your writing, you use the information that is already there, but you put it into a different order. The result is that your writing is easier to read and it makes more sense. Rearranging may involve as little as switching two words in a sentence. Sometimes rearranging involves moving phrases, sentences, or even whole paragraphs of information.

SECTION 1
The Writing Process

EXAMPLE Compare these sample sentences.

We excitedly watched as the shark ate and caught a piece of food.

We watched excitedly as the shark caught and ate a piece of food.

Rearranging the words *watched* and *excitedly* helps the sentence flow more smoothly. Rearranging *caught* and *ate* puts the events in better order.

Try It!

Improve these sentences by rearranging the information.

The dolphins swam around the tank in circles. Some of them jumped through the air and out of the water.

Revising • The Writing Process

A Revising Checklist

Below is a checklist you can use to make your writing better. It will help you think about what you have written and how to improve it.

Ideas

- Can I add information to make my writing clearer?
- Have I left out important information I need to add?
- Can I delete material unrelated to the topic or inappropriate for my audience and purpose?

Organization

- Does my opening sentence attract the reader's attention?
- Do I need to change the order of my sentences or paragraphs?
- Do I have a thoughtful conclusion?

Voice

- Does it sound like I wrote it?
- Have I involved the readers and made them care about the topic?
- Have I used language that is appropriate for my audience and purpose?

Word Choice

- Can I substitute words and phrases that are more exact?
- Have I painted "word pictures" for my readers?

Sentence Fluency

- Can I delete repeated or unnecessary words, phrases, or sentences?
- Can I use more variety in my sentences?

Conferencing with Classmates

During the revision process, you may wish to share your writing with fellow classmates. Called **peer conferencing,** these discussions can often provide you with additional ideas to improve your writing. This type of sharing can occur between two writers or within a small group.

Tips for Successful Peer Conferencing

Here are some things to keep in mind when you have been asked to read and comment on someone's writing.

- Avoid general comments such as "That wasn't very interesting" or "That was good."
- Make specific comments such as "I really liked the part where the wind blew the door open," or "I think it would be great to hear a description of the campsite."
- Always begin your comments with something positive before offering a suggestion for improvement.

Peer conferencing can be an effective tool for predicting your audience's response to your writing, but it will help to improve your writing only if you follow up on the comments made. Take notes on your classmates' responses. After the conference, carefully consider the reactions before making any changes. Do not change your writing just because a suggestion was made. Think about the suggestion and decide for yourself whether or not it would improve your writing.

Reading Your Writing

Writing takes a lot of time and effort. Sometimes your writing is not clear to your audience. Revising, staying on topic, adding variety, and conferencing are all ways that you can make your writing better. It is also a good idea to have peers or adults listen to and comment on your writing.

SECTION 1

The Writing Process

STEP 4 Editing/Proofreading

At the **editing/proofreading** stage, all of your writing mistakes should be corrected. On your draft, where you also marked your revising changes, you'll carefully make sure that spelling, punctuation, and usage mistakes are corrected. A dictionary is helpful during this step for checking spelling and definitions of vocabulary words you used.

Read your work out loud to yourself in a soft voice. Listen to how it *sounds* as you read it. You'll be able to catch many more problems this way.

Another editing aid is a pencil eraser. While reading your draft, be sure to use your eraser to point to each word as you say it. Doing this will ensure that you read *only* the words that have actually been written down instead of unintentionally filling in sentences with the words that your mind knows should be there.

> **EXAMPLE** You might easily overlook a missing word unless you point to and say each word softly.
>
> *I enjoy going the lake on hot, humid days.*
>
> You also could easily overlook an extra word unless you point to and say each word softly.
>
> *It's impossible to predict if if lightning will strike a certain location.*

Proofreading Marks

To make editing clear, quick, and neat, proofreading marks are used to indicate corrections.

Here's a list of proofreading marks and their meanings.

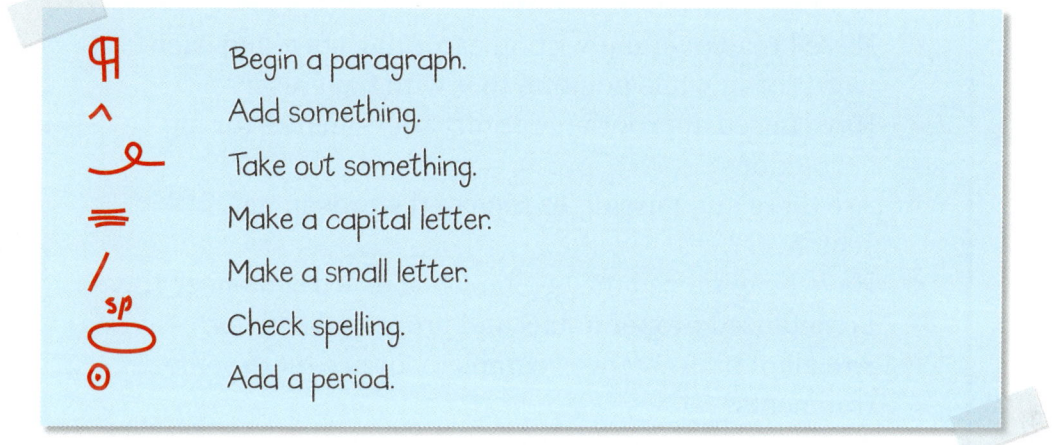

Mark	Meaning
¶	Begin a paragraph.
∧	Add something.
⌒	Take out something.
≡	Make a capital letter.
/	Make a small letter.
sp ◯	Check spelling.
⊙	Add a period.

Using Proofreading Marks

Use these marks in a different color to fix your paper quickly. Look carefully at the examples for each mark.

¶ Begin a paragraph.
¶ It is the easiest sandwich to make. First you get the cheese, the bread, and the butter together.

∧ Add words.
Had the house been there for ^many^ years?

⌒ Take out, or delete, words or punctuation.
The dog ~~dog~~ ran away.

≡ Change to a capital letter.
washington, D.C., is the nation's capital.

/ Change to a small letter.
Harley hid behind the old Tree.

sp Check spelling; write the correct spelling above the word.
Tad wore a green (cotten) cotton sweater.

⊙ Add a period.
The dog ran quickly across the road⊙

Editing/Proofreading • **The Writing Process**

An Editing Checklist

Below is a checklist that you can use to check the conventions in your writing.

- ▶ Have I read over my writing carefully, speaking each word softly while pointing to it with my eraser?
- ▶ Have I used appropriate proofreader's marks for my corrections?
- ▶ Are there any missing or repeated words in my sentences?
- ▶ Have I capitalized the beginning of every sentence? Have I capitalized proper nouns and proper adjectives?
- ▶ Are all of my sentences complete, or are there some fragments?
- ▶ Are there any run-on sentences?
- ▶ Are any punctuation marks missing or used incorrectly?
- ▶ Are there any misused verbs, modifiers, or pronouns?
- ▶ Do my subjects and verbs agree?
- ▶ Have I confirmed the definitions of words about which I am unsure?
- ▶ Have I misspelled any words?
- ▶ Have I written in paragraphs of appropriate length?
- ▶ Have I indented my paragraphs?
- ▶ Did I use a variety of words?
- ▶ Have I varied my sentence lengths?
- ▶ Is my language appropriate for my purpose? Have I used academic English for formal papers?
- ▶ Am I positive that I have fulfilled the detailed requirements of the assignment?

Writing on a Computer

Although computers can help with certain writing functions, their usage, punctuation, and spelling checks are not very accurate. These computer aids should be used only as possible suggestions for corrections.

Tips for Writing on a Computer

- First, label your document with the title of your writing. Save this file in a location that you will remember.
- Type your rough draft (including revisions) carefully. Say the words as you type them.
- Increase the font size to make it easier to read. Also try increasing the document size to 150 percent.
- Open your document to fill as much of your computer screen as possible.
- Save your work often. Remember that if your computer crashes, anything you've written since the last time you saved your work will be lost.
- Make corrections as you see them.
- After you've completed your corrections, read aloud what you've written directly from the computer screen.
- Finally, print your work and read it again. Looking at the printed version can alert you to mistakes missed when you were reading from a computer screen.

Reading Your Writing

Editing is the process of correcting any mistakes in your writing. An error-free paper will make reading it a breeze.

SECTION 1

The Writing Process

STEP 5 Publishing

Publishing is the last phase in the writing process. This is the step where you will prepare your writing to be shared with its intended audience. You will make certain that the *presentation* of your paper is pleasing to the eye of the reader. This means making certain the paper is neat and free from erasures. You can also consider adding graphics, such as illustrations, charts, or diagrams, to make your paper look more appealing.

Publishing is also the step during which you'll decide *how* your writing will be shared. Will you *mail* the letter you've written? Will you *perform* your writing in front of an audience? Will you transform your writing into a *booklet, pamphlet,* or *folder,* complete with pictures, illustrations, or charts? Will you use a desktop-publishing computer program to design and lay out your work like a *magazine article?*

Continue reading to find out about different ways you might choose to publish your work.

Mail Your Work

Some of your writing can be published through the mail. You can write letters to family members, friends, celebrities, politicians, and even to newspapers, television, and radio stations. If you write these letters by hand, you should follow appropriate friendly or business letter formats, and the letters should be neat and free from errors. If you are using a computer for the final copy, see if the program has an automatic letter format. Learn the correct way to fold your letter before placing it in an envelope, and be sure to address the envelope correctly and neatly.

Present Your Work Orally

Oral presentation is an exciting way to share your writing. You'll need to practice your oral delivery, making sure you can be easily heard. Try practicing in front of a mirror, or have a friend or family member videotape your practice. Ask yourself which audiences would most appreciate your performance and subject matter. Think about different types of audiences, such as your class, a younger or older class, adults at a faculty or PTA meeting, your after-school club, or relatives at a family reunion.

SECTION 1
The Writing Process

Try It!

What audience would most likely appreciate an oral presentation of the following topics?

- an original fairy tale you wrote
- educational websites
- your family's history

Print Your Work

If you decide not to perform your work, there are still lots of other opportunities for sharing it. Think of all the different types of printed material you come across in just one week: newspapers, magazines, brochures, booklets, fliers, comics—the list goes on and on.

Page Layout

Page Design Elements

text	pictures	illustrations
diagrams	charts	graphs
borders	captions	titles

Many publications rely heavily on a combination of the written word and graphic design elements. An important part of an article's graphic design is its *layout*, or the way these different graphics and words are arranged on a page. Scan through this book. Are there some pages that catch your attention more than others? What is it about these pages that makes them interesting to view? Try using some graphic design elements in your work. For example, use colorful boxes to set off special parts, or put important phrases in italics or other type styles. They will add to the *presentation*, or eye appeal, of your paper. You may be surprised by the impact that graphics can have on your project.

Paste-Up

If you don't have a computer to design and print your completed pages, do it the way newspapers and magazines have for hundreds of years—use paste-up. Start by gathering the elements that you want to appear on a page. Cut out columns of text, pictures, charts, and even separate titles and captions. Then, using a blank page of the same size as your project, experiment with arranging the cut-out pieces into a clear and attractive whole page. Think of it as a jigsaw puzzle. When you've decided on a layout for that particular page, lightly mark (with pencil) the position of each cut-out piece on the blank page. Then, apply glue or rubber cement to the back of the first piece you intend to paste up, and carefully rub it down onto the marked position. Continue pasting up each piece until you're finished.

Computer Page Layout

Today, many student-friendly page layout programs are available for your computer. To find one, try your media center or computer lab. If you have a computer at home, ask your parents what page layout programs they might have. If you can't locate one, use your computer to print all the page design elements, then use the paste-up technique outlined above.

Tips for Computer Page Design

Here are some ideas you can use with or without paste-up.

- Choose the page size of your final product.
- Decide on a color design for the elements of your page. Avoid putting too many colors on one page.
- Choose a font, font size, and color for your body text.
- Choose a number of columns for your body text.
- Choose a font, font size, and color for your titles.
- Choose a font, font size, and color for your pictures, illustration, or *captions*, which are short identifications or descriptions of graphics.
- Choose a style, size, and color for frames or borders that you want to place around text, graphics, titles, pictures, or photos.
- Experiment with a variety of layouts, fonts, font sizes, colors, and borders until you find design combinations that are visually clear, strong, and appealing.

Bind Your Work

Stories, reports, poetry, and other types of finished pieces can be published in a number of ways. Directions for the binding of homemade books can be found in your school media center or library, where your work might be exhibited. Perhaps you could loan your piece to a class studying an issue related to your topic or enter it in a school, district, or state contest.

Submit Your Work for Publication

If you think your work is appropriate for publishing in a newspaper, magazine, or other periodical, you'll have to *submit*, or send, your work to the publication's editor. Although few submissions are selected for publication in magazines, your project may prove to be special and appropriate enough to be published. You'll never know if you don't try!

The first thing to do when submitting your work is to find out the publication's requirements. You can visit a library and check for specific guidelines. You can also write to the magazine, journal, or website to which you want to send your work. In your letter, ask what the requirements are for submitting your work. Some publications will ask you to type and double space your writing. Some may require that you use a certain number of words in your piece. Be sure to follow the instructions that are given so you can increase your chances of having your writing published.

Reading Your Writing

Publishing is the part of the writing process when you show your work to the world. Choose the publishing option that is best for what you have written, and your audience will be sure to respond.

SECTION 1

Following the Writing Process

Now that we've explored each of the stages of the writing process, it's time to put all this information to good use on another project. This time, let's imagine that Alec Levy's class has been involved with a unit on *consumerism*. The students have been focusing on customer service and protecting the consumer. For example, they learned that television commercials for toys sound really good, but sometimes when you get the toy home, it is not all that the advertisement promised. In other words, the class learned how *not* to be cheated, and their assignment was to publish a piece of writing on some aspect of consumerism.

STEP 1 Prewriting

Consumerism is a broad topic. The wide range of options makes it difficult to choose a specific topic. Alec started by asking some questions: What do I already know about consumerism? Do I know anyone who has had to take consumer action? Do I have any reason to take some sort of consumer action?

With all these thoughts in his mind, Alec decided to make a topic web to brainstorm for a focused topic.

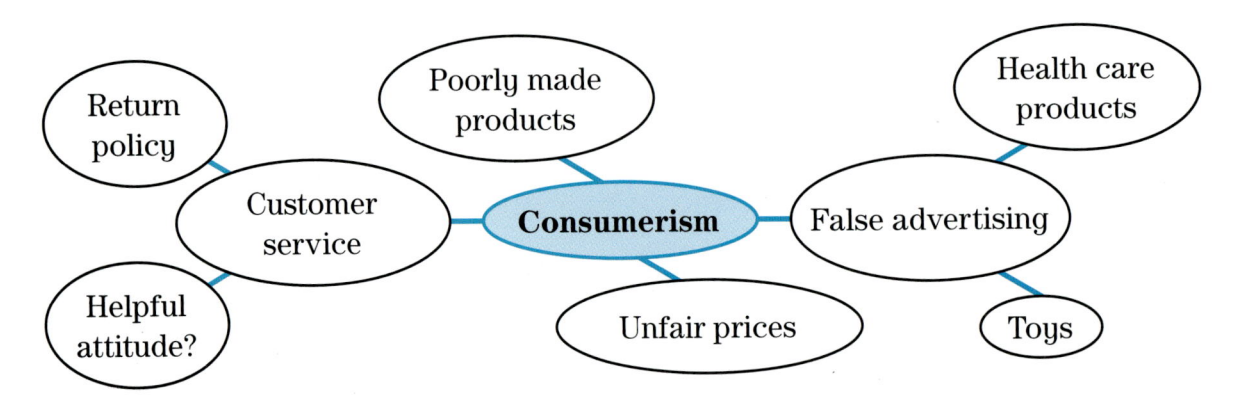

Topic web centered on "Consumerism" with branches to: Return policy, Customer service, Helpful attitude?, Poorly made products, Unfair prices, Health care products, False advertising, Toys.

Decisions before Writing

While making his web, Alec realized that he could fulfill the requirements of the writing assignment *and* stand up for his own consumer rights at the same time. Alec remembered that the DVD player he had gotten for his birthday had stopped working, so he and his dad took it back to the electronics store to exchange it for a new one. The salesperson said that the store did not exchange defective products and that Alec would have to mail it to the manufacturer for repair. Because he had it for only a week, and it would take weeks or months for the repair to be completed, Alec decided to look into another way of resolving the problem. Alec chose to write a **persuasive letter** to ask for a new DVD player.

Alec's purpose was to persuade someone at the electronics store to exchange his defective DVD player for a new one. He next had to decide on his audience. He asked himself who at the store would be the best person to whom to address his letter. Because a salesperson couldn't make the exchange, Alec decided to address his letter to the store's manager. He got the manager's name and the store's address by asking his dad to call the store.

Alec then made a plan for his letter. He decided to use a *business letter* format because he wanted to politely present his problem and ask for a replacement for his DVD player.

Alec knew that the first step in writing a *letter of complaint* was to set up the *heading, inside address,* and *salutation.* You can find out how to do this by turning to pages 74–79.

The second step in Alec's process was to plan out what he wanted to say. First he would introduce himself and say why he was writing. Next he would explain his problem and the solutions that he tried to fix the problem. Then he would ask for what he wanted and thank the reader for his or her time.

SECTION 1

The Writing Process

SECTION 1: The Writing Process

STEP 2 Drafting

EXAMPLE Alec used the plan he made in the prewriting step to help him draft this letter to the store manager.

Heading ▶
111 Wyandotte Ave.
Atlanta, ga 30305
October 30 2016

Inside Address ▶
Linda Reynard, Manager
The electric shop
222 biltmore Place
atlanta ga 30306

Salutation ▶
Dear Ms. reynard

Body ▶
My name is Alec Levy and I am writing about a DVD player that my parents bought for me.

I got the new DVD player for my Birthday and when I set it up and tried to play a movie nothing hapened. I took the DVD out. I saw the DVD was not turning in my player. I thought maybe my DVD was messed up when I put it in so I tried another one and the same thing happened again.

My dad and me went back to your store. We talked to the salesperson who sold it to my parents. She said the store would not xchange my DVD player and that I would have to send it in for repare and that it might take two to four weeks.

I should not have to wait two to four weeks to get my DVD player repaired since it was broke when I got it. I hope you will be able to exchange it for me.

Thank you for reading my letter.

Please call me at 404 555-5555 if you have questions.

Closing ▶

Sincerly,

Alec Levy

SECTION 1

The Writing Process

Try It!

Before moving on, read the letter again and look for words, phrases, or sentences that can be revised to make the letter better.

SECTION 1
The Writing Process

STEP 3 Revising

EXAMPLE This is a revised copy of Alec's letter.

Heading ▶
111 Wyandotte Ave.
Atlanta, ga 30305
October 30 2016

Inside Address ▶
Linda Reynard, Manager
The electric shop
222 biltmore Place
atlanta ga 30306

Salutation ▶
Dear Ms. reynard

Body ▶
My name is Alec Levy and I am writing about a DVD player that my parents bought for me ^from your store.

Adding ▶

Consolidating ▶
I got the new DVD player for my Birthday and when I set it up and tried to play a movie nothing hapened. I took the DVD out, ^and I saw the DVD was not turning in my player. I thought maybe my DVD was messed up when I put it in so I tried another one and the same thing happened again.

SECTION 1

The Writing Process

Clarifying ▶	My dad and ~~me~~ went back to your store. We talked to the salesperson who sold it to my parents. She said the store would not (xchange) [sp] my DVD player, and that I would have to send it in for
Clarifying ▶	broken for a new one repare and that it might take two to four weeks.
	I should not have to wait two to four weeks to get my DVD player repaired since it was broke when I got it. I hope you will be able to exchange it for me.
	Thank you for reading my letter. Please call me at 404 555-5555 ~~if you have questions.~~
Deleting ▶	to tell me if you can allow an exchange.
Closing ▶	Sincerly, Alec Levy

Try It!

Read the letter again now that the revisions have been made. Can you see any changes that you would make for the editing/proofreading stage?

SECTION 1 — The Writing Process

STEP 4 Editing/Proofreading

EXAMPLE This is a copy of Alec's revised and edited letter. Look for the proofreading marks that Alec used.

Heading ▶
111 Wyandotte Ave.
Atlanta, ga 30305
October 30 2016

Inside Address ▶
Linda Reynard, Manager
The electric shop
222 biltmore Place
atlanta, ga 30306

Salutation ▶
Dear Ms. reynard;

Body ▶
My name is Alec Levy and I am writing about a DVD player that my parents bought for me.

Adding ▶
from your store

I got the new DVD player for my Birthday and when I set it up and tried to play a movie nothing

Consolidating ▶
sp
(hapened) I took the DVD out, I saw the DVD was
and
not turning in my player. I thought maybe my DVD was messed up when I put it in so I tried another one and the same thing happened again.

My dad and ~~me~~ went back to your store. We
             I
talked to the salesperson who sold it to my
parents. She said the store would not (exchange) my *sp*
                      broken   for a new one
DVD player, and that I would have to send it in for
sp (repare) and that it might take two to four weeks.

I should not have to wait two to four weeks to get
my DVD player repaired since it was broke when I
                                           n
got it. I hope you will be able to exchange it for me.

Thank you for reading my letter. Please call me at
404 555-5555 ~~if you have questions~~,
              to tell me if you can allow an exchange.

Closing ▶   *sp* (Sincerly,)
                Alec Levy

SECTION 1 — The Writing Process

STEP 5 Publishing

This is Alec's letter after all the changes have been made.

> 111 Wyandotte Avenue
> Atlanta, GA 30305
> October 30, 2016
>
> Linda Reynard, Manager
> The Electronics Shop
> 222 Biltmore Place
> Atlanta, GA 30306
>
> Dear Ms. Reynard:
>
> My name is Alec Levy and I am writing about a DVD player that my parents bought for me from your store.
>
> I got a new DVD player for my birthday but when I set it up and tried to play a movie nothing happened. I took the DVD out and saw that the DVD was not turning in my player. I thought maybe my DVD was messed up when I put it in so I tried another one and the same thing happened again.

My dad and I went back to your store and talked to the salesperson who sold it to my parents. She said the store would not exchange my broken DVD player for a new one and that I would have to send it for repair and that it might take two to four weeks.

I should not have to wait two to four weeks to get my DVD player repaired since it was broken when I got it. I hope that you will be able to exchange it for me.

Thank you for reading my letter. Please call me at (404) 555-5555 to tell me if you can allow an exchange.

Sincerely,
Alec Levy

SECTION 1

The Writing Process

Reading Your Writing

The writing process has transformed this letter from an idea to a persuasive letter that is sure to grab the attention of the reader.

SECTION 2
Forms of Writing

Personal Writing 68

Informative Writing 86

Narrative Writing 134

Descriptive Writing 188

Opinion Writing 224

Poetry 240

Timed Writing 252

The purpose of writing is to communicate a message. When you write, it is important to choose a form of writing that fits the message you want to convey. Sometimes the message is very simple. Other times, the message is more complex. You have many choices about how to communicate the message. In this section you will learn about the different forms of writing: personal, informative, narrative, descriptive, opinion, and poetry. Think about how and when to use them when you write.

Personal Writing

Do you write notes to your friends? Do you make lists to remind yourself to do things? Do you write in a journal? These are all examples of personal writing. In these kinds of writing, you can express yourself in a more personal, or individual, way.

Some kinds of personal writing, such as lists and notes, are very practical. Others, such as journals, are more reflective. Think about how you can use each of them.

SECTION 2

Forms of Writing

Lists and notes are just two examples of personal writing. Other examples of personal writing include the following:

- Friendly Letters
- Business Letters
- Journals
- Learning Logs
- Literature Response Journal

EXAMPLE Here is a page from Ted's journal.

> October 7—I brought my pet gerbil 'Roo to school today. The class liked to watch him eat. Taylor made a loud noise and 'Roo jumped out of his cage. We found him in the gymnasium. It took 10 of us to find him.

Continue reading this section of the Handbook to see additional examples and to find out more information about personal writing.

SECTION 2

Forms of Writing

Friendly Letters

You can send a **friendly letter** to a friend, a relative, a pen pal, or someone you just met and want to get to know better. Include any or all of these things in a friendly letter.

- Updates on the interesting things you've been doing
- Questions for the person receiving your letter
- Tips on good books, movies, and videos
- Stories, poems, and jokes that you want to share

Parts of a Friendly Letter

Heading

This is your address and the date. It goes in the upper-right corner.

Salutation

Use the word *Dear,* followed by the name and a comma. The salutation goes by the left margin. Double-space or leave one line space between the heading and salutation.

Body

This is the message part of the letter. Double-space between the salutation and body. Indent each paragraph in the body of your letter.

Closing

Yours truly and *Sincerely* are commonly used as a closing. Double-space between the body and closing, and place the closing by the left margin. Capitalize just the first word, and use a comma at the end of the closing.

Signature

Sign your name under the closing.

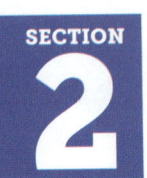

SECTION 2 — Forms of Writing

EXAMPLE Jason replies to a letter from Tyrone, a friend he made on vacation.

Heading ▶

4992 Illini Avenue
Rockford, IL 61109
May 21, 2006

Salutation ▶

Dear Tyrone,

Body ▶

It was great to hear from you. I really miss camping at Huntington Beach too. Can you believe all the baby crabs we caught in the ocean stream? I'm glad we threw them all back because my teacher told me that some crabs are getting scarce. The fiddler crabs up on the beach were pretty funny. I still think about how they ran across the sand and disappeared at the slightest noise.

My dad and I have been doing a lot of fishing where we live. We catch mostly sunfish and bluegills, but last weekend I caught a smallmouth bass. Do you ever go fishing? Wouldn't it be great if we could get our dads to takes us on a fishing trip together?

What do you like to do for fun in Kentucky? Is it warm down there now? It's still pretty cold where we live. We've been riding our bikes a lot and playing with scooters, but we will probably have to wait until the middle of June before we can go swimming.

My mom finally said I could take Tang Soo Do lessons. It's kind of like karate only it's Korean. Do you do any martial arts?

Write soon and tell me what you're doing.

Closing ▶

Your fishing buddy,

Signature ▶

Jason

SECTION 2

Forms of Writing

Personal Writing • Friendly Letters

E-Mail

E-mail stands for "electronic mail." Many people use e-mail messages in place of friendly letters. Writers use e-mail addresses to communicate by computer e-mail. An e-mail message is sent through the Internet.

EXAMPLE Below is an e-mail message sent by Jack Bodo to his favorite author, Jerry Spinelli.

> Dear Mr. Spinelli,
>
> My name is Jack Bodo. I like your books very much, especially <u>Maniac McGee</u>. Is it true that you got some of your ideas from growing up in Norristown, Pennsylvania? I live right near Norristown.
>
> Are you working on anything new? I might become a writer someday. What other kinds of jobs did you have before you won the Newbery Award?
>
> Your biggest fan,
> Jack Bodo

Tips for Writing a Friendly Letter

STEP 1 Prewriting
- Choose a friend or relative to whom you wish to write.
- List questions you want to ask and jokes, stories, and ideas you want to share.

STEP 2 Drafting
- Work on the body of your letter. Include everything you want to say. Refer to your prewriting ideas.
- After drafting the body of your letter, add the heading, the salutation, the closing, and your signature.

STEP 3 Revising
- **Organization** Make sure your letter has five parts.
- **Sentence Fluency** Make sure your reader can understand your ideas and that they flow well.
- **Voice** Check your tone. It should be friendly and not too stiff or formal.

STEP 4 Editing/Proofreading
- **Conventions** See pages 70–71 to make sure you used the proper format. Use a comma after the salutation, and indent paragraphs.
- **Conventions** Make sure you capitalized

STEP 5 Publishing
- **Presentation** Neatly type or write your final copy.
- **Presentation** See page 78 to find out how to address your envelope.

SECTION 2
Forms of Writing

Personal Writing • Friendly Letters

Business Letters

A **business letter** is a formal letter written to a company, organization, or professional person for a specific reason. Your tone should be less personal and even more polite and direct than that normally used for a friendly letter.

Heading

The heading consists of the sender's address and the date. It goes in the upper-left corner. Leave four to seven lines between the heading and inside address.

Inside Address

The inside address includes the name and address of the person receiving the letter. Leave one line space between the inside address and salutation.

Salutation

The salutation is the greeting. Put a colon after it. Double-space between the salutation and body.   **Dear Ms. Frederick:**

You may use salutations like this when you don't know the person's name: **To Whom It May Concern:**

Body

The body includes what you want to say. Be brief and polite but not overly formal or stiff. Begin the body two lines below the salutation. Leave a single line of space between each paragraph. Do not indent. Leave one line space between the body and closing.

Closing

The closing goes two lines below the body, at the left margin. Put a comma after it.   **Yours truly,   Sincerely,**

Signature and Typed Name

Leave four lines between the closing and your typed name. Sign your name in between.

The Three Types of Business Letters

You will have different reasons for writing business letters. Your purpose will determine which of the three types of business letters you write.

A Letter of Request asks for information.

You write to an amusement park to find out about the safety of its rides and whether it has any record of accidents.

A Letter of Concern states your concern about an issue that affects a group of people such as your school, your neighborhood, or the general public.

You write a letter to the editor of your local paper to raise awareness about the lack of community parks in your area.

A Letter of Complaint complains about a policy, a product, or a service.

You write a letter to a nearby rock-climbing gym to complain about its inconvenient hours.

Try It!

Which of the three types of business letters is each of these?
- A letter to the governor about the lack of bicycle trails in your state.
- A letter to a bicycle catalogue company telling them about a problem with the bicycle accessories they sent you.
- A letter to the state parks department asking them to send you bicycle trail maps.

SECTION 2

Forms of Writing

EXAMPLE This is a letter of complaint that Kevin Chang wrote to the makers of the Super Whiz-Bang Zoomer.

Heading ▶ 147 Mayfield Street
Campbell, FL 67043
November 3, 2008

Inside Address ▶ Karen Nelson, Customer Relations Coordinator
The Sky's the Limit, Inc.
3300 Atmosphere Ave.
Star City, KS 17970

Salutation ▶ Dear Ms. Nelson:

Body ▶ I am writing about the Super Whiz-Bang Zoomer made by your company. Last week I gave one to my brother for his seventh birthday. Just a few hours after I gave it to him, the Whiz-Bang broke. The store where I bought the toy didn't have any left. They offered me a refund, but my brother really wants another Whiz-Bang Zoomer.

I am sending you the original store receipt along with the broken pieces in this package. I have also included a receipt for the postage to mail this back. Please send us another Whiz-Bang Zoomer along with a check to cover the postage.

Thank you for your attention to this matter. You can write to me at the above address.

Closing ▶ Sincerely,
Signature ▶ Kevin Chang

The Business Letter Body

Use these checklists for writing the body of a letter of complaint, a letter of request, or a letter of concern.

Letter of Complaint

- ▶ Explain the problem.
- ▶ Describe the product, service, or policy.
- ▶ Tell what you think is the cause of the problem.
- ▶ Explain what you expect of the reader—whether a replacement, a refund, a change of policy, or other outcome.
- ▶ Thank the reader for looking into the problem.

Letter of Request

- ▶ Introduce yourself and explain why you are writing.
- ▶ Include any specific questions you want answered.
- ▶ Inform the reader of any dates or deadlines you must meet.
- ▶ Thank the reader for his or her help.

Letter of Concern

- ▶ Describe the issue or situation and give your opinion.
- ▶ Explain how you would correct the problem or change the situation.
- ▶ Tell the reader how your suggestions or solution will work.
- ▶ Ask that action be taken to change the situation.

Mail Your Business Letter

After you have checked and corrected your letter, you are ready to send it. First you will need to fold your letter and put it in the envelope. Then you need to address the envelope.

- ▸ In the center, just slightly to the left, write the name and address of the person receiving the letter.
- ▸ In the upper-left corner, write your name and address. When addressing your envelope, you should write in only capital letters and leave out all punctuation. This makes it easier for the Postal Service to process mail.
- ▸ Put the stamp in the upper-right corner.

Reading Your Writing

Write a business letter when you want to make formal contact with a company or professional person. Be sure to use the correct format so your reader can easily read your letter.

FUN fact

Will your letters be worth something someday? The highest price paid for a signed letter is $3.4 million. The letter was written by Abraham Lincoln.

Tips for Writing a Business Letter

STEP 1 Prewriting
- Refer to the checklist on page 77 to plan the body of your business letter.

STEP 2 Drafting
- After drafting the body, add the heading, inside address, salutation, closing, and signature.

STEP 3 Revising
- **Organization** Make sure your letter has six parts.
- **Organization** Delete sentences that stray from the central idea of each paragraph.
- **Voice** Check your tone. It should be polite and straightforward.

STEP 4 Editing/Proofreading
- **Conventions** See page 74 to make sure you correctly formatted your letter. Use a colon after the salutation, and do not indent paragraphs. If you are writing your letter on a computer, use the automatic business letter tool to set up your letter for you.

STEP 5 Publishing
- **Presentation** Neatly type or rewrite your final copy.
- **Presentation** See page 78 to find out how to address your envelope.

SECTION 2
Forms of Writing

Journals

You can use a **journal** to write about your thoughts, feelings, ideas, and observations. Many people find it helpful to write in their journals every day because it helps them organize and understand their thoughts and ideas. When you add to your journal, you write a **journal entry.**

A journal keeps good ideas from getting away and can be a wonderful resource for a writer. You can use a journal to store the interesting and meaningful things that catch your attention throughout the day. You might use your Writer's Notebook as a place to collect ideas and write journal entries.

Your journal writing can be useful for other writing you do. You may have written a few lines that can be expanded into an essay, or you may have written a description of an unusual person that could become the basis of a short story. You won't use everything in your journal, but a journal can serve as a valuable writer's tool.

Journals come in many shapes and sizes. A spiral-bound notebook keeps everything in one place and can be taken anywhere. A loose-leaf binder allows you to add and subtract pages. Folders with pockets allow you to insert things you've collected, such as magazine clippings, songs, poems, and pictures. You can also keep your journal on a computer.

SECTION 2

Forms of Writing

EXAMPLE

September 5, 2015

It is so strange how the weather changes right after Labor Day. It's almost like the weather knows that swimming and the other fun stuff of summer are over and that we have to get back to the business of going to school. Mom thinks that we will get some hot weather again, but I feel a change in the air. The trees don't look as green, and I've seen some apples on the trees.

The weather isn't the only thing that's different. My clothes feel different. I finally got to wear the new shoes we bought last week for starting school. I like them, but they make my feet sweat. My new jeans feel funny, too.

Try It!

For which type of writing might a student incorporate the above journal entry?
- ▸ historical fiction
- ▸ business letter
- ▸ personal narrative

Personal Writing • Journals

Although your journal entry should be readable, it does not have to have all of the elements of a finished piece of writing. Journals give you the chance to be freer and more creative. Some of your best ideas can begin in your journal.

Other Kinds of Journals

Some journals have more specific uses. They may overlap in use with your personal journal, but each type has a different focus.

Dialogue Journal

In this kind of journal, two people write back and forth to each other as if they are having a conversation or dialogue. Topics may include books, movies, people they've met, ideas they've thought about, and other experiences. You can share a dialogue journal with a teacher, a parent, or a friend. In this dialogue journal, a student and teacher discuss a story that was read in class.

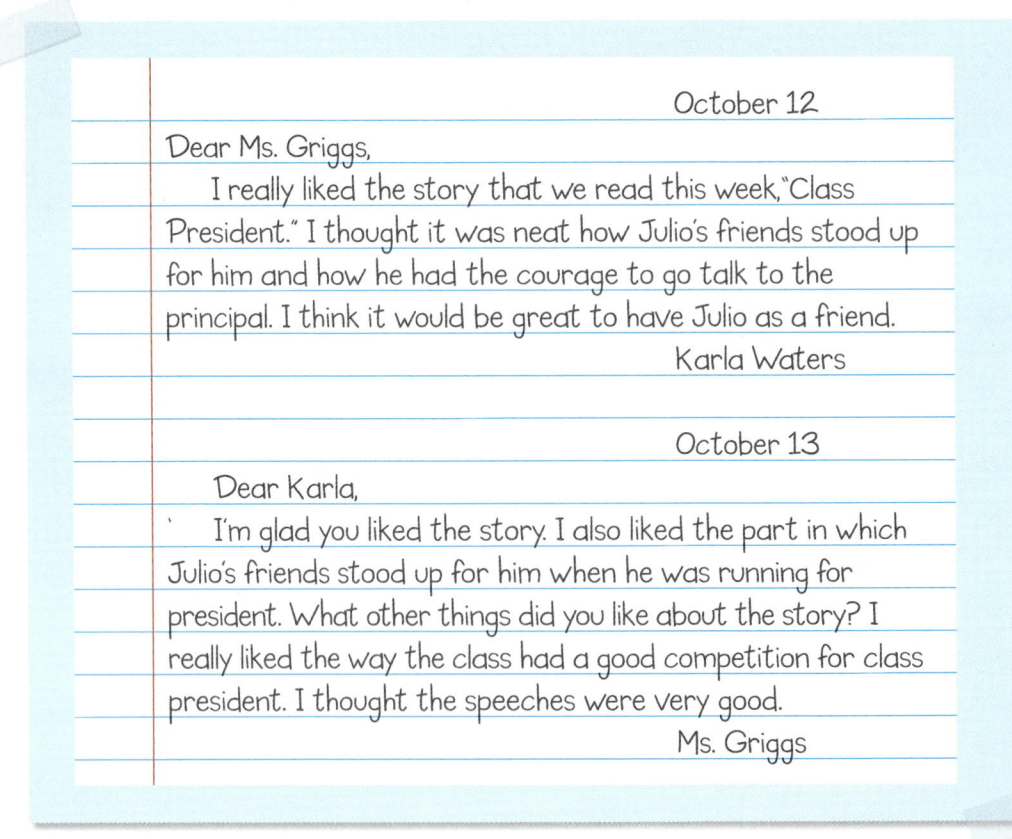

October 12

Dear Ms. Griggs,

   I really liked the story that we read this week, "Class President." I thought it was neat how Julio's friends stood up for him and how he had the courage to go talk to the principal. I think it would be great to have Julio as a friend.

Karla Waters

October 13

Dear Karla,

   I'm glad you liked the story. I also liked the part in which Julio's friends stood up for him when he was running for president. What other things did you like about the story? I really liked the way the class had a good competition for class president. I thought the speeches were very good.

Ms. Griggs

SECTION 2 — Forms of Writing

Learning Log

You can use a **learning log** to take notes as you learn about something. You may find it helpful to write about subjects that you wish to understand better. Suppose something doesn't make sense in science. You may want to write down your questions so you can research them later or ask your teacher. In reading, you may want to list vocabulary that you don't understand.

Karla wrote this entry in her learning log when she had a question about something she learned in class.

> Science
>
> We are studying butterflies in science. Mr. Nanapush told us that monarch butterflies that live east of the Rockies migrate 2,000 miles south to one village in Mexico. I think I can understand how a bird can migrate this far, but how can something as light and slow-moving as a butterfly do it?

Here's Karla's entry in her learning log after she experimented with some new ideas with her camera.

> Photography
>
> I took pictures A-1 and A-2 of our dog Leo with my camera. I was standing in the sun, and Leo was sitting in the shade. The photos turned out too dark. Leo is just a fuzzy shadow. I took A-3 and A-4 when we both stood in the sun. The camera shutter must have let in just the right amount of light, because Leo came out clear and colorful.

SECTION 2

Forms of Writing

Personal Writing · Journals 83

Other Ways to Use Learning Logs

Summarize
Make a list of key words or see if you can come up with a sentence that summarizes what you've learned.

Question Box
Write down any questions that you may have for your teacher or another expert. Some tough questions might require research when you have time.

Visual Cues
Drawing a diagram, a word web, or a simple picture may help you understand and remember your subject.

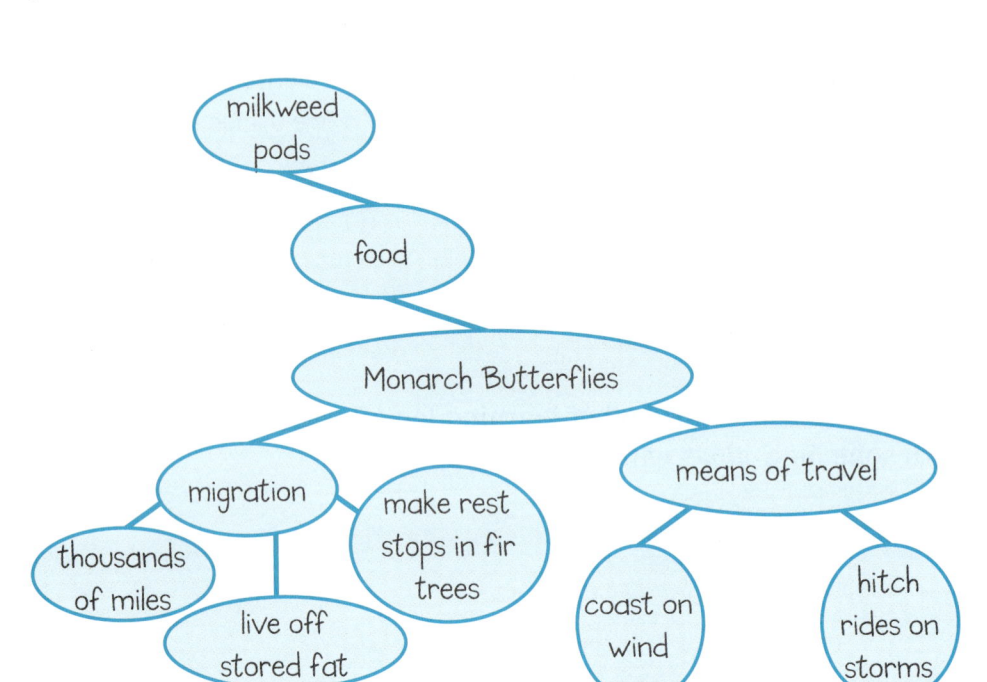

Hints for Keeping a Learning Log
Use separate, small notebooks for each subject or one large notebook that can be separated into sections. Write the date before each entry. Focus on ideas and questions you have about the subject.

84   Personal Writing • Journals

Literature Response Journal

This type of journal is similar to a learning log, but it deals with the special problems and questions related to reading a book. Here are some things to think about as you write.

Characters: Write down each character's name and take notes to record character's traits, actions, motives, and so on.

As You Read: Are there things you don't understand about the plot? Have the characters changed? Are things turning out differently than you expected? What do you think might happen? Do certain characters or events remind you of anything you've experienced? Are there important themes you want to track?

Wrapping Up: Did the book end in the way you expected or hoped? How did the main characters change? Did the book cause you to grow or change your views? Would you recommend the book to a friend?

SECTION 2

Forms of Writing

EXAMPLE David had trouble remembering who was who in the story "The Marble Champ," so he described the characters in his response journal.

> Lupe Medrano—shy, smart, hard-working, ambitious
> Lupe's brother—encouraging, helpful
> Lupe's mother—worried, nervous
> Lupe's father—supportive, encouraging, proud

Reading Your Writing

Most journals are meant for your eyes only and are used to write personal ideas, thoughts, and concerns.

SECTION 2

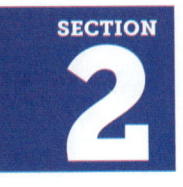

Forms of Writing

Informative Writing

Informative writing does two things. It explains how to do something, or it presents information about something. The steps in the explanation are arranged in a logical way so that the reader can follow the procedure or repeat the activity. When information is presented, it is clear, correct, and well organized.

Much of the writing you do for school is informative. This section can help you improve your reports and essays. Also, you can use this section to try different types of informative writing that may be new to you.

Example of informative writing include the following:

- ▶ Summary
- ▶ Research Reports
- ▶ Problem-and-Solution Essay
- ▶ Responding to Literature: Character Analysis
- ▶ Responding to Literature: Setting Analysis
- ▶ Responding to Literature: Plot Analysis
- ▶ Responding to Literature: Literary Criticism

SECTION 2
Forms of Writing

EXAMPLE Here is a paragraph Nick wrote to tell first graders how to plant a seed. Notice how he used order words.

> Let me tell you how to plant a seed. First, break up the ground. Next, make a hole. Poke your finger into the ground up to your first knuckle. Then, put the seed in the hold. Then, cover it with dirt. Finally, water the seed.

Continue reading this section of the Handbook to see additional examples and to learn more about informative writing.

Informative Writing   87

Summary

When someone asks you about a movie you saw, do you tell them every single thing that happened in it? Of course not! You give a **summary,** or a condensed version of the movie, highlighting the main events, ideas, and characters.

A summary is used as a way to communicate in a brief and to-the-point manner. Summaries on the back covers of paperback books are written to grab your interest and make you want to read the book. At other times, summaries help us decide whether we wish to explore more detailed information. Internet search engines, for instance, often feature summaries of recommended websites.

Often, we summarize the main points of a reading selection to help us remember what we feel is most important.

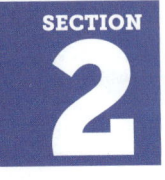

EXAMPLE Read the following section of text from "John Muir: America's Naturalist." Tessa used these paragraphs to write a summary.

> Muir left behind a legacy that still benefits Americans today. Although he was not responsible for the creation of the agency, he is often called the "Father" of the National Park Service. Because of his efforts, leaders of the country realized the importance of setting aside land as parks. Muir's writing led to the creation of a number of national parks. In addition to Yosemite, these include Sequoia, Grand Canyon, Glacier, and Rainier.
>
> The Sierra Club is another important aspect of Muir's legacy. This club is the oldest and largest "grassroots" environmental agency—one run by ordinary citizens. Today, the Sierra Club has more than one million members. The club sponsors adventures such as rock climbing and river rafting. Its purpose is more than just giving people exciting experiences with nature. It is also to make them aware of the beautiful and amazing places that exist. When people see these places, they are more likely to want to protect them.
>
> Today, Muir is also remembered by places that bear his name. Muir Glacier in Alaska and Muir Woods in California are two examples. Every year, millions of people visit these and other parks and preserves to get closer to nature. That is what John Muir would have wanted.

SECTION 2

Forms of Writing

Tessa's Notes

While looking for the main points of the passage, Tessa wrote down her ideas for her summary. Here are her notes.

> "John Muir: America's Naturalist" Notes
> 1. Muir called "Father" of the National Park Service.
> 2. Muir's work led to the creation of many national parks.
> 3. Sierra Club is another legacy of Muir's.
> 4. Places named after John Muir.

Here is Tessa's summary of the selection. Notice how she organized the summary based on the notes she made.

> John Muir, a preservationist, was passionate about the environment, and his work still benefits Americans today. Muir's writings led to the creation of many national parks, including Yosemite, Sequoia, Glacier, and Rainier. In fact, he is often called the "Father" of the National Park Service. Another important contribution by Muir was the formation of the Sierra Club. Today, the Sierra Club has over one million members and it is the oldest "grassroots" environmental agency. Millions of people every year visit places, such as Muir Glacier in Alaska and Muir Woods in California, which are named after Muir. John Muir's work has helped millions of people get closer to nature.

Reading Your Writing

A summary is a quick look at a longer piece of writing. It should tell your reader what the piece is about, without giving too much away. It should be brief and to the point. Be sure to use your own words.

Tips for Writing a Summary

STEP 1 Prewriting

- Read the material you are summarizing and figure out the main idea.
- Locate the supporting details.

STEP 2 Drafting

- Start with a sentence that states the main idea of the selection you are summarizing.
- Use your own words. Don't copy from the book.

STEP 3 Revising

- **Organization** Arrange your sentences logically so the reader can follow along with your summary.
- **Voice** Make the summary sound like *you* wrote it.
- **Organization** Have you left out any important details or added things that aren't necessary?
- **Sentence Fluency** Read your paper out loud to make sure the sentences flow together well.

STEP 4 Editing/Proofreading

- **Conventions** Proofread for spelling errors.
- **Conventions** Check for mistakes in punctuation and capitalization.

STEP 5 Publishing

Presentation Neatly type or write your paper if you are turning it in for an assignment.

SECTION 2
Forms of Writing

Research Reports

A **research report** is written to give in-depth information about a specific topic. Information should be obtained from many different sources.

Let's make our way through a research report, from beginning to end.

Targeting Your Subject

The first thing to do is to choose a topic. In many cases, your teacher may give you the overall subject and it will be up to you to choose the topic within that subject. Be sure to choose a topic that interests you, or you might find yourself becoming bored with your topic.

Imagine that your teacher has assigned the broad subject of *health* for your paper. Your task is to decide on a topic that relates to health. Start by brainstorming all the ideas you can think of related to health. You might want to make a web like this one to list your ideas.

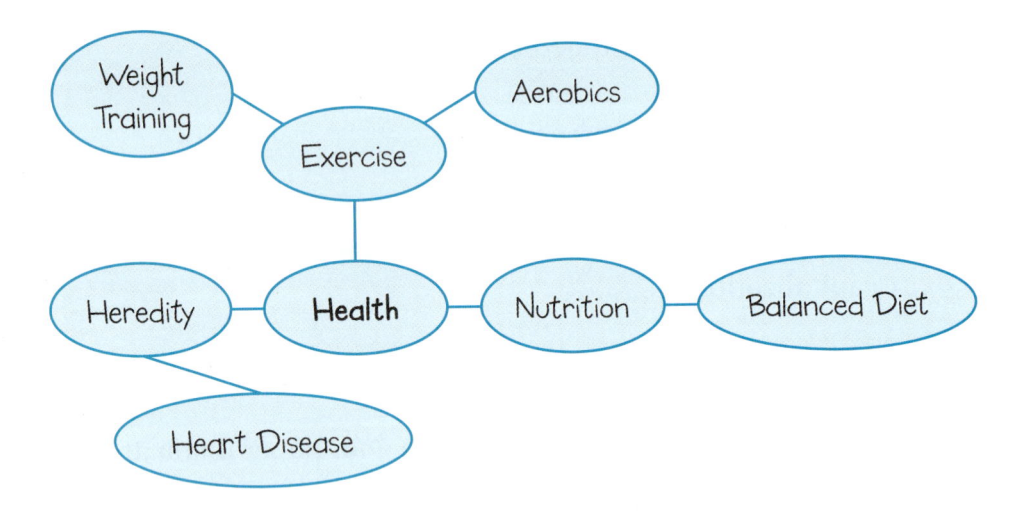

SECTION 2
Forms of Writing

Study your web for ideas for your report. As you look through the possible topics, *balanced diet* catches your eye. Your next task is to come up with some questions you think your report should answer.

Write the Questions

- What do our bodies need to keep going?
- What's in the different foods we eat?
- What different nutrients do our bodies need?
- What happens when our bodies don't get the right stuff?
- How can we balance the bad stuff with the good?

Find the Answers

Detailed answers to these questions may come from a variety of sources, including the following.

- books, magazines, encyclopedias, dictionaries, almanacs, atlases, videos, and newspapers
- personal interviews, museum visits, and brochures from businesses or organizations
- research findings from experiments you conduct at school or at home
- information from the Internet

Ask yourself these questions when choosing a research source:

- Can I trust this source to provide me with accurate and thorough information?
- Does this source provide enough information?
- Is this information up to date? Check the copyright to see when it was published. Get the most recent data available.

SECTION 2

Forms of Writing

Informative Writing · Research Reports

Finding Information Fast

Here are some tips for finding important information fast, without reading an encyclopedia entry or magazine article word for word.

Skimming Tips

- Search for words or phrases printed in CAPITALS, *italics*, or **bold** lettering.
- Search for clues in section headings.
- Read the article's introduction to decide whether it has information you need.
- Read the topic sentence of each paragraph to discover if the information applies to your targeted topic.
- Read the captions of photos, charts, graphs, and illustrations.

Key Words

As you take your notes, make a separate list of any key words that sound like they'll be important for the reader to know. If they are not included in your text's titles or section headings, these words are often *italicized*, **bolded**, or frequently repeated in the text. If your research doesn't already provide it, use a dictionary to find the definition of each key word.

Note Cards

Take notes on index cards to record information you think will be important to your report. Be sure to use your own words rather than copying straight from your source, unless you intend to include a direct quotation in your report. Don't write full sentences—only words and phrases. Use one card for each time you get an answer or part of an answer to one of your questions. Experiment with organizing them under headings and into an order that suits your plan and provides your report with a beginning, middle, and end section.

SECTION 2

Forms of Writing

Minerals

For bones – blood – to make body parts strong
Calcium – milk – cheese – yogurt – broccoli
Iron – red meat – whole grain breads – cereals – eggs – seafood – nuts

Informative Writing • Research Reports

The Final Plan

Finally, plan your report. Using a TIDE graphic organizer is a good way to put the information you have gathered in order. In the **T** box, write your **topic sentence** that tells what you are writing about. In the **ID** boxes, list three **important details** about the topic. In the **E** box, write a good **ending** that sums up the information about the topic.

T	**Topic Sentence** The food you eat affects your health.

ID	**Important Detail**
	 Body needs different kinds of food.
	   Protein—fish, chicken, turkey, nuts, eggs, meat, cheese, milk
	   Carbohydrates—pasta, noodles, potatoes
	   Fats—slow, steady energy but can cause heart problems because of cholesterol

ID	**Important Detail**
	 Vitamins and minerals are important to stay healthy.
	   Vitamins—fruits, vegetables, carbohydrates, protein, fats
	   Minerals—calcium from milk and cheese, iron from red meat, eggs, cereal

ID	**Important Detail**
	 Eat a balanced diet.
	   Eat balanced foods from each group
	   Stay away from too much sugar
	   Burgers and pizza: too much fat!

E	**Ending** Eating right is a balancing act, but worth it for your health.

EXAMPLE You can use the notes in your TIDE graphic organizer to write your report. Notice how the example below has a clear introduction, an organized body with details, facts, examples, explanations, and a reflective conclusion.

Eating the Right Thing—A Balancing Act

The food you eat affects your health. Eating nutritiously is a matter of balance and choices; the more you know about it, the better prepared you'll be to eat healthfully.

The body is a food-processing factory that needs different kinds of food to get all that you need. To start off, you can't live without protein from foods such as fish, chicken, turkey, nuts, eggs, meat, cheese, and milk. Your hair, muscles, bones, brain, and teeth are mostly made of protein.

Carbohydrates provide nearly all of your energy. They come from noodles, potatoes, bread, peas, beans, cereal, and fruit. These foods also provide fiber for a healthy heart and good digestion. Carbohydrates can also come from sugar, but sugar is not the best choice because it doesn't have any fiber or other nutrients. Your body will store leftover carbohydrates as fat. Some fats are good for you, providing a slow, steady source of energy. There's fat in all foods labeled as protein. There is also fat added to food, such as butter on toast and oil used to cook meat and vegetables.

Scientists have discovered that too much of the wrong kinds of fat can lead to heart problems. This happens when the wrong kinds of fats and a substance called cholesterol work to clog your arteries (one of the types of "roadways" in your body that circulate blood). For a healthy heart, choose fish or chicken (without skin) instead of hamburgers or steak. Limit butter, and if you drink whole milk, try switching to 1 percent fat or nonfat milk. You may not even taste the difference!

SECTION 2

Forms of Writing

To stay healthy, you need vitamins. Vitamins from fruits and vegetables help with basic body functions such as changing food into energy. Carbohydrates, protein, and fats also contribute to your daily dose of vitamins.

You need minerals, too. Minerals make your bones, blood, and other body parts strong. Most people need extra calcium and iron. Sources of calcium include milk, broccoli, cheese, and yogurt. Iron is found in red meat, seafood, nuts, eggs, and whole-grain breads and cereals.

A balanced diet means eating foods from each of these different groups to give your body all the different foods it needs to work well. Eating too many carbohydrates and fats or skipping your fruits and vegetables could overload your body's system. Then you might not feel well or have enough energy to get through the day. Eating right is a balancing act that will keep your body factory running smoothly.

Reading Your Writing

A research report is a paper that gives in-depth information about a topic. Use different sources such as nonfiction books, magazines, encyclopedias, and multimedia sources such as DVDs and the Internet to add variety to your research and provide your reader with the most up-to-date information.

Bibliography

A **bibliography** is a list of the research materials used and referred to in the preparation of an article or report. Placed at the end of your report, each entry identifies the name, author, title, publisher, date published, and sometimes the page numbers of the source. Each type of entry has a specific format that must be followed. Readers often want to know the source of the author's information or where they can read more about the subject. Here are some bibliography entries.

BOOK: Author (Last Name, First Name). <u>Title of book</u> (or italicized). City of publication: Publisher, Copyright date.

Important note: Follow the city of publication with the state abbreviation if the city is not a major city or could be confused with another city of the same name.

Kaplan, Francine. <u>The Kid's Guide to Nutrition</u>. Chicago: Snoopy Press, 2004.

MAGAZINE OR NEWSPAPER ARTICLE: Author (Last Name, First Name). "Title of Article." <u>Title of Newspaper/Magazine</u> (or italicized). Date of publication (month day, year): Page numbers of article.

Martin, Patricia A. "Eat to Live." <u>The Nutrition Guide</u>. February 26, 2007: 3–7.

ENCYCLOPEDIA ENTRY: Author (Last Name, First Name). "Title of entry." <u>Title of Encyclopedia</u> (or italicized). Edition or version.

Important note: If no author is given, begin with the title of the entry.

"Nutrition." <u>The Children's Encyclopedia of Health</u>. 2002 ed.

SECTION 2

Forms of Writing

Informative Writing • Research Reports

> **INTERNET:** "Title of page or post." <u>Title of Site</u> (or italicized). Year of post date or last update. Owner of site. Date accessed. (month day, year). <URL>.

> **INTERVIEW:** Person interviewed (Last Name, First Name). Type of interview. Date (month day, year)
>
> Clark, Sally. Personal Interview. October 20, 2008.

Pay close attention to the exact format and punctuation used in your bibliography. Ask your teacher about the required format for other types of sources, such as CD-ROMs, video clips, and musical recordings. As you do your research, list your source entries on a proposed bibliography sheet. Later, you can choose which ones need to be included on your final list. Avoid having to go back and find the information needed for the bibliography after you've already returned materials to the library.

Try It!

A URL is the electronic address of a website. When you record bibliographic information for a website, make sure you are recording the URL for the specific page you are using. If you are referencing many pages from a whole site, you may use the URL of the home page. Be sure to look at the URL closely and correctly record all punctuation, or else your reader will be unable to locate the page. Go to a government sponsored site, such as the NASA site, and practice recording URLs from various pages.

Tips for Research Reports

STEP 1 Prewriting

- Know your focus and intended audience.
- Use note cards to plan your report. Use an outline or a graphic organizer.

STEP 2 Drafting

- Each paragraph should have a topic sentence followed by sentences that contain important supporting details.
- Give your report an introduction, body, and conclusion.

STEP 3 Revising

- **Ideas** Make sure your main ideas and subtopics are clear to the reader by using strong topic sentences and plenty of supporting details, facts, examples, and explanations.
- **Organization** Tie the end of one paragraph to the beginning of the next.
- **Organization** Give your readers an ending that will make them think!

STEP 4 Editing/Proofreading

- **Conventions** Make sure you've spelled the names of people and places correctly.
- **Conventions** Double-check all facts used.
- **Conventions** Make sure your bibliography is accurate.

STEP 5 Publishing

- **Presentation** Consider including illustrations or other visuals in your report.

SECTION 2 Forms of Writing

Problem-and-Solution Essay

A **problem-and-solution essay** explains a problem and presents ways to solve the problem. A good problem and solution essay first carefully describes the problem so readers understand why it is a problem. Then it clearly explains how one or more solutions could solve the problem.

Why Write a Problem-and-Solution Essay?

Many people write problem-and-solution essays every day. Reporters might write articles describing a problem in their community and ways they can solve it. A person working in an office might write an essay for his or her supervisor presenting various ways to solve a problem the company is experiencing. Government workers might write problem-and-solution essays when they want to pass a new law. Scientists and medical professionals also write problem-and-solution essays. For example, a doctor might write an essay about a disease and list several ways to treat that disease.

A good problem-and-solution essay requires logic, imagination, and creative thinking. Some problems cannot be solved easily. A problem might need to be looked at from many different perspectives before a solution can be found.

Try It!

Can you think of a problem that you could write a problem-and-solution essay about? Is it a problem at your school or in your neighborhood or your community, or is it an even larger problem? What solutions would you suggest?

Organizing a Problem-and-Solution Essay

Introduction

The **introduction** begins the essay. The introduction is usually short and uses an attention-grabbing lead like a question or description to draw in the reader. It also briefly describes or provides background about the problem and introduces the possible solutions. In addition, the introduction might have a final sentence that states what the writer is going to suggest or which solution he or she supports.

Body

The **body** is the main part of the essay where details, facts, examples, and explanations are presented. First, the writer specifically describes the cause(s) of the **problem.** Facts and figures to explain the problem should be given (for example, "75% of American children do not get enough exercise").

Solutions

Then the writer presents the **solutions** to the problem. The writer may list the solutions from most important to least important, in chronological order, or by type. Writers should also use facts such as statistics and survey results, examples from experience, and expert opinions to support their solutions. Some problem-and-solution essays also look ahead to possible pitfalls of a solution or address opposing sides.

Conclusion

The **conclusion** is the end of the essay. The conclusion of a problem-and-solution essay should end on a strong note. It may summarize the points already made, reflect on how the problem relates to the individual, society, or the world, offer a new and unique perspective on the issue, or ask for the reader's support. Some essays might end with a quote or statement for the reader to consider.

SECTION 2

Forms of Writing

Informative Writing • Problem-and-Solution Essay

Problem-and-Solution Essay Model

Here is a problem-and-solution essay that Markus wrote. Identify the problem and each solution that Markus suggests.

Leave a Message

Last week, Maria Robbins was driving to work. Suddenly, her cell phone rang. Maria was not expecting a phone call, but she decided to answer her phone anyway. She took her eyes off the road to see who was calling. At the same time, another car pulled out in front of her. Maria was too distracted with her cell phone to notice. A few seconds later... crash! Maria was now using her cell phone to call a tow truck.

Cell phones are a part of our everyday lives. Unfortunately, as more people buy cell phones, more people use them while driving. This problem has to stop, and if we do not stop it now, more drivers will get hurt. To solve this problem, we need to require drivers to use hands-free cell phones, create designated stopping points for phone calls, or ban cell phone use on the road.

Driving and using a cell phone is a dangerous combination. To use a cell phone, you need to take your eyes off the road to dial a phone number or answer a call. It is easy to become distracted and lose your concentration. Last year alone there were more than 750 accidents citywide involving people who were talking on their cell phones while driving. Surveys show that with the new trend of text messaging, more drivers than ever are taking their attention off the road and likely causing increased traffic problems and accidents.

One solution to this problem would be to force drivers to use hands-free cell phones, headsets, or speaker phones that leave the driver's hands free on the road. Unfortunately, this solution is not fail-safe. Only a portion of accidents occur because the driver does not have his or her hands free to control a car. The majority of accidents occur because of lack of concentration. Even with a hand-free cell phone, the driver is still distracted by the conversation.

Another solution would be to have designated stopping points along the road for people who need to make and receive phone calls. Many people claim that they need to use a cell phone while driving because of their job. For example, some public utility workers have to be on the road throughout the day, call ahead before appointments, and respond to calls from an office or from customers. Stopping points would benefit these workers. In addition, people with minor emergencies or needs such as calling their destinations to ask for driving directions could also benefit. Creating designated stopping points would allow drivers to safely make necessary phone calls while keeping other motorists safe.

Cell phone advocates claim people need to use their cell phones while driving in emergencies. However, studies actually show that many people stop their cars when reporting an injury or an accident anyway. Furthermore, these calls do not need to be made while the car is in motion; it is just as easy, and safer, to pull over.

A final solution would be to ban cell phone use while driving altogether. Many states have already passed a similar law that extends even to hands-free phones. To many people, this solution may seem extreme. However, this solution is the only one that guarantees driver safety.

Using a cell phone while driving is simply dangerous. I know that stopping cell phone use on the roads will not prevent all car accidents. However, by making some important changes—requiring drivers to use hands-free cell phones, creating designated stopping points on the road, or banning cell phone use while driving—we can make a difference. We must do whatever we can to help protect our families and friends on the road.

Analyzing the Model

Introduction

The introduction of "Leave a Message" is two paragraphs. Markus grabs the reader's attention by using a lead that vividly describes a dramatic scene—a car accident caused by someone using a cell phone. He states the problem in the following paragraph, gives background, and presents the solutions he will examine so the reader knows his purpose.

Body

- In the first body paragraph, Markus analyzes the problem in more depth and provides details in the form of statistics and survey results to support his view of the problem—that driving while using a cell phone is dangerous.
- In the rest of the body, Markus uses one paragraph to describe each solution he is proposing. He explains his solutions simply so the reader can understand them. He uses clear topic sentences to signal each new idea and supports them with logically ordered supporting details.
- Notice that in the first body paragraph, Markus admits that hands-free cell phones may not really fix the problem. He also uses the third body paragraph not to describe a new solution, but to present an opposing argument to the solution he suggested in the previous paragraph.
- Markus saves his most extreme solution for the last body paragraph, leaving the reader with a strong impression of how serious the issue is.

Conclusion

The conclusion of the essay ends on a powerful note. Markus restates the problem, summarizes the solutions he suggested, and reflects on the problem in an emotional appeal.

Problem-and-Solution Essay Tips

STEP 1 Prewriting

- List some current issues that deal with your personal life, school, community, or the larger world.
- Choose a subject that you feel strongly about and decide exactly what your viewpoint is.
- Decide your audience and purpose.
- Use a graphic organizer or outline to help you decide how to organize your arguments or supporting points.

STEP 2 Drafting

- Grab the reader's attention in your introduction. State your subject and your opinion clearly.
- Use facts, examples, and explanations like statistics and expert opinions to support your main ideas.
- End on a strong note. Summarize your ideas, and give the reader something to consider.

STEP 3 Revising

- **Ideas** Are your message and purpose for writing clear?
- **Ideas** Are your facts accurate and your supporting details convincing?
- **Voice** Does it sound like you care about your subject?

STEP 4 Editing/Proofreading

- **Conventions** Double-check the spelling of proper nouns, and make sure your grammar, capitalization, and punctuation are correct.

STEP 5 Publishing

- **Presentation** Consider preparing handouts or a digital projection that outlines the main points of your report.

SECTION 2
Forms of Writing

Responding to Literature: Character Analysis

Robin Hood. Alice in Wonderland. Peter Pan. All of these characters have captured readers' imaginations for years. But what do these characters have in common? They are well-rounded and developed characters.

A **character** is an individual in a story, poem, or play. Characters can drive the action in a story or try to keep the hero from reaching his or her goal. Some characters are heroic and strong, while others need to use their wits to defeat the villain. Characters also come in all shapes and sizes. Some characters, like Frodo Baggins in J.R.R. Tolkien's *Lord of the Rings* trilogy, are small. Other characters, like the giant in *Jack and the Beanstalk*, tower over everyone else.

However, no matter their size or appearance, characters almost always have human personality traits, whether they are animals, robots, or vegetables. Authors give nonhuman characters human traits to help their readers relate to them.

> **Responding to literature** can mean expressing your personal opinions, thoughts, or feelings about a story. But when you respond to literature by *analyzing*, you must do more than that. To *analyze* something means to look closely at its parts or elements and figure out what they mean. When you analyze a story, you must support your ideas and opinions about it with evidence and examples from the text. Some aspects of a story you might analyze are: character, setting, plot, theme, and literary devices.

SECTION 2
Forms of Writing

There are many types of characters to explore, many aspects of an individual character to examine, and many ways to gather support for your ideas about a character. When planning and writing your character analysis, it will help you to know some basic terms, tools, and elements of characterization.

Types of Characters

Although all fictional characters have human traits that the reader can understand, they do not have the same role or importance in a story. Some characters are main characters, but others appear only a few times. Some characters are appealing to the reader, while others are meant to be unlikeable. And while some characters are dull and unchanging, others go through many struggles and changes over the course of a story.

The following are some classifications of characters that will help you with your analysis:

- **protagonist:** the main character; the character who sets the plot in motion
- **antagonist:** usually the villain; the character who blocks the protagonist
- **subordinate character:** a secondary character who is not the main actor in the plot
- **dynamic character:** a character who changes during the course of a story
- **static character:** a character who does not change much during the course of a story

Try It!

Think of one of your favorite characters in a book, movie, or play. Is that character a protagonist or an antagonist? Is he or she a dynamic or a static character?

Ways to Analyze a Character

There are many ways to analyze a character. Some aspects of a character you can focus on are:

- ▶ character traits (King Arthur was a courageous man with a generous heart.)
- ▶ physical traits (Molly was an energetic girl with long pigtails and freckles.)
- ▶ motivation (Josie longed to see her grandma's homeland and relatives in Africa.)
- ▶ changes they undergo (Piki is a dynamic character because the competition makes him finally realize his worth.)

Traits are the qualities a character has. Because they are easy to pick out, looking at traits is a common approach to character analysis. Keep in mind that character, or personality, traits usually reveal more than physical traits.

Motivation is the reason a character acts, thinks, or feels a certain way. For example, why does the hero leave his home in search of the enchanted sword? Knowing a character's motivation helps the audience understand the character.

Sometimes, the mismatched motivations of two characters or a character's own confusion about motivation lead to the **conflict** in a story. Another way to analyze characters is to look at how they deal with their conflicts. This will also help you understand how they change.

Sometimes, the conflict is connected to the **theme,** or overall message, of a story. In a character analysis, you might also explain how a character and his or her actions represent a theme.

Try It!

Think about your favorite character from a story, book, or movie. What are some of the character's traits? What is the character's motivation? How does the character deal with conflict?

How to Gather Ideas about a Character

You can analyze the aspects of a character by looking at the author's techniques of characterization. **Characterization** is a way to show what characters are like by telling what they do, say, think, and feel. Some techniques of characterization include:

- direct description (Lancelot was a tall, handsome knight with a magnetic charm.)
- dialogue ("I'm not going!" Lukas screamed, stamping his foot. "I'm not, I'm not!")
- inner dialogue (*I don't want anyone to know how scared I really am,* Jose thought.)
- what other characters say or think ("Vidas is a hard worker," Sharon told Sue.)
- the character's actions (Renaldo took the injured stray dog to the veterinarian.)

What do the above techniques tell you about a character? Dialogue tells you what a character thinks and feels and how he or she relates to other characters. A character's way of speaking can also give you clues about his or her personality. For example, it reveals whether he or she is shy or outgoing, or proper or laid back. Inner dialogue directly tells you what a character thinks and feels. A character's actions show traits, interests, and desires, while what other characters say provides outside opinions.

Try It!

Read the following sentences. What techniques does the author use to describe Garrett?

> Garrett stood out from the rest of his teammates because he was tall and lanky. He was also shy around strangers. That's why many people called him "the gentle giant."

SECTION 2

Forms of Writing

Informative Writing • Responding to Literature: Character Analysis

Planning a Character Analysis

A good way to gather ideas for your character analysis is to take notes about a character on a learning log, note sheet, or character web as you read a story. You might focus on the character's traits, actions, feelings, motivations, conflicts, relationships, changes, or any other aspect.

The following details are from Kyle's note sheet for Danny Flores, a character in "Just 17 Syllables!"

EXAMPLE

Danny Flores from "Just 17 Syllables!"

Actions: pays attention to cell phone; almost cries at the smell of the autumn air; sits in back row on the bleachers; shows respect by bowing to Professor Nakano and turning off cell phone when his teacher notices; carefully checks his work before turning it in

Thoughts: thinks about going back to Ohio; realizes poetry can be interesting; wonders if he can write haiku; enjoys the haiku

Feelings: sad, misses his friends from Ohio; disinterested in poetry; nervous about writing a poem; feels proud of his poem

Details: first school year in Japan; new to International School in Tokyo; likes hockey; warm pumpkin bread; corn mazes; from Ohio

Character Analysis Model

EXAMPLE Here is Kyle's character analysis of Danny Flores in "Just 17 Syllables!" How are the details from the note sheet included?

Learning to Adjust: Danny Flores in "Just 17 Syllables!"

The main character in "Just 17 Syllables!" is Danny Flores. Danny Flores is from Ohio, likes hockey, warm pumpkin bread, and corn mazes, and now lives in Tokyo, Japan. The story begins with Danny and his classmates from the Andrews International School on a trip to the Rikugien Gardens in Tokyo.

At the beginning of the story, Danny is sad, misses his friends from Ohio, and is disinterested in what the class is doing at the Gardens. While in the Gardens, Danny does not pay attention to the teacher, but instead, is interested in his cell phone and thinks about all of the things he left behind in Ohio. Danny almost cries just thinking about the hockey rink and his friends from Ohio. As the class sits down on benches in the center of the Gardens, Danny sits down in the back row and continues to check his cell phone.

Although Danny is sad, he shows respect when he bows to Professor Nakano and when he turns off his cell phone after his teacher glances at him. After Danny puts his cell phone away, he begins to pay attention to the professor's presentation on haiku, and even becomes interested in some of the facts he is learning about haiku and Basho.

As Danny and his classmates are writing their own haikus, Danny is nervous and unsure if he can write one. However, Danny thinks of himself as a samurai haiku writer, and becomes inspired and starts typing. Danny is proud of his haiku and enjoys when the professor reads his poem aloud. At the end of the story, Danny ends up enjoying his day at the Gardens.

Danny is a likeable and interesting character. He is a typical boy who is afraid of change and is unsure of his new home. However, as Danny begins to learn more about his new home, he starts to accept the changes and even begins to like it.

SECTION 2

Forms of Writing

Analyzing the Model

Title

The title tells the audience simply and creatively which character will be analyzed in the essay.

Introduction

The introduction is simple and concise. It opens by telling who the main character is. It also gives background information on the character, and tells how the story begins.

Body

Each of the three body paragraphs describes how Danny's character traits progresses throughout the story. The paragraphs have clear topic sentences so the reader will know what the paragraph is about. They also have several supporting details in the form of evidence from the story. The evidence includes references to Danny's actions, thoughts, and feelings.

Conclusion

The conclusion states the writer's view of the character and summarizes the main ideas discussed in the essay.

Try It!

Look at "Just 17 Syllables!" in your **Student Anthology**. What are some quotes or other evidence from the story you might have included in the model essay? What main points would they support?

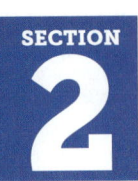

Tips for Writing a Character Analysis

STEP 1 Prewriting

- Record details about different aspects of your character on a chart or note sheet. Include descriptions, quotes, actions, and so on.
- Decide which aspects or traits of the character you will analyze. Find some details or quotes that you could use for support.

STEP 2 Drafting

- In the introduction, name the story, author, and character you are analyzing. State your interpretation of the character and the main ideas you are going to look at.
- Use your plans to draft the body. Use vivid descriptions to bring your character to life.

STEP 3 Revising

- **Organization** Does each paragraph present one main idea or trait of the character? Do your paragraphs have clear topic sentences? Did you stay on topic?
- **Ideas** Do you use enough examples from the story to support your points?
- **Sentence Fluency** Have you varied your sentence lengths and beginnings?

STEP 4 Editing/Proofreading

- **Conventions** Did you capitalize and correctly spell all proper nouns, like place and character names?

STEP 5 Publishing

- **Presentation** Consider illustrating your character analysis with a depiction of your character in a scene.

SECTION 2

Forms of Writing

Informative Writing • Responding to Literature: Character Analysis

Responding to Literature: Setting Analysis

Are there trees or buildings where you live? Is there a community spirit? What was your neighborhood like a hundred years ago? What will it be like a hundred years from now? These questions relate to **setting**, which is when and where a story takes place. Setting includes the background and environment of the characters. It also includes the values and beliefs of the characters that live in it.

The setting may change many times during a story, or it may stay the same. It can be very general, like Boston in the 1770s, or very specific, such as a certain town square in Boston on July 4, 1776. A setting may be an exotic place born from the imagination, like a Martian colony, or a familiar place as common as an American small town.

When you respond to literature by analyzing setting, you study how the author uses it to affect the reader or create meaning. You look closely at the role of setting in the story. For example, the setting might be used to create mood, to create conflict, or to reveal character.

Setting and Mood

Mood is the feeling a story creates in the reader. Authors purposefully describe their settings with images, sensory details, and word choices that will create a specific mood. For example, an author might describe a basement as "dark and musty" but a festival as "bright and lively."

> ### Try It!
>
> Read this paragraph. How does the description of setting create mood?
>
> Amanda held the flickering candle as she crawled into the heart of the ancient tomb. Long, sinewy cobwebs brushed her face, and she heard rats skittering over the dusty stones. Suddenly, the door slammed behind her. An icy wind blew out her candle, plunging the temple into darkness.

Setting and Conflict

Authors also use setting to establish **conflict** in a story. Conflict is the main problem the characters face. In an external conflict, a character struggles against an outside force. This force is sometimes the environment the character is in. Man-versus-nature stories are examples of how the setting creates the conflict.

> ### Try It!
>
> Read this paragraph. How does the setting provide the conflict?
>
> Braddock pulled the last of the supplies from the smoldering wreckage of the airplane. Strange sounds came from the jungle around him, sounds never before heard by humankind. Braddock studied the map. He guessed it was a fifty-mile walk to the nearest village. Suddenly, a rumble shook the ground. Braddock turned and gaped at the spewing volcano in the distance. It looked ready to erupt any second. He had better hurry.

Setting and Character

Setting often affects how the characters in a story think and act. Sometimes, authors use the setting to show the background that a character comes from. Other times, authors use the setting to reveal how a character reacts in a certain situation.

> ### Try It!
>
> Read the following paragraph. What does the setting reveal about the character?
>
> Renaldo walked into his bedroom and tossed his jacket into the corner. Piles of dirty laundry covered the floor. Dirty plates and never-opened school books littered his desk and nightstand. Renaldo jumped into bed and fell asleep.

SECTION 2
Forms of Writing

Informative Writing • Responding to Literature: Setting Analysis

Planning a Setting Analysis

A good first step to understanding a story's setting is to make a setting chart. Look at Clara's setting chart for "A Year on the Bowie Farm."

EXAMPLE Setting of "A Year on the Bowie Farm"

Winter	Spring	Summer	Fall
snowy	harvest alfalfa	hot	produce stand
gather eggs	ducks and ducklings	pick vegetables	herd cows
prune orchard	thick grass	herd cows	corn harvest
paperwork	plant seedlings	swim for fun	planting alfalfa
	pluck weeds		pumpkin patch

Setting Analysis Model

EXAMPLE Clara used her chart to write her setting analysis.

The Importance of Setting in "A Year on the Bowie Farm"

"A Year on the Bowie Farm" takes place on a farm. The farm and the farm activities are described for each season of the year. *Where* this story takes place—a farm, remains constant throughout the story. *When* this story takes place—each of the four seasons, changes throughout the story. The story shows how each of the four seasons affects the daily routines of the farm.

The story begins in the winter when it is cold and snowy. The farm is quiet, but there are still a few chores to be done, such as gathering eggs, cleaning the poultry coops, and training a new puppy.

As winter becomes spring, the activity on the farm picks up. Many more chores are needed as the farm begins to spring to life. Some of the chores include harvesting the alfalfa, taking care of the ducks, planting seedlings, and plucking weeds.

As the summer heat beats down on the farm, the vegetables and fruits are ripening and are ready to be picked. The family spends days picking and canning the produce. The summer routine on the farm is fairly mundane—milking the cows, herding the cows to the pasture, and milking the cows again,. To break the monotony of the summer days, the kids go fishing or swimming in the creek or chase rabbits and chipmunks out of the garden.

As the autumn days become cooler, the routine on the farm does not slow down. Fruit drops from the trees and the kids open up a produce stand. Just as in the spring and summer, the cows are milked and herded to the pasture. As October comes, corn is harvested, alfalfa is planted, and pumpkins are picked and sold. Autumn leads to winter and the cycle begins again.

The farm routines described in each season help the reader clearly understand the daily life on the farm and the impact each season has on the farm and the activities. How do the seasons affect your daily activities?

SECTION 2

Forms of Writing

Informative Writing • Responding to Literature: Setting Analysis

Analyzing the Model

Organization

- The introduction provides background information on the setting and states directly what the writer is analyzing—how the seasons affect the daily life on the farm.
- The body is organized based upon the four seasons and describes the farm routines in each of the seasons. Each paragraph has a clear topic sentence that tells what seasons the paragraph will be about.
- The conclusion restates the essay's main point, and provides a concluding sentence that draws the reader into the text.

Ideas

- The purpose, or main idea, of this essay is to show how the setting (the four seasons) affects the characters' actions.
- The writer chose several interesting details from the story that support the main points.
- The writer's analysis is fresh and original—it shows what she thinks about the setting. For example, she shows how the time of the story affects the characters' actions.

Voice and Word Choice

- The writer not only picks interesting details from the story, but also uses her own descriptive language to liven up her essay—"Many more chores are needed as the farm begins to spring to life." and "As the summer heat beats down on the farm, the vegetables and fruits are ripening and are ready to be picked."
- The writer ends with a question to get the reader involved in the text.

Tips for Writing a Setting Analysis

STEP 1 Prewriting

- Record details about the time, place, and ideas and values on a setting chart.
- Decide how you want to organize your analysis. What will each body paragraph be about?

STEP 2 Drafting

- In the introduction, name the story and author and give background. Include a direct statement of what your essay will say about the setting.
- Use your plans to draft the body. Include quotes and vivid descriptions of the story's setting.

STEP 3 Revising

- **Organization** Does each paragraph present one main idea? Do your paragraphs have clear topic sentences? Did you stay on topic?
- **Ideas** Are your ideas fresh and original? Do you use enough details from the story to support them?
- **Voice** Do you use an interesting lead and thoughtful concluding statement?

STEP 4 Editing/Proofreading

- **Conventions** Did you capitalize and correctly spell all proper nouns, like place names? Did you correctly indent paragraphs?

STEP 5 Publishing

- **Presentation** Consider illustrating your setting analysis with a depiction of the story's setting.

SECTION 2
Forms of Writing

Informative Writing • Responding to Literature: Setting Analysis

Responding to Literature: Plot Analysis

Plot refers to what happens in a narrative, or the key events that take place from the beginning of the story to the end. All narratives, whether they are short stories, books, or episodes of your favorite television show, have a plot. For example, in every episode of *Star Trek*, the crew of the starship deals with a problem. It could be aliens on the attack, aliens in trouble, or a conflict between crew members. The captain and crew members solve the problem before flying off into space for next week's episode.

In a mystery, the hero must solve a crime or riddle. He or she must work out the problem before the villain gets away. In the end, the crime is solved in a dramatic fashion. The villain goes to jail, and the hero lives to solve another crime.

In a legend, the hero might go on a quest to solve a problem. Along the way, the hero faces many dangers, such as horrible monsters or life-threatening traps. In the end, the hero completes his or her quest, and everyone lives happily ever after.

> **Responding to literature** can mean expressing your personal opinions, thoughts, or feelings about a story. But when you respond to literature by *analyzing*, you must do more than that. To *analyze* something means to look closely at its parts or elements and figure out what they mean. When you analyze a story, you must support your ideas and opinions about it with evidence and examples from the text. Some aspects of a story you might analyze are character, setting, plot, theme, and literary devices.

Plot Structure

The plot in a story usually has the same parts.

Beginning

In the beginning, or **exposition**, of a story, the setting is established and the main characters are introduced.

Conflict

The **conflict**, or main problem the characters face, can be an external struggle between two characters or forces or an internal struggle inside one character's mind. Some common conflicts involve a character struggling against another character, against himself or herself, against society, against nature, or against a supernatural force.

Rising Action

Rising action refers to the key events in the middle of the story. The action builds as characters deal with the conflict, and this creates tension and suspense.

Climax

The **climax** is the turning point and the most exciting part in the story, when the action reaches its highest point and the conflict is about to be resolved.

Falling Action

Falling action refers to the events that occur as the plot winds down after the climax.

Resolution

The **resolution**, or ending, tells how the problem is solved. The crew members have saved their starship, the mystery is solved, the villain is put behind bars, or the hero has defeated the monster and won the day!

Planning a Plot Analysis

One way to plan a plot analysis is to complete a plotline diagram. You can record the key events of the entire plot, including conflict, rising action, climax, and resolution.

EXAMPLE Here is a plotline diagram from "Alejandro's Gift" by Richard E. Albert. Notice how the diagram includes major events but excludes minor details.

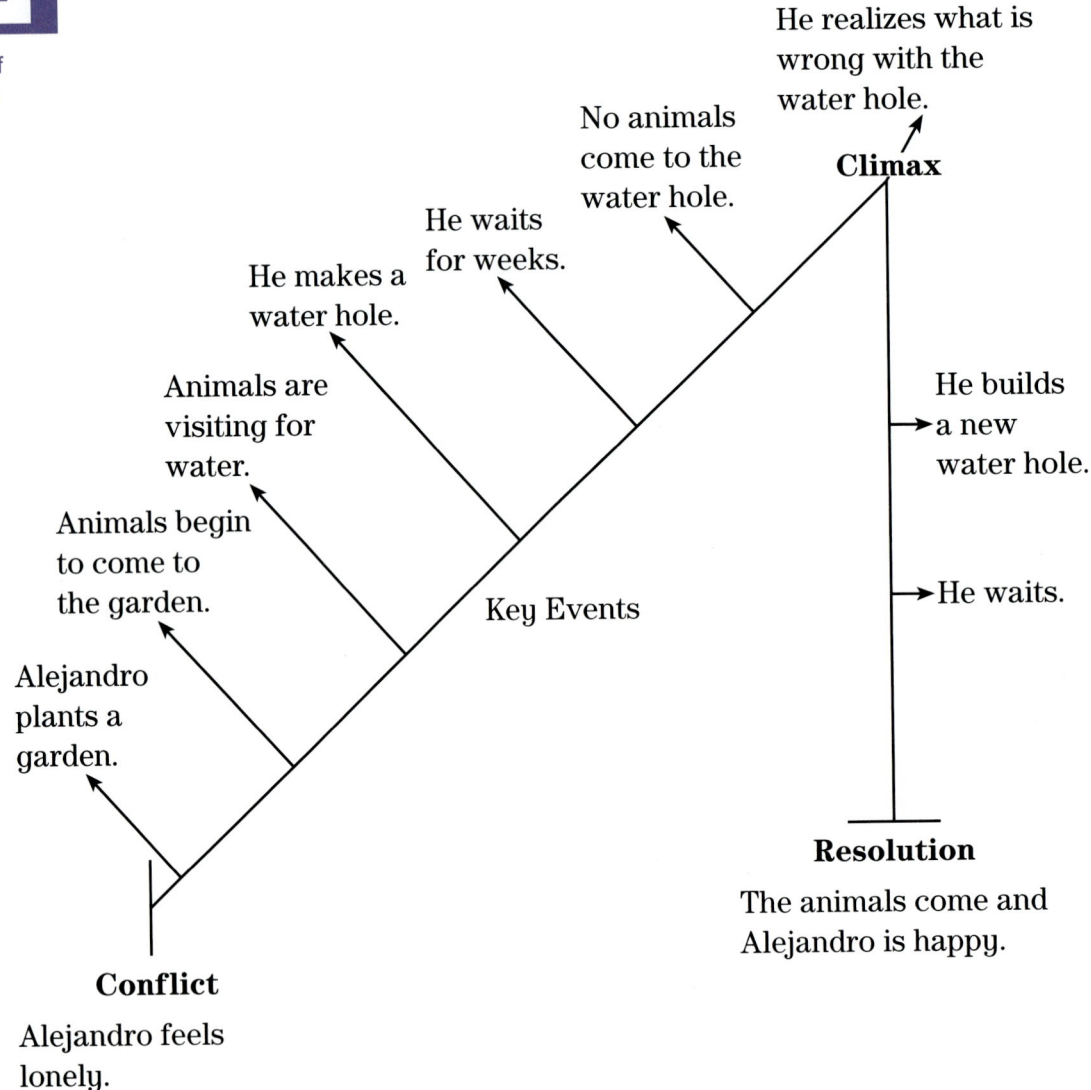

Climax
- He realizes what is wrong with the water hole.

Key Events (Rising Action)
- No animals come to the water hole.
- He waits for weeks.
- He makes a water hole.
- Animals are visiting for water.
- Animals begin to come to the garden.
- Alejandro plants a garden.

Falling Action
- He builds a new water hole.
- He waits.

Conflict
Alejandro feels lonely.

Resolution
The animals come and Alejandro is happy.

124 **Informative Writing** • Responding to Literature: Plot Analysis

Plot Analysis Model

> **EXAMPLE**
>
> "Alejandro's Gift" by Richard E. Albert takes place at Alejandro's small adobe house in the desert. Alejandro is alone in the desert and has only his burro for companionship.
>
> The conflict is apparent right from the start—Alejandro is lonely. His house stands beside a lonely desert road and very few visitors stop by. This conflict sets the events in motion. To pass the time, Alejandro plants a garden filled with delicious vegetables—carrots, beans, onions, tomatoes, corn, squash, red peppers. One day a ground squirrel approaches his garden and drinks some water. More animals begin to visit the garden and Alejandro begins to think of the animals as friends.
>
> In the middle of the story, Alejandro finds that time is passing more quickly because of the animals that come to his garden. Alejandro soon realizes that the animals are coming to his garden for water, and he decides to dig a water hole for the animals. Alejandro spends many days in the hot desert sun digging the water hole, and is pleased when he finishes the hole for his desert friends. Alejandro is patient and waits for days, but no animals come to his water hole. He wonders what he did wrong.
>
> Suddenly the climax occurs: Alejandro realizes that he dug the water hole too close to his house. Right away, he digs a new water hole that is far from his house and screened by heavy desert growth. Alejandro doesn't have to wait long before the animals discover his water hole.
>
> Finally, Alejandro's problem is solved. Although he cannot see the animals, Alejandro can hear the sounds of the animals as they visit the water hole. Alejandro is no longer lonely as he sits and listens to the sounds of his desert friends.

SECTION 2

Forms of Writing

Analyzing the Model

Introduction

The introduction tells the reader what story will be analyzed and who its author is. It also describes the setting, names the main characters, and gives a brief summary of what the story is about. This will help the readers understand the plot analysis (remember that your reader may not have read the story).

Body

The body analyzes the events of the plot. It is important to do more than summarize or retell the story in a plot analysis. In the model, the conflict, rising action, climax, and resolution are clearly pointed out. The strong topic sentences highlight the part or aspect of the plot that the writer is analyzing. For example, in the fourth paragraph, the writer describes the climax and how the character responds. The supporting sentences include examples of events in the story that support the writer's points.

Conclusion

The final paragraph concludes the analysis by telling the reader how the conflict of the story is resolved.

Try It!

A well-written plot analysis explains the conflict, the way action rises or builds tension, the climax, and the resolution of a story. Where are these explained in the model?

SECTION 2
Forms of Writing

STEP 1 Prewriting

- Record the conflict, climax, resolution, and key events of your story on a plotline diagram.
- Find some events, details, or quotes in the story that you could use to support your points.

STEP 2 Drafting

- Draft an introduction that gives your readers background on the story.
- Use your plotline diagram to draft the body. Analyze the full plot structure.
- Leave your reader with an interesting reflection. Perhaps you can connect the story's plot to characterization, theme, or to your readers' own lives.

STEP 3 Revising

- **Organization** Do you analyze the plot in chronological order? Are any of the events you mention out of place?
- **Organization** Do you have clear topic sentences that tell what each paragraph analyzes?
- **Ideas** Do you use enough examples from the story to make the plot, and your points, clear?

STEP 4 Editing/Proofreading

- **Conventions** Did you capitalize and correctly spell all proper nouns, like place and character names?

STEP 5 Publishing

- **Presentation** Consider illustrating your plot analysis with an exciting scene from the story.

SECTION 2

Forms of Writing

Informative Writing • Responding to Literature: Plot Analysis

Responding to Literature: Literary Criticism

Do you like to talk about stories with your friends? **Literary criticism** is the study and interpretation of literature. It asks the question "What is this story about?" However, it is more than just a book review or statement of your personal opinion. In literary criticism, the reader tries to examine and understand the deeper meanings in a story.

Do you sometimes disagree with your friends and classmates about what a story means? Most stories do not have one "correct" meaning. In reality, there might be several meanings or interpretations of one story. To discover those meanings, the reader has to analyze the story. This means that he or she will look closely at how the author uses certain passages of text or specific words and phrases to affect the reader and create meaning.

When you write a literary criticism, you might

- analyze how the author's use of one or more **literary devices** relates to the meaning of the story.
- analyze how a story reflects a certain **issue, topic,** or **question**.

Try It!

Sometimes, a writer might have to research the culture or era when a story was written to gain a better understanding of some issues or questions about the story. What are some sources you could use to research different cultures or eras? Make a list of the sources to keep on hand for future research.

> **Responding to literature** can mean expressing your personal opinions, thoughts, or feelings about a story. But when you respond to literature by *analyzing*, you must do more than that. To *analyze* something means to look closely at its parts or elements and figure out what they mean. When you analyze a story, you must support your ideas and opinions about it with evidence and examples from the text. Some aspects of a story you might analyze are character, setting, plot, theme, and literary devices.

SECTION 2

Forms of Writing

Response, Analysis, and Literary Criticism

There are many elements of literature that you can study for a literary criticism. Some of the major narrative elements you can analyze include character, setting, and plot. But keep in mind that not all responses to literature or analyses of such elements are literary criticism. In literary criticism, you *absolutely must* show how what you are analyzing connects to the story's deeper meaning. For example, a character analysis that simply describes the major traits of a character is not a literary criticism. Instead, you would have to explain how the character traits relate to the meaning of the story. For more information on character, setting, and plot analysis, turn to pages 108–127.

Literary criticism can also look at other elements of literature. Sometimes, writers look at patterns and symbols that occur in many different texts throughout history and across cultures. Other times, they look at how authors use certain techniques, like illustrations in a picture book or figurative language, to influence the reader's perspective of a story.

Informative Writing • Responding to Literature: Literary Criticism

Analyzing Other Literary Devices

Figurative Language

Analyzing how **figurative language** is used to affect the reader or create meaning is a common approach to literary criticism. **Figurative language** is imaginative words or groups of words with an intended meaning that is different from the actual meaning. Some common types are simile, metaphor, personification, and hyperbole.

- A *simile* compares two things that are not alike by using the word *like* or *as*.
- A *metaphor* compares two unlike things without using the word *like* or *as*.
- *Personification* is a figure of speech in which an object or idea is given human qualities.
- *Hyperbole* is a type of extreme exaggeration used for humor or emphasis. Often the quality of one thing is compared to a more extreme quality in another.

Try It!

Decide whether each sentence is a simile, a metaphor, personification, or hyperbole.

- The old tree is like a wise grandmother.
- The wind beat its gusty fits on my door.
- My stack of homework is bigger than a horse.
- The playground bully was a tornado of terror.

SECTION 2
Forms of Writing

Imagery

Analyzing how imagery affects the reader and connects to deeper meaning is also very common. Put simply, **imagery** is "word pictures." It is the vivid descriptive language and concrete sensory details an author uses to make a story or poem come alive for the reader. Imagery can refer to any of the five senses.

Try It!

Read the following sentences. How do the sentences affect your sense of sight, smell, taste, and touch?

> My sore feet sank into the soft, hot desert sand. Harsh rays of golden sunlight attacked my sweating skin and blinded me. My throat was dry, sore, and longed for water. All was silent as a strange burning smell overcame me.

Symbolism

Studying the connection between symbolism and meaning is also a popular type of literary criticism. **Symbolism** is a technique in which an author uses objects or images to represent ideas. A **symbol** can be a person, place, or thing, but it must represent something beyond itself. You can draw a picture of a symbol, but you probably will not be able to draw a picture of what it means.

Thinking about common symbols that you see in daily life might help you understand symbolism. For example, a skull and crossbones is a symbol that something is poisonous. You might see it on product labels. Most people know what it means—the image immediately represents a certain idea to them. You could draw a picture of this symbol, but it would be hard to draw a picture of the concept of "poisonous." Other common symbols people know are the smiley face, the recycle symbol, and images from road signs or flags.

SECTION 2

Forms of Writing

> ## Try It!
>
> Remember that symbols usually stand for ideas. Some common symbols you might be familiar with are a sword standing for *war*, a rose standing for *love*, an eagle standing for *freedom*, a dove standing for *peace*, and an owl standing for *wisdom*. What are some other symbols that you have seen in stories? What symbols could you use in your own stories to represent beauty, friendship, heritage, and work?

SECTION 2
Forms of Writing

Planning Your Literary Criticism

Because literary criticisms usually include complex ideas and a lot of examples and quotes from the story, it is very important that you have a written plan before you begin writing. Make sure that you have looked very closely at the story and recorded the most important details and quotes that support your main idea. For example, if you are analyzing metaphors and similes, make sure you have a lot of examples of each in your notes before you make your plan. The type of organizer you use to plan your literary criticism will depend on the literary device or topic you are exploring. Consider using topic webs, charts, or outlines to record your ideas.

Tips for Writing a Literary Criticism

STEP 1 Prewriting

- Decide what you want to analyze. Will you examine figurative language, symbolism, or imagery?
- Look closely at the story to find examples and details of the literary device you are analyzing. Think hard about how these examples connect to the story's meaning or affect the reader.
- Decide how you will organize your essay. What will each main idea in your body be about?

STEP 2 Drafting

- In the introduction, name the story and author, and give background information. Include a direct statement of what your essay is analyzing and how it connects to meaning or affects the reader.
- Use your plans to draft the body. Include quotes and vivid details from the story.

STEP 3 Revising

- **Organization** Does each paragraph present one main idea? Do your paragraphs have clear topic sentences? Did you stay on topic?
- **Ideas** Are your ideas fresh and original? Do you use enough details from the story to support them?
- **Voice** Do you use an interesting lead and thoughtful concluding statement?

STEP 4 Editing/Proofreading

- **Conventions** Did you capitalize and correctly spell all proper nouns, like character or place names? Did you correctly indent paragraphs?

STEP 5 Publishing

- **Presentation** Type your literary criticism, and share your ideas with your classmates.

SECTION 2

Forms of Writing

Informative Writing • Responding to Literature: Literary Criticism

Narrative Writing

Narrative writing tells a story. The story can be true, such as a biography or autobiography. These stories are about real people and real events. The story can be fictional, or make-believe. Some fiction stories can be realistic, with characters and events that could really happen. Others, such as fantasy and science fiction stories, contain characters and events that could never really happen.

When you do narrative writing, you are telling your readers what happened. Narrative writing has a plot with a beginning, a middle, and an end. It also needs a setting, a conflict and resolution, and characters. It may also need dialogue. Look on the following pages for some different kinds of narrative writing.

SECTION 2

Forms of Writing

Examples of narrative writing include the following:

- Fictional Narrative
- Biography
- Autobiography
- Tall Tale
- Historical Fiction
- Science Fiction
- Fantasy
- Play

EXAMPLE Here's part of a fictional narrative that Hiro wrote about some brothers who are very different.

> Mateo was only five when the family moved into the yellow house on Dickens Street. He learned English very quickly. Now he could speak it as well as kids who were born in the United States. He was very friendly and laughed a lot. Mateo was also curious about everything.
>
> Bruno was seven when the family got to the United States. He learned English more slowly than Mateo. Sometimes he still couldn't remember how to make his sentences work. That made school hard for him. Bruno was quiet and a little shy.

Continue reading this section of the Handbook to find out more information about narrative writing.

SECTION 2

Forms of Writing

Fictional Narrative

A **fictional narrative** is a story that is invented or make-believe. Some fictional stories are realistic, with characters that exist and events that could really happen. Others, such as fantasy and science fiction stories, contain characters that cannot exist and events that could never happen.

All fictional narratives have a beginning, a middle, and an end. They also contain the elements of *story grammar*, including setting, plot, and characters.

Setting

Setting is when and where a story takes place. The setting in a fictional narrative can be anywhere. It can be a Spanish galleon sailing across the Atlantic Ocean in 1803 or a spaceship orbiting Neptune in 3012. A setting can be familiar to the reader or a place that was born from the writer's imagination.

Writers often use **descriptive writing** to establish the mood of the story and to create a vivid picture for their readers. For example, in a mystery, a writer might describe a city as "dark and sinister." In a piece of historical fiction, he or she might focus on the cobblestone streets in Boston to make the city come alive and seem more realistic.

Characters

A **character** is an individual in a fictional narrative. Depending on the genre characters can be super humans, animals, other creatures, or regular people you might meet at the grocery store. They can also have many varied roles and character traits. Some characters drive the action in a story, and others try to stop the hero from reaching a goal. Some are heroic and strong, and others use their wits to defeat the villain. Although you can create many different kinds of characters, all characters need to be developed so the reader can relate to their conflicts and situations.

Plot

The **plot** is the series of events that take place in a story. In the beginning, the setting, characters, and conflict are introduced. The **conflict** is the main problem that the characters face. It can be an external struggle between two characters or forces or an internal struggle within one character's mind. Some common conflicts involve a character struggling against another character, against society, against nature, or against a supernatural force.

In the middle of the story, the characters attempt to deal with the conflict. The tension builds, and the events get more exciting. When this tension reaches its highest point, the story reaches its **climax**, or turning point. After the climax, the action winds down as the plot comes to an end. The story's **resolution** shows how the problem is solved.

Point of View

Point of view is the position from which the story is told. In the **first-person point of view**, the narrator is one of the characters (usually the main character) in the story. The narrator uses the pronouns *I, me, my, we, us,* and *our* to describe what he or she says, does, and thinks. In the **third-person point of view,** the story is told from outside the action of the story. The narrator is an outside observer instead of a character. The third-person pronouns *he, she, they, him, her,* and *them* describe what the characters say, do, and sometimes think.

Fictional Narrative Model

The Soccer Field

Jose heard people cheer as he ran up the front stairs to his house. He didn't even have to see the television to know what had happened.

Ricardo Rodriguez had scored another goal.

Rodriguez was the best soccer player in Brazil. He played in all the major tournaments and was loved by everyone in the country.

Jose opened the door and ran inside. Someone called his name from the dining room. "Jose!"

It was his older sister, Esmeralda. She was sitting on the floor with her friends. She was holding a soccer ball. "Did you see Ricardo kick that goal?" Esmeralda asked. "That was incredible!"

"You think all of his goals are incredible," Jose said. "What are you doing here? I thought you had a soccer game this afternoon."

Esmeralda looked at her friends. At the mention of the soccer game, all of their smiles had suddenly vanished. "There's no soccer game today," Esmeralda said. "I think the entire season is cancelled."

"Cancelled?" Jose exclaimed. "Why? What happened?"

"The referees said the field is unsafe," Ursula, one of Esmeralda's friends, responded. "There's a giant puddle in the middle of the field. And there's garbage everywhere. The referees think we're going to get hurt if we play there."

Jose knew the soccer field was in horrible condition. The grass was overgrown and the holes in the ground were nearly a foot deep. It was only a matter of time before someone twisted an ankle.

"When are they going to fix it?" Jose asked.

"Who's going to fix it?" Esmeralda said with a shrug. "People don't care about a soccer field in the middle of nowhere, Jose."

That night, Jose lay in bed thinking. There had to be something he could do. Jose played baseball on the same field. If they cancelled his sister's soccer season, they might cancel his baseball season, too.

Suddenly, Jose had an idea! Jose grabbed a piece of paper and a pen and started writing . . .

One week later, Esmeralda and her friends stood in the middle of the soccer field, waiting for Jose. He had told them to show up with some work gloves and safety goggles. "Where's your brother?" Ursula asked, annoyed.

Esmeralda shrugged. "I don't know. I thought he'd be here by now." Suddenly, Esmeralda saw Jose walking toward them. He had a huge grin on his face. "What are you smiling about?" Esmeralda asked. "You're late."

Jose glanced at his watch. "Actually, I'm right on time. Look!"

Jose pointed down the street at three large pickup trucks heading toward the soccer field. The trucks were filled with lawn mowers, rakes, shovels, and paint. Esmeralda and her friends stared in disbelief as the trucks pulled into the parking lot and stopped. "Who is that?" Esmeralda asked. Jose said nothing.

The front door of the first truck opened. It was Ricardo Rodriguez!

"Oh my gosh!" Esmeralda nearly screamed. "Is that...?"

"Hello, my friends," Ricardo said, smiling widely. "I heard you needed to fix up your soccer field!"

Esmeralda and her friends sprinted across the field and surrounded Rodriguez. Rodriguez laughed a booming laugh that carried across the length of the field. In the parking lot, several workers piled out of the pickup trucks and began lugging the lawn mowers onto the field.

Jose smiled to himself. All it took was a friendly letter to his favorite soccer player. Judging by the gigantic smile on his sister's face, it was all worth it.

Try It!

Continue the story of Jose, Esmeralda, and Ricardo Rodriguez. How did they fix the field? Do you think Jose and Ricardo became friends? How did Ricardo's help affect Esmeralda?

Analyzing the Model

Setting

This fictional narrative takes place in Brazil. The first part of the story takes place in Jose's house. The second part of the story takes place in Jose's room. The third part of the story takes place on a run-down soccer field, which was described with clear details.

Characters

All of the characters in this story are realistic. Jose is a young boy who has an older sister, Esmeralda. Esmeralda plays soccer, and Jose plays baseball. Jose and Esmeralda are fans of the best soccer player in Brazil, Ricardo Rodriguez. Jose's actions show us he is dedicated and ambitious.

Plot

The conflict is introduced when Jose discovers his sister's problem in the beginning of the story. The soccer field is in horrible shape. Unless the field is fixed, her soccer team will be forced to cancel the entire season. Not only that, but Jose's baseball season might be cancelled too because they play on the same field. The climax of the story occurs when Ricardo Rodriguez appears at the soccer field. The problems are resolved in the end, when they start working together to clean the field.

Reading Your Writing

Reread the dialogue in the model narrative. Does it sound natural and like conversations children would have in real life? If you include dialogue in your fictional narrative, read it aloud. This will help you be sure that the ideas and word choices sound like things people in your story would say.

Tips for Writing a Fictional Narrative

STEP 1 Prewriting

- Brainstorm, and refer to your Writer's Notebook for story topics and ideas.
- Plan the setting and character(s) of your story, as well as the conflict and how it is resolved. Use a story map or plotline diagram to record your plans.
- Decide whether your story will be told in the first person or the third person.

STEP 2 Drafting

- Refer to your graphic organizers, story map, or notes to write your story.
- As you describe the setting and characters, focus on descriptive detail and dialogue.

STEP 3 Revising

- **Ideas** Is your story original? Are your characters believable?
- **Organization** Is the order of events in your story logical, interesting, and fun to read?
- **Organization** Did you include the elements of plot structure? Is there an obvious conflict with a resolution at the end?
- **Organization** Is the point of view of the story clear? Are you using the correct pronouns?
- **Sentence Fluency** Are sentences put together well? Do they flow together and vary in length?

STEP 4 Editing/Proofreading

- **Conventions** Proofread your fictional narrative for spelling, punctuation, and capitalization. Did you punctuate your dialogue correctly?

STEP 5 Publishing

- **Presentation** Neatly type or rewrite your final copy.
- **Presentation** Consider illustrating your story.

Biography

A **biography** is the story of a real person's life that is written by *another* person. Unlike a story written about a fictional character, all the events in a biography are supposed to be true. Unlike a research report, which is written on a specific topic, the subject of a biography is always a person.

A biography contains important information about a person's life. It includes the major events. It may also include information about how the person thinks and feels about things. Biographies often include what other people have to say about the subject. A biography may cover a person's life from birth to the present, or it may focus on an important period in a person's life.

Biographies usually organize events in chronological order, or the order in which the events occurred in time. A biography that focuses on just one period may order events from a key event and go backward.

Gathering Information

The sources you use will depend on your subject. If your subject is no longer living, encyclopedias and other reference books may provide you with the most information. For well-known living subjects, use reference books, magazines, websites, and video and audio clips. If your subject lives nearby, you may be able to interview both your subject and the people who know him or her. If you arrange an interview, be sure to come prepared with a list of questions. You may wish to record the interview. No matter which type of source you use, remember to write down where you got your information. For more information on documenting your references, see pages 99–100 on bibliographies.

Organizing Your Information

A graphic organizer such as a time line may help you focus on key events as you gather information. The dates used in this model are years only. You may want to include exact dates such as the day, month, and year of the event. Dates help the writer put the events in order.

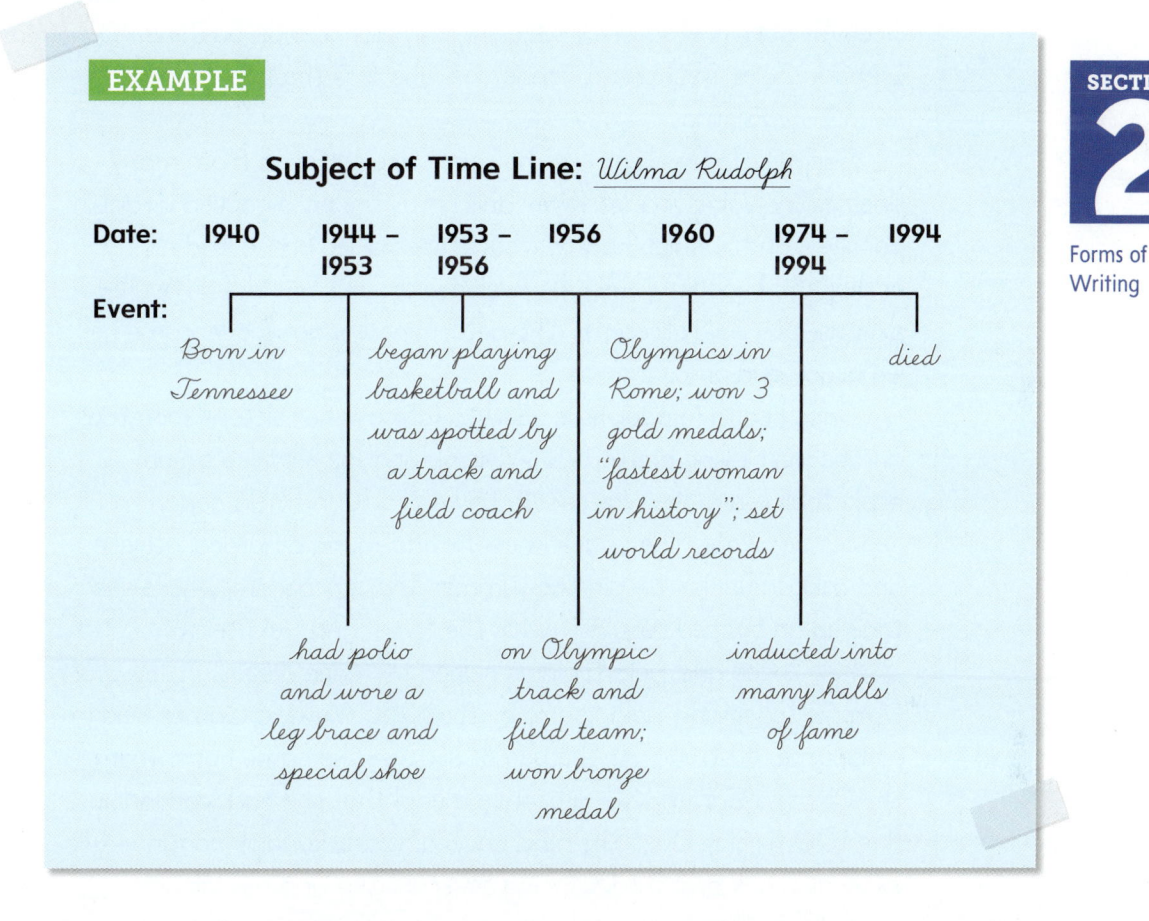

EXAMPLE

Subject of Time Line: *Wilma Rudolph*

Date:	1940	1944–1953	1953–1956	1956	1960	1974–1994	1994
Event:	Born in Tennessee	had polio and wore a leg brace and special shoe	began playing basketball and was spotted by a track and field coach	on Olympic track and field team; won bronze medal	Olympics in Rome; won 3 gold medals; "fastest woman in history"; set world records	inducted into many halls of fame	died

SECTION 2

Forms of Writing

Narrative Writing • Biography

Biography Model

Wilma Rudolph

Wilma Goldean Rudolph was an American track and field star. She was born prematurely, weighing only 4.5 pounds, on June 23, 1940 in Saint Bethlehem, Tennessee. She was the twentieth of twenty-two siblings.

Early life for Rudolph was not easy. She suffered from many illnesses, including scarlet fever and polio. The polio caused infantile paralysis and Rudolph had to wear a special leg brace and an orthopedic shoe until she was twelve years old. She did difficult exercises to build strength. The determined Rudolph overcame her leg brace and polio.

Once healthy, Rudolph decided to follow in her sister's footsteps and began playing basketball. While playing for her high school basketball team, she was spotted by a track and field coach from Tennessee State. The coach knew he had found a natural athlete and asked Rudolph to join the summer track program, where she trained and raced regularly with the track and field team.

Her track and field training helped her earn a spot on the U.S. Olympic track and field team for the 1956 Olympic Games held in Melbourne, Australia. At the age of sixteen, she came home from the Olympic Games with a bronze medal that she had won in the 4 x 100m relay. Over the next several years, Rudolph continued to excel at track and field, winning several titles and medals.

In 1959, Rudolph won the Association of American Universities 100m title and defended it for four consecutive years. She also won gold and silver medals at the 1959 Pan American Games.

Once again, Rudolph qualified for the U.S. Olympic track and field team, and participated in the Summer Olympics held in Rome, Italy. Along with setting an Olympic record in the 200m dash and a world record in the 4 x 100m relay, Rudolph won three gold medals at the Olympic Games, something no American woman had ever done. At the age of 20, Rudolph was labeled "the fastest woman in history". Over the next few years, Rudolph participated in various races, set additional running records, and won numerous awards, including the Associated Press Woman Athlete of the Year in 1960 and 1961. Rudolph decided to retire from track competition in 1962 at the age of 22. In 1994, at the age of 54, Rudolph was diagnosed with a brain tumor and died a few months later.

In recognition of her accomplishments as a track and field star, Wilma Rudolph was given many awards and honors. She was inducted into the National Black Sports and Entertainment Hall of Fame, the National Track and Field Hall of Fame, the U.S. Olympic Hall of Fame, and the National Women's Hall of Fame. In addition, a stretch of highway in Clarksville, Tennessee was named after her and a postage stamp was issued in her honor. Wilma Rudolph will always be remembered as one of the fastest women in track and as a source of great inspiration for thousands of athletes.

Try It!

What is the main thing the author of this biography wants the reader to know? What did you find interesting about Wilma Rudolph's life?

Analyzing the Model

Choosing a Key Issue

When gathering your information about the person, you may want to focus on a key issue related to the person. Notice how the model includes information about Rudolph's early struggles with illnesses. This helps the reader see the obstacles Rudolph had to overcome to become a great athlete.

Organizing the Information

Now go back to the time line on page 143 and see how each event listed on the time line is included in the biography. While you are gathering your information, you may find it helpful to use a time line or chart to list dates and events. It will keep you on track as you take notes. It will also help you organize your writing chronologically.

Making It Readable

As with other forms of writing, a biography should also have an introduction and a concluding paragraph. In the model, the introduction tells us who the subject is, what she is known for, and where and when she was born. The conclusion tells us the impact Rudolph made and the honors she was given. The rest of the biography sticks to the events in Rudolph's life.

Reading Your Writing

A biography is the true story about a person that is written by another person. When writing a biography, use a time line of events to help you keep events in order. This will make it easier for the reader to follow along.

Tips for Writing a Biography

STEP 1 Prewriting

- Pick your subject. Think of a person who interests you and about whom you would like to know more.
- Find reliable sources of information about your subject.
- Make a time line to help you focus on key events.

STEP 2 Drafting

- Use your time line to write the biography.
- Focus on details that interest you and will interest your readers.

STEP 3 Revising

- **Ideas** Are events accurately described? Does what you included relate to the things for which the subject is known?
- **Organization** Do events and ideas connect, and do most paragraphs end with transitional sentences? Do you tell about events chronologically?

STEP 4 Editing/Proofreading

- **Conventions** Proofread the biography for spelling mistakes.
- **Conventions** Check to make sure the names of the people in your subject's life and any other proper nouns are capitalized.

STEP 5 Publishing

- **Presentation** Neatly type or rewrite your final copy.

Autobiography

An **autobiography** is a story that you write to tell about your own life. It covers a string of events, sometimes from your birth to the present. An autobiography is like a personal history written by you. It is different from a biography, which is a story about a person's life written by someone else.

Like a personal narrative, an autobiography may include details about how the writer thinks and feels about things. An autobiography differs from a personal narrative by focusing on a longer period in a person's life instead of on just one event or experience. An autobiography may tell about one important period, or it may cover the whole lifetime of the writer.

For example, for your autobiography, you might choose to write about the major events from kindergarten through fifth grade, or you could write about just one year of your life. However, an autobiography usually covers a longer period.

Gathering Information

If you're writing an autobiography that begins at your birth, you will need to interview your family members. They can give you information and details about your early days. They may have a baby book or photo album that tells about where you were born, when you walked, and what your first words were. Ask them about any funny or unusual things that you did. As with other types of writing, the details will make your autobiography interesting to your readers.

SECTION 2
Forms of Writing

Organizing the Information

An autobiography that covers an entire life is most often told in chronological order, the order in which the events occurred in time. Another way to organize would be to begin with a key event in the present, such as winning an athletic tournament, and then go backward in time telling about each event in the last few years that led to the recent accomplishment. Whichever way you organize your autobiography, you will want to make sure your method makes sense. You may find it helpful to list key events on a chain-of-events graphic organizer such as the one shown here.

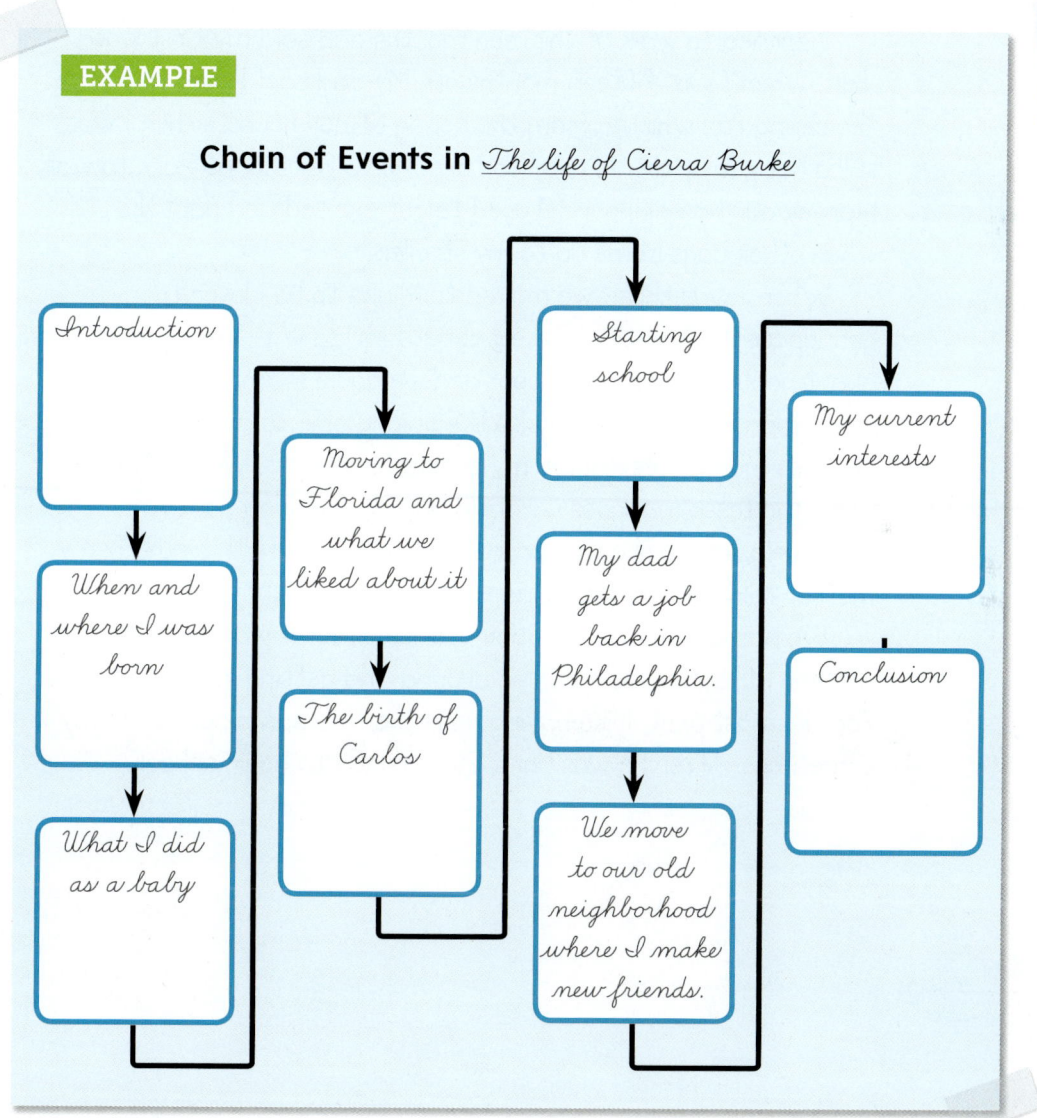

SECTION 2 — Forms of Writing

EXAMPLE

Chain of Events in *The life of Cierra Burke*

- Introduction
- When and where I was born
- What I did as a baby
- Moving to Florida and what we liked about it
- The birth of Carlos
- Starting school
- My dad gets a job back in Philadelphia.
- We move to our old neighborhood where I make new friends.
- My current interests
- Conclusion

Narrative Writing • Autobiography

Autobiography Model

My Life: Florida and Back by Cierra Burke

I was born during a huge ice storm on January 25, 1993, at Thomas Jefferson Hospital in Philadelphia. When my mother was ready to have me, my parents had to walk to the hospital because taxis couldn't get through all of the ice and snow in the streets. I weighed seven pounds exactly.

I learned to walk at thirteen months and said my first word, "fan," when I was fifteen months old. My dad said I liked to watch the ceiling fan whirling from the ceiling of our house. When I was still a baby, my parents used to take me to Fairmount Park to walk Harvey, our basset hound. I used to get excited and pant like a dog when other dogs came up to my stroller.

When I was three, we moved to Miami to be closer to my grandparents. The thing I liked about Florida was the weather. Our apartment complex had a pool, and we could swim in it just about every month of the year. I also liked being able to pick lemons and oranges from trees right in my grandparents' backyard. My mother loved the fresh mangoes we could buy. It reminded her of Venezuela, where she was born. Soon after my fifth birthday, my mother told me she was going to have a baby.

We named my baby brother Carlos, after my grandfather. In no time at all, he was crawling around and getting into my stuff. For the most part, I like having a brother. He can be pretty funny sometimes. After he was born, I was ready to begin school.

I started kindergarten at Mangrove Elementary School. My first teacher's name was Mrs. Cavendish. The main thing I remember about her was a shirt she always wore. It was aqua with pink seahorses and bubbles. I went to that school through third grade. Then we moved back to Philadelphia. My dad got a really good job with a big bakery here. It was hard to leave our grandparents, but the place where my dad worked in Florida was shutting down.

We moved back to Spring Garden, our old neighborhood. We bought a three-story house, so we were all very excited. I started going to Greentree Elementary School in fourth grade and made some new friends. My mom said my best friend, Alicia, is actually an old friend that I don't remember! My interests include listening to music, drawing, and riding my bike. In fifth grade, I started taking Spanish. I'm hoping to be able to surprise my grandparents next time we visit them in Florida. They speak Spanish and so does my mother, but she never taught me much.

I'm glad I got to live in Florida, but I like my life here, too. I guess the saying is true— Philadelphia really is "the place that loves you back."

SECTION 2

Forms of Writing

Try It!

Think about the events that have shaped your life. What would you choose to focus on in your autobiography?

Analyzing the Model

Organizing the Events and Connecting the Ideas

Do you see how this autobiography is organized in chronological order? In the first paragraph, the author tells about her birth. Each paragraph after that moves us forward one to three years in time until the present.

Notice how the paragraphs are connected. The last sentence of most paragraphs provides the transition to the next. Transitional sentences make it easier for readers to follow the sequence of events.

Introduction and Conclusion

Just as with any form of writing, this short autobiography has an introductory paragraph and a concluding paragraph. In the introductory paragraph, the student captures the readers' attention with an interesting first sentence. In the concluding paragraph, she reflects on the major events in her life: moving to Florida and then back to Philadelphia. Her concluding sentence, ". . . Philadelphia really is 'the place that loves you back,'" echoes her title, "My Life: Florida and Back." Her autobiography isn't simply a telling of events from birth to the present. It is also a comparison of the two places Cierra has lived and a reflection on moving away and back to the original place.

Reading Your Writing

An autobiography is a true story that a person writes about himself or herself. To keep the reader's interest, be sure to use only the most interesting facts, not every little detail about your life.

Tips for Writing an Autobiography

STEP 1 Prewriting

- Interview your family to learn interesting and important facts about your background, birth, and early years.
- List the major events of your life. Include topics on which you might want to reflect and possibly a theme that may tie it together.
- Use a chain-of-events graphic organizer or just list events chronologically on a piece of paper.

STEP 2 Drafting

- Use your chain-of-events organizer or your list to write your autobiography.
- Focus on interesting details in your autobiography.

STEP 3 Revising

- **Ideas** Are events accurately described? Will the things you chose to write about be interesting to your reader?
- **Organization** Do you write about events chronologically? Do the events and ideas connect, and do paragraphs end with transitional sentences?
- **Voice** Does your writing involve readers, providing them with a sense of who you are?

STEP 4 Editing/Proofreading

- **Conventions** Proofread your autobiography for spelling, punctuation, and capitalization errors.

STEP 5 Publishing

- **Presentation** Neatly type or rewrite a final copy. Include family photos, baby pictures, and other images or artifacts from your life.

SECTION 2

Forms of Writing

Tall Tale

A **tall tale** is a uniquely American fictional story that uses exaggeration and hyperbole to explain the creation of a geographic feature, describe extreme weather, or tell of amazing accomplishments and improbable events. The characters, plot, and setting of a tall tale are not merely unrealistic; to create humor, they are presented as being far beyond the limits of believability.

Setting

The setting of a tall tale is most often a well-known area of the United States known for its unique geographic features. The story of Paul Bunyan takes place in the lake-spotted woods of Minnesota. Pecos Bill rides a bucking tornado in the flat lands of the west.

Plot

In tall tales there is usually an impossible problem that is solved in a unique, creative, and humorous way. Pecos Bill rides the biggest, meanest tornado until it finally rains itself out, causing so much water that the Grand Canyon is carved out. Sometimes the whole life of the character is told and other times there is just a major event, such as the wedding of Pecos Bill and Slew-foot Sue.

Characters

The main characters in tall tales are larger than life in physical appearance or abilities. Some are exaggerated versions of real people, such as John Henry and Calamity Jane. Other tall-tale characters are purely fictional, as with the story of Paul Bunyan, who was so large that his footsteps made the lakes in Minnesota. Slew-foot Sue is another fictional character who could ride a catfish while standing up and shoot holes in the clouds to make pretty patterns.

Hyperbole

A hyperbole is an extravagant exaggeration. It is a statement that is so outlandish and recognizably unbelievable that it is humorous. The statements are not presented as boasts but rather stated simply as facts. The humor comes in because the statements are so obviously fictional.

Brainstorming

Keep a journal to write ideas for tall tales, humorous hyperbole, or creative answers to unusual problems. It may be helpful to ask your friends and your family what super powers they would like to have or amazing things they would like to do..

SECTION 2

Forms of Writing

Reading Your Writing

With its colorful language, humor, and friendly voice, tall tales lend themselves very well to oral presentations. Reading aloud also helps to make the narration smooth and to catch mistakes that can be missed with silent reading.

FUN fact

The word *hyperbole* comes from the Greek words *hyper* to exceed and *ballein* to throw. A hyperbole then is an extreme exaggeration, an excess that goes way beyond.

Tall Tale Model

Sky Lynn Aurora McKallis Borealis, Baby Extraordinaire

Sky Lynn Aurora McKallis Borealis was born in the dusty little town of Dry Gulch, Montana. This town made the bodacious claim of having the most spectacular aurora borealis shows (better known as the northern lights) in the whole country. The night little Sky Lynn came crying into the world, the sky was really showing off, putting on the most incredibly phenomenal display that folks thought maybe a thunderstorm was coming. But since Dry Gulch had never ever even had enough rain to brag about, much less a thunderstorm, folks figured the sky was just celebrating the arrival of li'l Sky Lynn with its natural fireworks of the northern lights.

As soon as Sky Lynn got their attention away from the northern lights, they all took major notice of how truly amazing this new baby was. She was truly the most adorable baby in the whole state of Montana. Not only was she adorable, she was so alert, looking around at people with unusual purple eyes and smiling right off at everyone. Why, folks just lit up looking at her!

The folks in Dry Gulch needed that cheering up, too. While Dry Gulch was legendary for its dryness, recently there had been the most severe drought ever recorded in Montana. All the crops had dried up and blown on over to North Dakota. Yep, folks were sure ready for a little cheering up.

It wasn't until the nurse handed Sky Lynn to her mom that anyone got a hint of just how truly amazing this little baby really was. The flowers that Sky's daddy had sent in all the way from California stood up straight and bloomed their hardest! The buds that hadn't quite opened just yet burst forth in full flower glory. Why, even the flowered wallpaper brightened up and bloomed!

When Sky's mom brought her outside to take her home, the grass grew so long folks had to cut it five minutes later. The leaves on the trees unfolded, and flowers bloomed wherever Sky passed by. The apple trees leafed out and apples formed and ripened!

The neighbors couldn't help but notice that the yard around the McKallis Borealis' farmhouse was in full summer greenery that first day in March when li'l Sky Lynn and her mom came home from the hospital. It looked just like an oasis in the desert, better than the agricultural displays at the Sunscorch County Fair!

When Sky's mom took her out for a stroll, the whole neighborhood started greening up. By the time Sky had toured the town, it had become so overgrown with green plants that folks had to change the name of the town from Dry Gulch to Evergreen.

Three months later, the government finally got wind of Sky's amazing ability and they sent over Special Agricultural Agent John Q. Horticulture from the National Department of Agriculture's office. His mission was to thoroughly investigate these unbelievable claims of green growth coming out of this previously-known-to-be-driest-place-west-of-the-Sahara. After witnessing first-hand what had happened in the newly named Evergreen, Agent Horticulture wrote up his report in triplicate and recommended that li'l Sky be strolled around all the dry spots in the whole United States of America.

First on the list was the Everdusty Desert in Florida. After just two days, the place had become such a swampland they had to rename it The Everglades!

Of course by now the news of little Sky had traveled all over the world. Brazil was first to invite her to come be strolled around their Great Amazon Desert. So li'l Sky Lynn and her mom and dad packed up the stroller and headed out for South America, spreading greenery and good cheer all along the way.

Last I heard those Brazilians were thinking of renaming their desert The Great Amazon Rainforest.

SECTION 2

Forms of Writing

Try It!

Where do you think Sky's parents should stroll her around next? Brainstorm a second chapter in the life of Sky Lynn. Be sure to include extravagant adjectives, hyperbole, and humor in your continuation.

Narrative Writing • Tall Tale

Analyzing the Model

Point of View

The point of view of the tall tale is the third person. The narration is in an informal voice with a friendly manner, much the way a family member who is adept at storytelling might tell a tale. The narrator gives background information and tells the action of the story without being a part of the action.

Word Choice

In the tall tale about Sky, the extreme descriptions and hyperboles require the use of extravagant, colorful, superlative adjectives. Writers of tall tales can let their imaginations run and use their most embellished vocabulary, with good-natured humor as the goal.

Setting

The setting is a tiny rural town in the state of Montana with the unusual features of incredible displays of northern lights and an extreme drought problem. Most tall tales are American in origin, but the genre could be used in other settings and cultures to explain extreme weather or tell of amazing feats in foreign lands.

Characters

All the characters are ordinary people with the exception of the main character, Sky Lynn, a beautiful, cheery baby who possesses the unusual ability to make plants grow at an unbelievable rate.

Plot

In this tall tale, Dry Gulch has an extreme drought problem that is solved by a baby's effect on plants. When news of Sky's ability reaches other places, her family is asked to stroll their little one around their dry spots.

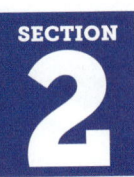

SECTION 2
Forms of Writing

Tips for Writing a Tall Tale

STEP 1 Prewriting

- Brainstorm ideas about a larger-than-life character.
- Use a story map to plan the introduction of the character, the problem and the unique way of solving the problem.

STEP 2 Drafting

- Refer to your story map and other notes to write your tall tale.
- Let your ideas and humor flow. With this type of story, the more outlandish the ideas, the funnier the story can be.

STEP 3 Revising

- **Ideas** Are your ideas different, unusual, unique, and original? Will your readers find them humorous?
- **Organization** Does the story flow from the problem to the resolution? Do the exaggerations fit the character and work to solve the problem?
- **Word Choice** Do you use plenty of extravagant adjectives and adverbs?
- **Voice** Does your narrative capture the readers' attention and keep them laughing and interested in finding out what happens next? Is the voice friendly and engaging?
- **Sentence Fluency** Read your tall tale out loud to check for variety, flow, and humor. Reading aloud can help you catch mistakes easily overlooked by silent reading.

STEP 4 Editing/Proofreading

- **Conventions** Proofread your tall tale for spelling, punctuation, and capitalization.

STEP 5 Publishing

- **Presentation** Neatly type or rewrite your final copy.
- **Presentation** Consider giving an oral reading of your tall tale. With the informal, friendly voice and humor, tall tales make excellent read-aloud selections.

SECTION 2

Forms of Writing

Historical Fiction

Historical fiction is a story that takes place in an actual time and place in the past. When you write historical fiction, you give lots of details about the period in which your events take place.

Like other fiction, historical fiction must have a setting, a plot, and characters. However, in historical fiction, the specific time and place in which the story takes place play a major role in the events and in some ways control what the characters think, say, and do.

Setting

When you write historical fiction, you will need to include plenty of detail about the time and place. This often requires research. Information about the way that people talked, their points of view, the tools they used, what they ate, drank, wore, and did for fun all help make the story accurate and seem real. This information should be included in a way that fits with the telling of the story.

Elizabeth George Speare's *The Sign of the Beaver* is set in Maine in the 1700s. When Matt, the main character, meets the other central character, Attean, we learn some of the language of the native people of the area, the Penobscot. We find out what Attean and some other Penobscot think—that white people have taken over their hunting grounds. We also learn about Penobscot foods such as corncakes, nuts, and cakes of maple sugar when Matt receives them as gifts. When Attean teaches Matt native ways to trap and fish, we learn about Penobscot tools and also the plants and animals of the Maine woods in the 1700s.

Plot

The problems that characters face and their decisions and actions have to do with actual historical events. In *Number the Stars*, a novel by Lois Lowry that takes place during World War II, a Danish family copes with food shortages and the constant presence of soldiers. The action and suspense have to do with hiding Ellen, a Danish Jew, and the resolution of the book is safely getting Ellen's family to Sweden.

Number the Stars bases its fictional storyline on actual events. The Danish people really did smuggle most of the Jews out of their country to safety in Sweden.

Characters

Just as the plots may include actual events, some of the characters in historical fiction may be actual people. When famous people from the past are used, it is especially important to do careful research so that the thoughts and actions you create for them do not contradict what is known about them. You may find it easier and less limiting to write about minor historical figures or made-up characters whose everyday lives are affected by the events of the time.

Anachronisms

An anachronism is a person, thing, or event that is chronologically out of place. To avoid anachronisms in your story, it is important to have the characters in historical fiction act the way that people of the time would act. Don't make the mistake of including things that do not belong to the time. For example, a story that takes place during the Middle Ages should not have characters driving cars or using contemporary slang.

Historical Fiction Model

Golden Mountain

We were really scared. One of them had a shotgun, and it didn't look like they would see it our way. The five bearded men were searching for gold on the claim next to ours, and one afternoon they came with their picks and shovels to our side of the boundary. When we showed them our claim rights, they gruffly shoved us aside and laughed, saying California was their country and that we should go back to China. Believe me, I had thought of that plenty of times.

My name is Chang Hong. The year was 1853, and I was sixteen years old. My uncle, cousins, and I had been working our claim for four months without any luck. We had heard about Gaam San, which in Cantonese means "golden mountain," from relatives in China who said California was covered with gold. When we got here, we discovered that it was not what we imagined. We saw shacks and shanties everywhere. Back in our province in China, things were not much better, so we had no choice but to carry through with our plan to mine gold. We hoped to send for our families or at least bring some wealth home.

The tools needed for mining gold were very expensive, so we pooled what money we had and bought only what we really needed. Then we had to bargain for our mining claim.

Every day we dug in the hard earth and panned in a nearby stream. We saw only mud and rocks—no gold. When our bellies weren't twisting in pain from eating salt pork, beans, and other strange foods, they ached from hunger. It was hard to find the fresh vegetables and rice that we were used to eating. At least we had our tea. Sometimes we could buy rice and vegetables from other Cantonese carrying these provisions on bamboo poles. They traveled from mine to mine selling to Chinese and other hungry miners. We began to wonder if they were the ones striking it rich. As we spent our savings on food, we did not find the gold that would bring us more money. So when the five bearded men threatened to take over our claim, instead of fighting back, we packed up and left.

We had heard of other Cantonese setting up "chow chows" similar to the eating places in China, and we wanted to open one. We pitched our tent on the edge of San Francisco near where others from our province had settled in a village made of shanties and tents. We were able to buy just enough chickens and pigs to get started. Some villagers gave us seeds so we could plant a vegetable garden, and we soon had enough food to start our own "chow chow."

We chose a spot near the center of town that would attract Chinese and non-Chinese. We flew a triangular yellow flag so people would see that we were a "chow chow." Our prices were very low, and word got around that our food was good, so we quickly became busy. As long as we were making food (not competing for gold or other jobs), the non-Chinese left us alone.

Tending a garden, taking care of animals, and making and selling food is very hard work. It isn't why we came here, but it is a lot better than coming up empty-handed in the gold mines. At the end of the day, my belly is content, filled with rice, vegetables, and sometimes chicken or pork. I could do worse!

Try It!

If you were writing a historical fiction piece, what setting would you use? Would you include a real person from history or a fictional person who might have lived during that time?

Analyzing the Model

Point of View

Sometimes historical fiction is written as if it were someone's diary or journal. It takes this approach to encourage the reader to identify with Chang Hong and to provide a more personal view of what it may have been like to be a Chinese miner.

Setting

The story takes place in 1853, five years after gold was first found in California. The story includes many facts about the time and place, such as San Francisco being filled with the tents and shanties of miners. The Chinese did receive supplies from traveling Cantonese carrying food from bamboo poles. The story includes these details in a way that fits with the telling of the story.

Plot

The main struggles of facing prejudice, searching for gold without results, and surviving with little food are historically based. The details such as the five bearded men are fictional. The resolution is realistic. Selling food was a way for many Chinese, unwelcome in the mines, to make a living.

Characters

Chang Hong is a fictional character based on an actual person, Chang De-ming. Information about Chang De-ming is scarce. The author wrote about a fictional Chang Hong with whom it is easier to identify and match historical information.

Reading Your Writing

Historical fiction is a story that takes place in an actual time in the past. Don't make the mistake of putting a modern convenience in a story about the Old West or your reader will not believe your story.

Tips for Writing Historical Fiction

STEP 1 Prewriting

- Think of historical events or characters that interest you. Draw from a social studies learning log or textbook.
- Research historical details such as food, tools, and language that will make your story interesting and accurate.
- Consider using a story map or plotline diagram to plan your story.

STEP 2 Drafting

- Refer to your story map, plotline diagram, or other notes to write your historical fiction story.
- Focus on the struggle in the plot and the historical details.

STEP 3 Revising

- **Ideas** Are the events of your story interesting? Does it have plenty of historical detail, described in a way that fits with the story?
- **Word Choice** Did you choose just the right words to describe the time and place? Will your reader understand, through context or explanation, the words you used?

STEP 4 Editing/Proofreading

- **Conventions** Be sure to capitalize the names of historical events, characters, and any other proper nouns. Check punctuation and spelling.

STEP 5 Publishing

- **Presentation** Neatly type or rewrite your final copy.
- **Presentation** Consider illustrating and binding your story.

Science Fiction

Science fiction, or sci-fi as it is commonly known, is the genre of fictional stories that include science, technology, and futuristic settings. Many sci-fi stories also involve space travel and encounters with alien beings. The stories are imaginative and inventive, and usually contain adventure and suspense. Although the characters, plot, and setting of a sci-fi story may be very unusual, the stories have situations and character traits that readers can relate to.

Setting

Science fiction stories often take place in a future time or tell about a visit to a future time. The location is often a space ship, another planet, or a futuristic Earth. Different features such as the lack of gravity or breathable atmosphere, bizarre plants and animals, and the idea that any human characters are considered aliens on other planets will all affect the action and plot of the story.

Some sci-fi stories are set in familiar present-day locations. Bruce Coville's book *I Was a Sixth-Grade Alien* takes place in Syracuse, New York. Pleskit Meenon from the planet Hevi-Hevi is the first purple kid in Ms. Weintraub's sixth grade class. Betty Ballantine's book *The Secret Oceans* begins in the South Pacific. The explorers on the "Turtle," a high-tech submersible, journey to the Arctic and then the Amazon Delta.

Plot

The problems encountered by the characters in a sci-fi story have to do with exploring new worlds, space and time travel, technological advances, and interaction between beings of different worlds. Plots contain action and suspense. In Bruce Coville's book, human Tim and alien Pleskit stumble upon a plot to sabotage the peaceful intergalactic mission of the aliens.

The Secret Oceans tells of a race of super dolphins who guide a six-member crew of the "Turtle" on a tour of the oceans to impress upon them the fragility of the water world and the need to protect it.

Characters

The main characters in sci-fi stories can be animals, androids, or robots but are often humans or humanoid creatures. Even though the characters may be encountering alien life forms and strange planets, they have feelings and reactions that readers can relate to. In *I was a Sixth Grade Alien*, the preteen desire to fit in and apprehension of the main characters are handled with humor. The feelings are written in the first person narrative from both preteens, human and alien (translated from Pleskit's native tongue of Hevi-Hevi in the case of the alien). An advanced dolphin race with three-fingered fins are main characters working with the human crew in *The Secret Oceans*. Together they persuade readers to see the importance of preserving the health of the oceans.

Inspiration for Technological Inventions

Although the technology imagined by science fiction writers is not usually plausible at the time, sci-fi writers have inspired scientists to develop technology to reach goals achieved in sci-fi stories. In 1865, Jules Verne wrote *From the Earth to the Moon*. Considered to be the originator of modern science fiction, Verne proposed travel to the moon by being blasted out of a giant cannon. Such ideas led to visions of rocket travel. H.G. Wells wrote *The War of the Worlds* in 1898, about a Martian invasion. Before the inventions of cars, televisions, and airplanes, Wells had predicted tanks, nuclear war, gas warfare, laser-like weapons, and industrial robots. The Flash Gordon stories of the 1940's introduced the public to the idea of routine space travel that helped to inspire space shuttle travel.

Brainstorming

Keep a folder or write ideas for science fiction stories. It can be helpful to ask your friends and family what technological advancements they would like to see in the future or to read about new scientific and technological discoveries in the newspaper.

Science Fiction Model

The Star Light from the Past

Twelve-year-old Yona had suddenly tensed up every muscle as she sensed that she and her father were not alone in the meadow. They had come to this clearing in the rolling hills to see the stars, tiny brilliant jewels scattered across the black velvet curtain of night. But someone or something else was out there too.

Yona touched her father's arm. He looked at her and knew she had detected a presence. They froze in position. Every one of Yona's senses intensified as she strained to detect what the other presence was, where it was, and what its intentions were.

At the opposite end of the meadow, the presence was searching, that much Yona could sense. They waited, still and quiet. Then Yona smiled. The presence had been abruptly called away before it had found what it was looking for. Feelings of relief came over Yona and her father. They had not been discovered.

With the presence completely gone, they walked carefully over to where the presence had been. Her father was the first to notice a faint glimmer in the grass. They bent down to examine it and immediately recognized it as a tracking device. Looking closer, Yona gasped as she recognized the markings on the device.

"Resis," Yona said.

"We must communicate tonight," her father said shaking his head.

Yona located the Sirius Star and just south of it was the constellation Columba, also known as Noah's Dove. And on the tail of the Dove, the star was still there. It had taken light-years for the light from the star to get to her eyes. Even the light from Earth's sun had taken eight minutes to reach them. She knew she was looking into the past, but it was still reassuring to see the star.

Yona looked intently at the star, hoping it was still there. Together they sent a message of hope. Earth was a good planet. The atmosphere was breathable and the vegetation was edible. The Earthlings they had met were generally friendly and open.

Yona and her father added a warning: Take precautions, as the Resis are here too. Although, maybe this would finally be the place where the Resis would be reunited in harmony with them. After all, the Resis were from the planet Tov too. They had left long ago, determined to survive alone. They had taken a piece of the Treasure and disappeared, abandoning the rest of the Tovians.

Their planet, Tov, was in danger of being consumed by fire as their sun was growing bigger every year. Already the climate had gotten too warm by the time Yona and her father left. The reflector shields had been activated to keep the polar ice caps from melting. But it was only a temporary solution.

Tov had sent out 300 pairs of Tovians to travel through space to find a habitable planet. Meanwhile, the Tovians at home were in the process of equipping space ships to accommodate the long term travel of the entire population of Tov.

Yona and her father waited for a response from Tov. They looked at each other, hoping that the Tovians were able to complete their travel preparations before the planet burned up. Hoping they would be able to outwit any space pirates determined to steal supplies or the Treasure. It must be guarded well, as it was the gift for the planet that would give them sanctuary. Yona and her father pondered the potential for disasters. They had completed the mission entrusted to them. Now they must continue to hope.

Yona concentrated on being open to an answer. With so many light-years away, mental transmission was the most effective means of communication. Yona received an answer that was urgent and clear. The Tovians were on their way.

Try It!

Brainstorm an extended ending for the story. Do the Tovians encounter space pirates and outwit them? How are the Tovians treated when they arrive on Earth? What is the Treasure they will give as a gift? Answer these questions (or other questions you have).

Narrative Writing • Science Fiction

Analyzing the Model

Point of View

The story is told from the third-person point of view. This way, readers get background information as well as Yona's inner thoughts and the mental communication between Yona, her father, and the Tovians.

Setting

The setting is a meadow on Earth. It is a clear night in weather warm enough for green plants to survive.

Characters

All readers know about Yona at the beginning of the story is that she is twelve years old and is very sensitive to her surroundings. Readers find out later on in the story that she is actually an alien from the planet Tov. Yona also has special telepathic abilities. The Resis are rebel Tovians who have broken away from the planet Tov.

Plot

The plot has elements of surprise and suspense. Readers are not told right away who Yona and her father are. Suspense develops as Yona senses that they are not alone. As the story progresses, readers discover that Yona and her father are on a mission to find a habitable planet for Tovian immigrants. The presence is identified and communication is made with the home planet.

Futuristic Advancements and Inventions

The Tovians possess a form of mental telepathy that allows them to communicate over the vast light-year distances in space. Yona also has the ability to sense the presence of someone nearby and their intention. The Tovians have developed space travel to distant galaxies and solar systems

SECTION 2
Forms of Writing

Narrative Writing • Science Fiction

Tips for Writing a Science Fiction Story

STEP 1 Prewriting

- Brainstorm ideas for creating a science fiction story.
- Use a story map to plan the introduction of the characters, the conflict, and the resolution to the conflict.

STEP 2 Drafting

- Refer to your story map and other notes to write your science fiction story.
- Let your ideas develop from your imagination and notes.

STEP 3 Revising

- **Ideas** Are your ideas futuristic? Are there characters or situations that readers can relate to?
- **Organization** Does the story flow from the conflict to the resolution? Does the technology work to solve the problem?
- **Sentence Fluency** Read your science fiction story out loud to check for sentence variety and flow. Reading aloud can help you catch mistakes easily overlooked by silent reading.

STEP 4 Editing/Proofreading

- **Conventions** Proofread your science fiction story for spelling, punctuation, and capitalization.

STEP 5 Publishing

- **Presentation** Neatly type or rewrite your final copy.
- **Presentation** Consider illustrating your science fiction story with a drawing or creating an alien or space ship.

Narrative Writing • Science Fiction

Fantasy

A **fantasy** is any story containing things that do not exist or cannot happen in the real world. Fantasy stories allow writers and readers to use their imaginations. A fantasy has a setting, a plot, and characters just as in other kinds of fiction—but in fantasy, one or more of the elements are not realistic.

Setting

The setting of the story may be a world or place that does not exist. In *The Phantom Tollbooth*, by Norton Juster, Milo travels in the Lands Beyond to one impossible place after another. Two examples are the Doldrums where no one is allowed to think and Dictionopolis where words grow on trees and are sold in cases in the "word market."

Plot

A fantasy story has a beginning, a middle, and an end just like other stories, but in a fantasy, impossible events occur. In addition, the conflict or struggle may involve a problem that would not exist in the real world. In *Heartlight*, by T. A. Barron, the main character, Kate, and her grandfather travel to alternate worlds to discover why the sun is losing its pure condensed light. Neither the problem nor the way it is solved in a fantasy reflects reality, but it makes for fun writing and reading.

Characters

Some fantasies have characters that do impossible things or simply could not exist, such as dragons, ogres, talking animals, or tiny people. In *The Indian in the Cupboard,* by Lynne Reid Banks, Omri is amazed when a plastic toy comes to life as a miniature, but very real, Iroquois brave when placed in a cupboard that has magic powers.

SECTION 2

Forms of Writing

Things to Keep in Mind

Your story does not need to have every single feature of a fantasy. When you write a fantasy, you may wish to have only one unrealistic character or event.

Also keep in mind such things as character development and action. Even if your main characters are totally fantasy, you will want to develop their personalities so readers can identify with them. To make events interesting, you will want to add action, suspense, and surprise. Use your imagination and the tools of story grammar to create a fantasy story that involves readers and makes them want to pretend the story is real.

Coming Up with Ideas

You may wish to keep a folder, journal, or section of your Writer's Notebook with ideas for fantasy writing. You could create a chart like this. Title it *Wild Ideas*.

Wild Ideas		
Setting: An old barn in a new housing development.	**Setting:** The fifth grade section of an elementary school.	**Setting:** My house.
Characters: A bar family. Two human girls named Iesha and Sandra.	**Characters:** Two boys named Ashish and Rob.	**Characters:** The pixies and me.
Plot: A family of talking bats lives in the barn. The developers want to tear down the barn. The bats befriend Iesha and Sandra, who help the bats save their home.	**Plot:** Ashish and Rob find a secret locker. When they climb into it, they become someone else.	**Plot:** A family of tiny pixies lives in my house. Only I know about them. They create mischief such as scattering papers and spilling people's drinks. I often get the blame.

Fantasy Model

Unrealistic feature of setting ▶

The Secret Locker

It was really strange. They had never noticed it before. Toward the end of their row of lockers, between locker 97 and locker 98, was one more locker. The number on it was 97.6. Ashish and Rob agreed that they had never heard of lockers having numbers with decimals. They watched the locker carefully for the rest of the week. Nobody seemed to be using it. They talked about it by telephone over the weekend and decided that on Monday they would look inside.

The weekend finally ended, and they went back to school. Kids always seemed to be around so there was never a good time to look. Because neither Ashish nor Rob rode the bus, they were able to hang around at the end of the day. When the last locker banged shut and the hallway was empty, they walked over to the mysterious locker and opened it very slowly.

They looked inside and saw a strange glowing light. Ashish stepped in, and before he could say anything, he was sucked down a tube. He felt rushing air, darkness, and then a plop. He was watching a wide broom sweeping a floor. It looked just like the school hallway except that Rob was nowhere in sight.

Unrealistic event ▶

He heard someone whistling, and it sounded like it was coming from his own mouth. He didn't feel like himself. When he looked down at his hands, they were large, muscular, and very hairy. Then he heard a voice much deeper than his own saying to a janitor, "I'm almost finished with this hall. Let me know if you need help with the bathrooms." That was it. He was inside the body of the other janitor. He wished he could tell Rob. Then he wondered how he would get back, and he began to worry. He didn't have to worry long because the janitor sneezed. He felt rushing air and darkness, and he was back in locker 97.6. He stumbled backwards and fell out of the locker.

Rob was waiting. When Ashish told Rob about what happened, Rob wanted to try it, but then they saw someone coming. They decided to try the locker during recess the next day.

Recess finally came. After everyone went outside, Rob and Ashish met at locker 97.6. Rob was nervous. He was worried about getting back. Ashish assured him that a simple sneeze would bring him back. Still, what if whoever's body he was in didn't sneeze? Rob knew that if he wanted the experience, he would have to take his chances. ◀ **Unrealistic problem**

He stepped into the locker and was swept away. After the darkness and rushing air, he saw and felt his hand dribbling a basketball and shooting. He scored. Two minutes later he made another basket. Wow, he never knew what it was like to be this good at basketball! He heard someone yell, "Tony, I'm open." He was inside Tony Rivera, the best basketball player in fifth grade, and it was pretty great. Recess was almost over and Tony still hadn't sneezed.

Rob worried about getting back to class on time. Then the playground aide blew the whistle, and Tony headed back with all the other kids. How could he get Tony to sneeze? Tony approached the building—and still no sneeze. Rob concentrated very hard on getting Tony to kick up some fine dirt near the corner of the school. Then Tony started kicking up the dust, and Rob heard him say, "This is really weird. What is going on?" Finally, Rob heard "Achoo," felt rushing dark air, and smelled the metal of locker 97.6. He stumbled out and saw Ashish waiting. The two of them made it to class just in time. ◀ **Unrealistic power**

They decided to take a break from locker 97.6 for a while. Apparently the decision wasn't theirs to make, however. After school, locker 97.6 had a large brass lock hanging from its door.

Narrative Writing • Fantasy

Analyzing the Model

Setting

The setting of "The Secret Locker," a typical school, is mostly realistic. The locker with the unusual number suggests that something is different. Schools do not normally have lockers with decimal numbers. "The Secret Locker" is an example of a fantasy story set in the real world with one unusual feature.

Characters

The main characters are also realistic. Ashish and Rob are normal boys who have something very unusual happen to them. Although the story does suggest that Rob is able to use a special power when he gets Tony to kick up dust and sneeze, the characters in "The Secret Locker" could exist in the real world.

Plot

The story's plot contains much more fantasy. The impossible happens when Ashish and Rob are sucked down the tube into another person's body. These events cannot happen in the real world. The plot contains a conflict—getting back to one's own body. But the conflict would not exist in the real world. The main events, the conflict, and the way it is solved are what make this story a fantasy.

FUN fact

The word *fantasy*— the free play of the creative imagination— comes from a Middle English word spelled fantasie, which also means "fancy."

Reading Your Writing

Remember to develop the characters in your fantasy so that your reader will care about what happens to them.

Tips for Writing a Fantasy

STEP 1 Prewriting

- Think of how you could write about any of your own fantasies such as having special powers, visiting an imaginary world, watching toys come to life, or seeing and talking to fantastic creatures.
- Look in your folder or journal for possible story ideas.
- Use a story map to plan the parts of your story that will have fantasy elements. Plan the conflict, resolution, and any events containing fantasy.

STEP 2 Drafting

- Refer to your story map and other notes to write your fantasy story.
- Let your imagination run free as you write.

STEP 3 Revising

- **Ideas** Are your ideas original? Will readers find them interesting?
- **Organization** Do the story events make sense and fit together? Does your story have a problem or conflict that is solved?

STEP 4 Editing/Proofreading

- **Conventions** Proofread your fantasy for mistakes in spelling, punctuation, and capitalization.

STEP 5 Publishing

- **Presentation** Neatly type or rewrite your final copy.
- **Presentation** Consider illustrating your fantasy.

Narrative Writing • Fantasy

Play

A **play** is a story that is written to be acted out before an audience. What the characters say and do tells the story in a play. People called actors memorize and perform their parts, which are the words and actions written for their character.

Plays have the basic elements of other forms of literature. When you write a play, you will want to include setting(s), a plot, and characters.

Setting

The **setting** refers to the time and place where events occur. Plays often have more than one setting. These different settings are called **scenes.** Scenes are like chapters in a book. For example, a play based on *The Princess and the Pea* might have its first scene in the late afternoon at the castle gate where the princess appears during a storm. The next scene might be in the evening in the bedroom where the queen tests the princess by placing a pea under twenty mattresses. When describing the settings and scenes in a play, be sure to tell when and where the action takes place.

Plot

Plot refers to what happens in the play. It should include not only a beginning, a middle, and an end but also conflict and resolution. The audience finds out about the play's conflict or struggle through what the characters say and do. For example, in a play based on *Charlotte's Web*, you discover the central struggle in dialogue between the old sheep and Wilbur, the pig, when the old sheep tells Wilbur he is being fed so that he can be slaughtered for ham. The events and the resolution that follow (the actions of Charlotte, the spider) are based on the struggle to save Wilbur's life. When writing a play, be sure to include a conflict and a resolution.

SECTION 2
Forms of Writing

Characters

Characters refer to the figures that act and speak in the play. They are listed at the play's beginning as the **cast of characters.** For example, a play based on *Alice's Adventures in Wonderland* might list Alice, White Rabbit, Cheshire Cat, and Queen of Hearts as its cast. A character in a play may be a person, an animal, or even an object such as a car or a tree.

Dialogue

Dialogue refers to the words or lines spoken by the characters. In plays, words spoken by characters are not put in quotation marks as they are in other forms of writing. Instead, the character's name followed by a colon marks the lines or dialogue. This is how dialogue in a play based on *The Princess and the Pea* might look.

> **Queen:** How did you sleep, dear?
>
> **Princess:** Not very well. I felt something digging into my back all night.

Stage Directions

Stage directions describe just about everything going on in the play that isn't dialogue. They include where characters move, how they should express themselves, and also directions on how to use props, sound effects, costumes, and lighting. Place stage directions in parentheses or in brackets. You may also underline them or use italic type. See these stage directions for a play based on *Charlotte's Web*.

> **Charlotte:** *(talking in a quiet, soothing voice from a dark corner of the barn)* I'll be your friend, Wilbur.
>
> **Wilbur:** *(jumping to his feet)* But I can't see you. Where are you?

Play Model

This portion of a play was taken from "The Search for the Mysterious Patriot." Look for the features of a play such as stage direction and setting.

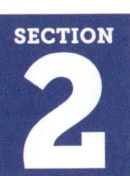

Scene 1

SETTING: The action of the play takes place in New York City in 1787.

AT RISE: A silversmith's shop in New York City, 1787. ABIGAIL peers intently at the inside of a clock on a table. A workbench sits nearby. FATHER enters.

FATHER: Are you still studying the insides of that clock, Abigail? I'm surprised your eyes don't hurt.

ABIGAIL: I want to know everything about clocks, Father. I want to know how the gears move, why it ticks, why these things are called hands...the workings of a clock are a mystery to me. As you know, I do love a good mystery.

FATHER: Then maybe you can solve the mystery of where your brother is? He was supposed to help me sweep up the shop.

(ALEXANDER HAMILTON enters.)

FATHER: Ah, how do you do, Mr. Hamilton? 'Tis so nice to see you again.

HAMILTON: Good morning, sir. I seem to have broken a silver buckle on one of my shoes. Could you repair it?

FATHER: Indeed! (*pointing to ABIGAIL*) Mr. Hamilton, I would like to introduce you to my daughter, Abigail. Abigail, this is Mister Alexander Hamilton.

ABIGAIL: Very nice to meet you, sir.

HAMILTON: The pleasure is mine, madam.

FATHER: Now then, Mister Hamilton, if you'll just follow me.

(*FATHER and ALEXANDER step to the workbench to examine the broken shoe buckle. SAMUEL enters in a huff. He carries a newspaper.*)

ABIGAIL: (*whispering hotly*) Samuel, where have you been? Father's been looking all over for you. You were supposed to sweep the shop!

SAMUEL: (*Ignoring her and holding up newspaper*) They've done it again, Sister!

ABIGAIL: They've gone and printed a newspaper. What ever will they think of next?

SAMUEL: No, Abigail. 'Tis not the newspaper I'm angry about. 'Tis what's *in* the newspaper.

ABIGAIL: You're in a mood today.

SECTION 2

Forms of Writing

SAMUEL: This is serious business, Abigail. This Publius fellow has written another article. Listen to this. (*reading from newspaper*) "Nothing is more certain than the indispensable necessity of government, and it is equally undeniable, that whenever and however it is instituted, the people must cede to it some of their natural rights in order to vest it with requisite powers."

(*Alexander Hamilton subtly turns to listen to Abigail and Samuel's conversation.*)

ABIGAIL: He's arguing for the ratification of the Constitution.

SAMUEL: How do you know that?

ABIGAIL: You're not the only one who reads the newspaper, Samuel. Do you think the Constitution should be ratified?

SAMUEL: (*proudly*) I'm an anti-Federalist. The Constitution gives too much power to the national government.

ABIGAIL: You don't think our national government should be powerful?

SAMUEL: A strong national government takes away the liberty of the people. It takes away the freedoms that people like Father fought for during the revolution.

ABIGAIL: No, the Constitution limits the power of the national government through checks and balances. (*off Samuel's look*) You're not the only one who reads books, Samuel.

SAMUEL: You speak like a Federalist.

ABIGAIL: Indeed. Perhaps that's because I am one.

SAMUEL: (*gasping*) My own sister, a Federalist? You better not let Father know.

ABIGAIL: I am allowed to have my own opinion.

SAMUEL: You think everyone should have your opinion.

ABIGAIL: (*laughing*) Come now, I'm sure we can find common ground. Like our shared interest in this Publius fellow.

SAMUEL: I wonder who it might be? Alas, we will never know his true identity.

ABIGAIL: (*thinking*) I say we test that statement.

SAMUEL: What do you mean?

ABIGAIL: I've been tinkering with this clock all day—studying the gears, the hands, the springs. All of these mechanics are clues to discovering how the clock works. Maybe if we study these papers and follow some clues, we can figure out the identity of the writer behind them? What do you say?

SAMUEL: I say that's the first thing you've said all day that I agree with.

(FATHER and ALEXANDER HAMILTON cross the stage.)

FATHER: Thank you for coming in, Mister Hamilton. I hope you didn't find my children's arguing too bothersome.

HAMILTON: Not at all. I have reserved a room above the meetinghouse while I am in town for business. I am leaving for Philadelphia the night after tomorrow. Will the buckle be ready by then?

FATHER: Aye, sir. I will deliver the buckle myself.

HAMILTON: Very good, sir. (*picking up the newspaper*) Is this Publius fellow writing again? He is a bit long-winded at times, don't you think? I wish you all a good day.

FATHER: Good day, Mister Hamilton. (*HAMILTON exits. FATHER turns to ABIGAIL and SAMUEL.*)

FATHER: Come on, you two. Stop that lollygagging and get back to work. And Samuel, grab that broom! Many hands make light work!

Analyzing the Model

Setting

Information at the beginning of the play and at the beginning of each scene should tell you when and where the action takes place. In this play excerpt, the setting is given after the heading for the scene.

Plot

How would you describe the plot? What is the conflict? How is it resolved? Through the character's words, we learn that they want to find out the identity of the writer of a newspaper article. The characters are going to study the newspaper article to determine the identity, but we do not find out the resolution in this excerpt.

Characters

How are characters developed? The play develops personalities through dialogue and action (described by stage direction). Through dialogue, we learn that Samuel is an anti-Federalist and believes that a strong national government takes away people's freedoms. On the other hand, we learn that Abigail is a Federalist and does not agree with Samuel.

Try It!

Can you think of any stories or books that you would like to make into a play? What would be the setting of the play? Who would be the characters? What kind of stage direction might you add?

SECTION 2
Forms of Writing

Reading Your Writing

A play is a story that is written to be performed for an audience. When writing your play, include good stage directions so the actors can understand what their characters should do.

Tips for Writing a Play

STEP 1 Prewriting

- Plan your setting and plot. You could make a chart listing *when* and *where* each scene occurs and *what* happens.
- Develop your characters. Plan what they will say and do.

STEP 2 Drafting

- Refer to your prewriting plan to write your play.

STEP 3 Revising

- **Ideas** Do your dialogue and stage directions show clearly what happens in your play?
- **Organization** Does your play have a beginning, a middle, and an end and also a conflict and resolution?
- **Word Choice** Do you have characters using words and language in a way that develops individual personalities?

STEP 4 Editing/Proofreading

- **Conventions** Check to make sure character names and other proper nouns are capitalized. Check punctuation and spelling.

STEP 5 Publishing

- **Presentation** Make neat final copies for each cast member to read and memorize.
- **Presentation** Present your play to an audience.

Descriptive Writing

Descriptive writing provides the reader with a clear, vivid picture of something or someone. Think about the best place you ever visited. What do you remember about the way it looked, sounded, and smelled? When you use sensory details in your writing, you help your readers see what you see, hear what you hear, and feel what you feel.

SECTION 2

Forms of Writing

Examples of descriptive writing include the following:

▶ Writing a Description
▶ Observation Report
▶ Magazine Articles
▶ Describing an Event
▶ Comparing and Contrasting

EXAMPLE Read the descriptive paragraph Chloe wrote. Look for the descriptive words she used.

> My Nice Surprise
> When I got home from school, I saw a rose on the table. It was my favorite color, dark red! It smelled better than the perfume my mom always wears. I touched a petal. It was soft and silky. The rose was in a smooth glass vase. It had lots of water in it for the rose to drink. Then I saw a little card beside the vase. It said, "Haley, I love you! Dad." My first rose!

Continue reading to see additional examples and to find out more information about descriptive writing.

SECTION 2

Forms of Writing

Writing a Description

Descriptions tell about how things and events look, sound, feel, smell, and even taste. If you write good descriptions, your readers can almost experience the things about which you are writing.

Descriptive Writing

Writing that is descriptive uses details to create a clear and interesting picture in the reader's mind. Unlike a story, descriptive writing does not usually contain events with a beginning, a middle, and an end. Descriptive writing, in the form of sentences or paragraphs, is usually found *within* another type of writing. Descriptive writing is used in many different kinds of writing, both fiction and nonfiction.

In your own writing, you might choose to write a paragraph to describe a setting, a character, an action, or an object. Descriptive paragraphs help readers create detailed mental pictures that make the descriptions seem real.

Good Description is in the Details

Sensory writing tells how something smells, tastes, feels, and sounds as well as how it looks. The sentences below engage the reader's memories of taste and smell.

> As I blew up the rubber raft, I could taste the salt of last year's trip to the ocean. The raft smelled like the moldy garden hose stored in our basement.

> ## Try It!
> Which senses do these sentences rely on for sensory description?
> - The aroma of banana and peanut butter sandwiches floated toward me.
> - Drills whirred and hammers clanged as sawdust filled the air.

Select the Right Word

Colorful adjectives such as *bumpy, spongy,* and *shrill* are an obvious choice for descriptive writing. Specific nouns such as *Big Ben, cicada,* and *No. 2 pencil* add interest, also. Precise action verbs such as *plunge, saunter,* and *singe* add energy and interest to your writing. Be creative and exact with your words. For example, the narrative sentence *My boots were getting stuck in the mud* becomes much more interesting when you add descriptive adjectives and verbs: *The brown-green mud sucked at my favorite boots as I wrestled to free myself.*

Tell How

Don't just tell *what;* tell *how* something looks or sounds. Similes and metaphors are great for describing *how.* For examples of similes and metaphors, see pages 330–331.

Organizing Your Descriptions

When writing a description, you will want to present the details in a way that makes sense to your reader. Avoid jumping from one unrelated detail to the next. Descriptions may be organized in any number of ways: from top to bottom, left to right, near to far, most recent to least recent, or any way that makes sense for what you are describing.

SECTION 2
Forms of Writing

Descriptive Writing • Writing a Description

SECTION 2

Forms of Writing

EXAMPLE The three descriptive models on these pages are each part of a longer piece of fiction. *Up on a Roof* describes the planets and the place where a girl sets up her telescope. The details are arranged from the nearest details to the ones farthest away. *Under the Sea* describes what a group of snorkelers sees under the water. The details are organized from top to bottom. *In the Gym* describes what the writer sees while looking for his friends. The details are organized from left to right.

Up on a Roof

Old newspapers, aluminum cans, and discarded rags littered the rooftop. A pungent tar odor from the roof filled Luisa's nose. The roof had been baking in the hot sun all day, and she could feel the warmth under the soles of her shoes. A soft, warm breeze fluttered the laundry hanging on nearby apartment balconies.

Farther out, a few wispy clouds floated by the silver glow of the moon. Overall, it looked like a clear evening, perfect for viewing the night sky. Luisa's grandfather had told her that four planets should be visible with her telescope that evening. Venus was the easiest to spot. Low in the sky, looking close enough to touch, it shone brighter than anything else. Jupiter was also easy to find. It appeared much higher, but it, too, was bright. Luisa scanned the sky for Mars and trained her telescope on a pinkish star. When she increased the magnification, she saw the object's roundness and knew it was the planet Mars. Last she searched for Saturn. She finally spotted something far away that did not seem to belong to the nearby constellation. It was Saturn. When she focused the lenses, she saw the spectacular rings circling the planet like a silver disk.

Under the Sea

A gentle breeze rippled the top of the water. Just under the surface, bubbles from other snorkelers floated to the top. The turquoise blue of the Caribbean deepened to a sapphire when we looked down. Tiny silver fish swam in schools just five feet below. Beneath them we saw striped fish, royal blue fish with black and yellow markings, and one silvery bronze fish with black spots.

As we dove toward the coral at the bottom, colder water surrounded our bodies. Shades of pink, orange, green, and purple tinted the vast array of coral on the seafloor. Small orange and white clown fish swam in and out of the formations. What was that in the sand? A large manta ray emerged from its spot and moved on, leaving us to our underwater exploration.

SECTION 2

Forms of Writing

In the Gym

As I entered the hall to the gym, I heard the loud buzzer announcing halftime. I wanted to find my friends. To the left of the bleachers was the drinking fountain with its usual small puddle of water on the floor in front of it.

Even though it was halftime, the bleachers were almost full. I could feel the heat of the crowd. On the left side of the bleachers sat a group of sixth graders. They were wearing red T-shirts that said, "Go Eagles." I saw some kids from my fifth-grade class sitting to the right of them and, farther to the right, lots of parents. Closer to the center, on an empty bleacher at the bottom, were water bottles and towels. A net bag held the extra basketballs. To the right of the bench was the scoring table, then the speaker's stand. On the right end of the bleachers, I saw fans from the other team waving their green banners.

Descriptive Writing • Writing a Description

Analyzing the Models

Up on a Roof

What do you notice about the first model? Do you see how the author first describes what is nearby and then describes what is farther away? Details in this description are organized from near to far. The description uses location words such as "near," "nearby," "close," "farther," and "farther out." Luisa first senses her immediate environment. She sees the litter, she smells the tar, and she feels the heat under her feet. The author tells about the laundry hanging "nearby" in Luisa's neighborhood. Next, the description moves "farther out" to the clouds, then to the moon, and finally to the planets farther out in the solar system. Saturn is described last as being "far away."

Under the Sea

The details in this piece are organized from top to bottom. Location words such as "top," "under," "down," "below," "beneath," "bottom," and "seafloor" guide the reader from the top to the bottom of the underwater scene. Organizing the description from top to bottom allows the reader to follow the snorkelers to the bottom of the sea.

In the Gym

This model describes a scene from left to right. Location words and phrases include "to the left," "left side," "to the right," and "the center." These words take the readers along with the speaker as they scan the bleachers from left to right.

> **Reading Your Writing**
>
> Descriptions use details to tell about objects, people, places, and things that happen. Organized descriptions help readers see a picture in their minds.

Tips for Descriptive Writing

STEP 1 Prewriting

▶ Figure out how you want to organize the details of your description, whether from top to bottom, near to far, or left to right.

STEP 2 Drafting

▶ Use your notes from prewriting to write your descriptive piece.

STEP 3 Revising

▶ **Ideas** Have you provided a lot of concrete sensory detail to make the scene real? If not, add more detail to your description.
▶ **Word Choice** Have you chosen descriptive words that are precise and have sensory appeal?
▶ **Organization** Is your piece written in an organized way that helps the reader understand what is described? Did you use location words?

STEP 4 Editing/Proofreading

▶ **Conventions** Proofread your descriptive writing to check for spelling mistakes. Check capitalization and punctuation, and make any corrections.

STEP 5 Publishing

▶ **Presentation** Revise your original story or nonfiction piece to include your description.

Explaining a Scientific Process

A well-written report is one of the most important parts of a science experiment. Communicating your results in writing is essential since, in most cases, your audience will not be present to observe the entire scientific process themselves. A report on an experiment includes information about what you did, how you did it, what you observed, and any conclusions you were able to draw.

SECTION 2 — Forms of Writing

Recording Data and Observations

Careful note taking is the first type of writing you will need to do for a science report. A learning log is an excellent tool for recording your questions, ideas, and observations as you complete the scientific process. Here are some excerpts from the learning log Lia used as she conducted her science experiment.

Saturday, February 6

Grandpa was bothered today when he dropped some blueberry pie on the rug. He said that blueberries leave the worst stain. I don't know if Grandpa was serious, but he made me wonder: Do blueberries stain fabric more than other fruits or vegetables?

Monday, February 8

I decided to conduct an experiment with blueberries and beets. Beets are dark red, and I think they probably leave a darker stain on fabric than blueberries do.

Tuesday, February 9

I put 1/2 cup of chopped beets and 1/2 cup of water in one pan. I put 1/2 cup of blueberries and 1/2 cup of water in another pan. I boiled each mixture for 15 minutes, then I soaked two 4" x 6" pieces of white cotton cloth in each pan.

The cloth turned a deep shade of orange-red after soaking with boiled beets for 1 minute. The cloth I soaked for 1 minute with boiled blueberries turned a medium shade of purple.

Parts of a Science Report

A report on a science experiment consists of three main parts. Your report should begin with an introduction that states your hypothesis. This is followed by a detailed description of the experiment and, finally, a conclusion.

1. Introduction

In the introduction, you should explain the purpose of your experiment and state your hypothesis. A hypothesis is an unproven statement that can be tested by an experiment. Your introduction can also include personal knowledge and background information about how you formed your hypothesis and why you chose to perform the experiment.

2. Experiment

This is where you turn to the careful notes you took in your learning log. This section of your report focuses on the details of your scientific process and includes the following information:

- a list of materials, including the quantity of each
- the steps of the procedure in the order they were performed
- the results of the experiment

3. Conclusion

The conclusion is where you tell whether the experiment proved your hypothesis to be true.

Presenting information in the correct order is especially important when reporting on a science experiment. A clear and logical order to your report will help your audience stay focused.

> **EXAMPLE** Using notes from her learning log and following the correct order for presenting information, Lia wrote this report on her science experiment.

> Beets vs. Blueberries: Which One Makes a Better Dye?
>
> This experiment was inspired by a dropped piece of blueberry pie. My grandfather looked at the blue splotch on his rug and stated that blueberries leave the worst stain. I decided to test this statement by comparing blueberries and beets as dyes. My hypothesis is that beets will make a better dye because of their dark red color.

Materials

- 1/2 cup fresh blueberries
- 1/2 cup chopped beets
- 9 cups water, divided
- 4 pieces of white cotton cloth
- 2 teaspoons laundry detergent
- 2 small plastic buckets

Procedure

1. Put the blueberries in a pan of water. Put the beets in a separate pan of water. Boil each mixture for 15 minutes.
2. Put two pieces of cloth in each pan and soak for 1 minute.
3. Hang the four pieces of cloth to dry for 24 hours.
4. Mix 1 teaspoon of detergent with 4 cups of water in two separate buckets. Wash one blueberry-stained cloth in one container; wash one beet-stained cloth in the other container.
5. Rinse each cloth and hang to dry for 24 hours.
6. Compare the washed and unwashed cloths.

Results

The blueberries turned the cloth a medium shade of purple, and the beets turned the cloths a dark orange-red. After washing and rinsing one of each stained cloth, I found that the beet-soaked cloth came almost totally clean, while the blueberry-soaked cloth still had a bluish-purple stain.

Conclusion

The blueberry-stained cloth kept more of its color than the beet-stained-cloth. Therefore, the results of the experiment do not support my hypothesis that beets make a better dye.

Tips for Explaining a Scientific Process

STEP 1 Prewriting

- Review the notes you made in your learning log, and think about the information that should be included in the report.

STEP 2 Drafting

- Make sure your report has the three essential parts: an introduction that states the hypothesis, a detailed description of the experiment, and a conclusion.
- Include a colorful graph, chart, or diagram to present your data and information.

STEP 3 Revising

- **Organization** Make sure the various sections of your report are presented in the correct order.
- **Word Choice** Is your report clear and detailed enough to thoroughly explain your project to someone who is not familiar with it?
- Give your report a catchy title that relates to the topic of your experiment.

STEP 4 Editing/Proofreading

- **Conventions** Check your report for correct sentence structure, spelling, and punctuation.
- Is your graph, chart, or diagram clearly labeled?
- Make a title page for your report.

STEP 5 Publishing

- Write or type the final version.
- Present your report at a science fair. Consider creating a display board to accompany your report.

Descriptive Writing • Observation Reports

Magazine Articles

A **magazine article** is usually a factual story that bridges the gap between a book and a newspaper. Magazine articles are longer than newspaper articles and shorter than books. Magazines usually include several articles about a particular subject. While a magazine article usually gives more in depth and more detailed information than a news story, magazine articles do share some of the same features. Like news stories, magazine articles often have a lead, body, quotation or callout, photo or diagram, caption, and a close.

Audience

There are magazines that cater to almost every audience and interest. For example, *National Geographic* has articles, maps, and photographs that feature places, people, and animals from all over the world. *Sports Illustrated Kids* contains action photographs, posters, activities, and information about all types of sports. Although *Cricket* is mainly a literary magazine, it also contains puzzles, crafts, recipes, and contests to motivate readers and writers. Knowing the age and interest of your audience is vital to writing magazine articles.

Purpose for Writing

The purpose of a magazine article can be to inform about a topic, to explain a process, to describe an event, person, or issue, or to persuade readers to a particular viewpoint. Magazine articles can be expository or persuasive essays, research reports that inform, or narrative writing that tells a story to entertain.

Human interest stories are another common and popular type of magazine article. Their purpose is to inform the reader about important issues or stories and bring about an emotional reaction. They sometimes describe a person or persons in a way that will bring about interest or sympathy in the reader. Often they describe the stories and people behind organizations, events, and meaningful historical occurrences, like natural disasters. In addition, they usually include vivid descriptions and interviews.

Research

Research for a magazine article depends upon your purpose for writing. Informational articles may require research from books, newspapers, magazines, encyclopedias, atlases, videos, and the Internet. Look for up-to-date, reliable sources. Research for explaining a process or a "How To" article may include an outline of the steps you take to do something, or an interview with someone who knows how to do it. For a persuasive magazine article, you will need to research facts and examples to support your argument.

Brainstorming

Start with interests that you have and things you know. Writing about subjects that are important to you will help your writing be more interesting to read. Your enthusiasm for the subject will help your readers to be excited about it too. Keep a folder or write ideas in a journal so you will have several to choose from when writing a magazine article.

SECTION 2

Forms of Writing

FUN fact

The word *magazine* comes from the Arabic word *makhzan* meaning "storehouse." *Magazine* can mean a building for storing ammunition, a supply chamber for camera film, or a periodical publication containing articles, stories, and often drawings or photographs. Magazine publications are like a storehouse for information.

Magazine Article Model

Lead ▶

Tips for Taking "Funtastic" Photos

Want to take "Wow!" photographs? You know, the ones that make you want a copy for yourself. It is not that difficult or expensive to do. Professional photographers do take award-winning photos with their cameras and lenses worth thousands of dollars, but you can take pictures to be proud of with even the simplest of inexpensive cameras. All it takes is careful observation and knowing a few tricks of the trade.

Body ▶

Be sure your camera lens is clean. Nothing is more discouraging than having an awesome photograph with a big lint squiggle in the middle. Even a small bit of lint on the lens will look big after the prints are blown up from the negative. Many cameras have a little plastic lid called a dust cover to help protect the lens from grit, dust, and smudges. Even with a dust cover, check your lens before shooting.

Now pick a subject: a person, place, or thing that you think will make a good photograph. Choose something that you will be able to spend some time with in order to allow for careful observation and thoughtful planning of your picture. Although great action shots look like they were just snapped off casually, photographers have usually been on the scene where the action is, trying different angles and composing many shots, to capture just the action they want.

Lighting conditions can make or break a photo. While taking pictures outside in sunlight, try to have the sun behind you so that it shines on your subject. If a bright sun is behind your subject, it will cause the background to be too bright and your subject to be too dark in the print.

Next, take a good look at your subject and the background behind them. A tree trunk directly behind someone's head will make it seem as if the tree is growing right out of their head! That may not be the look you are trying to capture.

Look through your lens and frame your picture. Center your subject so you are not clipping off the top of their head. Move around your subject to see what angle looks best. Try backing up, moving closer, or asking your subject to back up or move closer.

When taking photographs of babies, small children, or pets, try squatting down to their level, or even lying down on the floor to see the world from their point of view. Remember too that you can turn the camera to create a vertical or horizontal shot.

Now for some fun with trick photography. Here are a few ideas to help you get started. Besides your camera, you will need a willing accomplice and a brick or stone walk. Have your subject lie down on their stomach on the walkway and bend their arms, legs and hands as if they were climbing a brick or stone wall. Now you stand over your subject and bend your camera down so that you are taking the picture from a parallel angle to your lying-down subject. You may need to stand on a small step ladder or nearby stairs to get high enough over your subject to see their whole body.

For this next shot, you will need two agreeable volunteers and an outdoor location. Have one volunteer stand at a distance far enough away for you to see all of their body from head to toe. Ask them to hold out their arm to the side and their hand with the palm up and flat, as if they were holding a tray. Ask your second volunteer to move several yards behind the first volunteer. Position yourself and your second volunteer until they look like they are a tiny person standing on the hand of the giant first volunteer.

If you have a camera with a shutter timer, your can have some fun being in your own pictures. Set your camera up on a level ledge and look through the lens to see where you need to stand or sit to be in your picture. Set the timer lever, push the shutter down, and run quickly to position yourself in the photograph.

Close ▶

With a little thought and some careful observation, you can produce some memorable photographs. Remember that if you are having fun taking pictures, your viewers will enjoy looking at them. You may find yourself having so much fun with photography that it becomes a life-long hobby or a creative career.

SECTION 2

Forms of Writing

Try It!

Think of an activity you enjoy doing and know how to do well. Make a web or outline to list the steps involved in your activity. Imagine what pictures, drawings, or diagrams you would include in a magazine article about your activity.

Analyzing the Model

Titles and Leads that Capture Readers' Attention

An eye-catching title and intriguing lead are essential for capturing your readers' attention. Misspelling "fantastic" sets a humorous tone that says this article will be fun to read. The lead grabs the readers' attention by asking an obvious question and offering tips that will help the reader succeed.

Organization

The article is organized in the same sequence that one would use to take photographs. It begins with practical considerations, such as having a clean lens. The article advances from simple tips to trick photography. It closes with the suggestion that photography can become a lifelong hobby or career.

Close

An effective close leaves the reader wanting more information or wanting to try something for themselves. In the magazine article, the last few paragraphs about trick photography are designed to entice the reader into having fun with photography.

> **Reading Your Writing**
>
> Reading aloud helps to make your writing sound smooth. You may also catch mistakes in a sequence of events or steps that can be missed with silent reading.

Tips for Writing a Magazine Article

STEP 1 Prewriting

- Read issues of the magazines that cover subjects you are interested in. Pay attention to how long the articles are and if there are drawings or photographs to illustrate the articles.
- Brainstorm ideas for magazine articles. Choose a subject you are excited about.
- Use an outline or a web to help organize your article.

STEP 2 Drafting

- Refer to your outline and notes to write your article.
- Write without stopping to let the ideas flow. Later, you can correct grammar, spelling, and sentence structure.

STEP 3 Revising

- **Ideas** Are your ideas interesting and exciting?
- **Organization** Does the process or events of the article make sense in the order you have written them?
- **Word Choice** Do you use appropriate language that is clear and easy to understand? Do you explain any technical terms or unusual procedures?
- **Title, Lead, and Voice** Does your title capture the readers' attention and your lead draw the reader into the article? Does your voice keep the reader interested in your subject?
- **Sentence Fluency** Read your magazine article out loud to check for variety with word choices and sentences. Reading aloud can help you catch mistakes easily overlooked by silent reading.

STEP 4 Editing/Proofreading

- **Conventions** Proofread your magazine article for spelling, punctuation, and capitalization.

STEP 5 Publishing

- **Presentation** Neatly type or rewrite your final copy.
- **Presentation** Consider illustrating your magazine article with a drawing, photograph, diagram, or graph.

SECTION 2 Forms of Writing

Describing an Event

Have you ever seen a movie that depicted an event so well that you almost felt you were there? Perhaps it was a period film that depicted the first shot of the Revolutionary War, a historical drama that had scenes of a wagon train heading west, or a documentary with exciting images of the moon landing. When you describe an event, you should give your reader the same kind of vivid imagery and sense of "being there" that you get when you watch a great movie. You can do this by using the tools of descriptive writing, such as concrete sensory details and figurative language (similes, metaphors, personification, and so on).

Choosing an Event

You have several options when choosing an event to describe. You can pick a historical event that happened long ago, or you can write about a recent event you experienced yourself. You might describe a specific event that happened only once, like the Cherokee Trail of Tears or your sister's high school graduation ceremony. Or, you might describe what happens at a general event like a basketball game. Either way, you will need to know your subject well enough to describe it clearly and vividly for your audience.

> ### Try It!
>
> What events have you experienced that you would like to describe? A sporting event? A concert? What historical events have you read about in class that you would like to write about? Pick one event, and think of three vivid details you would use to describe it.

Gathering Ideas and Information

To paint an accurate picture of your event, you need to know its details inside and out. Before you plan your description, you should know the *who, what, when, where, how,* and *why* of your event. Unless you are already an expert on your topic, you will probably have to search to find this information!

There are many ways to gather information about an event. If you are writing about a historical event or something that happens in another country, you will likely need to do research at the library and on the Internet. You might seek firsthand accounts of the event in books or published diaries. If you are describing a recent event you experienced or something that happens close to home, you can gather ideas through visualization or observation. For example, if your topic is a "basketball game," you can go to a school basketball game and record what you see. You can also interview experts on your topic or the people who witnessed an event to gather details.

Taking Notes

It is important to take detailed notes as you gather information. Record sensory details that relate to each of the five senses, and keep a running list of exciting adjectives, adverbs, and action verbs you might use. Organize notes in a learning log with the date and source of information.

Try It!

Where might you find information and details about the following events: a family reunion, the Wounded Knee Massacre, the Running of the Bulls in Spain?

SECTION 2
Forms of Writing

Descriptive Writing • Describing an Event

Describing an Event Model

Here is a description of the Japanese tea ceremony.

A Ceremony to Remember

Imagine yourself stepping lightly on a dewy path through a garden full of rounded shrubs and beautiful flowers. You stop to wash your hands and mouth with cool water at a stone fountain and quietly wait on a straight wooden bench. Then, your host calls you, and you are about to step into a Japanese tearoom in the 1500s. Chanoyu, the Japanese tea ceremony, is an ancient and interesting ritual. The simple setting of the tearoom, the beauty of the rigid ceremony, and the respect given to its traditional equipment make it an inspiring event.

The typical Japanese tearoom is an inviting space perfect for the calming ritual. The room is small and plain. It has smooth *tatami* mats arranged on the floor for the guests to walk and sit on. A special area called the *tokonoma* contains a scroll hanging on a wall, a seasonal flower arrangement, and the only other decor. Being in the simple tearoom is like a peaceful daydream, an escape from the world outside.

The ceremony is a lengthy and refined event with many parts. Before guests enter the tearoom, they dutifully remove their shoes. They walk to the *tokonoma* to admire the scroll and are then seated *seiza*-style on the mats, sitting upright on their knees and resting back onto their heels. The practiced host serves tiny treats, which are eaten from special papers carried in the guests' bare or simply patterned kimonos. Next, the utensils are thoroughly cleansed in a specific order and set in an exact arrangement. The host then carefully places a measured amount of green tea powder into the bowl, adds hot water, and whisks the tea. During this time, guests relax quietly and enjoy the hissing sounds of water, the warmth of the fire, and the soothing smells of incense. Once ready, the bowls of tea are ceremoniously exchanged between the host and guest of honor, and then passed on to each guest with specific bows, positioning, and respectful words.

The utensils used in a tea ceremony sing of honor and tradition, and are treated with great care and respect by the guests. After everyone has savored the tea, the host cleans the dirtied utensils with *chakin*, long rectangular white cloths, and *fukusa*, square, colored silk cloths. He or she allows the guests to examine and admire the utensils. The ladle for scooping water has a long bamboo handle. The *chawan*, or handmade tea bowl, has unique imperfections in its design, and the short, round, and glossy tea caddy known as a *natsume* has a glossy surface smooth to the touch.

Imagine yourself at the end of a tea ceremony. You carefully hold tradition in your hands and feel a tranquil sensation. Maybe you feel you have entered another world or gone back in time. But you actually could experience all of this—Japanese tea ceremonies are still performed today. Those who wish to host tea ceremonies study their art for many years so others can experience the peaceful setting, beautiful ceremony, and ancient tools of the Chanoyu of the past. One can only hope they will continue to keep this inspiring event alive far into the future.

SECTION 2

Forms of Writing

Try It!

What are some of the best sensory details or descriptive words you can find in the model? Have you ever witnessed a ceremony or ritual? What details and words would you use to describe it?

Reading Your Writing

When you describe an event, it is important to use vivid concrete sensory details. Descriptive language helps to capture your readers' attention and helps them visualize and understand your subject. As you draft, picture your subject in your mind and try to choose the most exciting descriptive words and figurative language to describe it. When you revise, check your draft to see if you can add more precise words to your details. Remember that you can always use a thesaurus to find more interesting words.

Descriptive Writing • Describing an Event

Analyzing the Model

Title
The title tells the audience what will be described in a way that is straightforward and creative; it expresses the importance of the event by saying that it should be "remembered."

Introduction
The opening paragraph is descriptive and informative. It captures the reader's attention immediately with a vivid lead that places them in a dramatic scene: the setting of the event. Importantly, the introduction also clearly states the event and the main parts of it that will be described.

Body
The body provides information about the *who, what, where, when,* and *how* of the event. The major parts of the event that are described (the setting, the parts of the ceremony, and the equipment used) are organized logically—the writer arranged these main ideas chronologically and by topic. Each paragraph has a clear topic sentence stating the main idea and supporting details. But because this is a descriptive piece, the supporting details are not simple facts and evidence. Instead, they include colorful word choices, concrete sensory details, and figurative language that make the event come alive for the reader.

Conclusion
The conclusion draws the event to a close and returns to the opening by urging the readers to imagine themselves at the ceremony. The writer surprises the readers by informing them that tea ceremonies still occur today. The final sentences summarize the main ideas and include a thoughtful reflection on how the event relates to the individual, society, or the world.

Tips for Describing an Event

STEP 1 Prewriting

- Choose an event that will interest you and your reader.
- Conduct research, observations, or interviews to gather ideas and information. Keep notes in a learning log or notebook.
- Decide the parts of the event you want to describe. Will you organize them by topic, by chronological order, or by another system?

STEP 2 Drafting

- Use your notes to draft your description. Remember to use interesting words and sensory details. It may help to stop periodically and visualize the event.

STEP 3 Revising

- **Ideas** Did you include enough details so the event is clear? Will your description interest your reader?
- **Organization** Did you use transition words to make the parts of the event clear?
- **Word Choice** Did you use precise words and concrete sensory details to make the scene come alive? Use visualization or a thesaurus to add more vivid descriptions to your piece.

STEP 4 Editing/Proofreading

- **Conventions** Check your description for correct spelling, grammar, and punctuation. Did you capitalize all proper nouns and adjectives?

STEP 5 Publishing

- **Presentation** Consider adding a detailed drawing or photos of your event.

SECTION 2

Forms of Writing

Descriptive Writing • Describing an Event

Comparing and Contrasting

A **comparison** shows how two things are alike. A **contrast** shows how two things are different. In a compare/contrast essay, you examine the similarities and differences between two subjects. Your subjects could be objects, places, people, animals, events, or even ideas. You have many options, and there are many ways to organize your essay. However, there are some useful guidelines to follow.

A compare/contrast essay is informative and descriptive. You *inform* your readers about each of your subjects' traits and show them how they are similar and different. To help your audience visualize these traits, similarities, and differences, you clearly *describe* each subject with vivid details. It is important to choose two subjects that are enough alike. It would not be fun to read about the similarities and differences between a bear and a beach ball! However, an essay describing the similarities and differences between two different bears might be very informative and interesting.

Try It!

What are some things you would like to compare and contrast? What descriptive details would you use to make their similarities and differences obvious to your reader?

Reading Your Writing

It is important to use transition words to clearly connect ideas in your writing. Transition words help sentences and paragraphs flow smoothly together. They help the readers follow your train of thought more easily. Some transition words that show comparisons include *also, in the same way, like, likewise, both, just as, similarly,* and *too*. Some transition words that show contrast include *although, but, however, even though, on the other hand, otherwise, yet,* and *in contrast*. As you draft and revise your writing, make sure you are using transition words to help your ideas flow smoothly.

Comparing and Contrasting Two Events

To compare and contrast two events, you will have to describe what happened at each event clearly. You will have to make the similarities and differences of each event obvious to your reader. This means that you might need to break down the aspects or parts of the events that are comparable. For example, imagine you are comparing and contrasting two different battles of World War I. You could decide upon three topics, or parts of the battles, that you will describe. The three topics you choose to compare and contrast are the soldiers, the battle strategy, and the outcome.

Remember that it is important that the two events you choose can really be compared. While two battles of the Revolutionary War might be easily compared, you could not compare a battle and visiting the zoo. Although they are both events, there are no points of comparison. Make sure the events you choose to describe have a similar theme .

SECTION 2

Forms of Writing

Descriptive Writing • Comparing and Contrasting

Choosing Two Events

Did you think of two events that interest you and that have a similar theme? Are they also events that will be easy to describe and interesting for your reader? Remember that when you are deciding upon events, you have many options. You could compare and contrast two historical events that happened long ago. You could compare and contrast two current events you saw on the news or are learning about in school. Or, it might be interesting to compare two events from different time periods. If you wanted to choose battles, for example, you could compare and contrast a battle from World War I to a battle from the past decade. Similarly, you could compare and contrast two similar events that occurred in different places or cultures. It might be very interesting, for example, to analyze the similarities and differences between a wedding in America and a wedding in India.

Try It!

Think of some events that you have read about in a history book or a newspaper. Are there any events that stand out to you? Choose two events, and answer the following questions:
- What are three topics or points of comparison between these events that you could analyze?
- What are three reasons that these events might be interesting to your reader?

Organizing Information

Depending on the events you have chosen and how much you know about them, you may have to do research to find information. Make sure that you take notes and record vivid details to help you paint a picture of the event.

However, without a method for organizing your compare/contrast essay, you may end up with notes scattered throughout your page. A **Venn diagram** is a graphic organizer that is useful for comparing and contrasting two related subjects. For an essay comparing and contrasting two events, you can record your notes on the diagram to help you visualize the similarities and differences between them.

EXAMPLE This Venn diagram compares and contrasts the 1969 moon landing and the 1997 Mars landing.

Moon Landing
- explored by humans; Eagle landing module; communication with Earth through radio; module left moon, came back to Earth; first visit to moon

Both (center)
- explored a body in space; provided visual images of outer space; left mementos from Earth

Mars Landing
- explored by spacecraft; parachuted in from outer space; beamed pictures back to Earth; remained on Mars; second landing on Mars

See the sample essay on the following pages. Note how it uses the information from the diagram to organize ideas. Also notice the concrete sensory details and precise words in the description.

Descriptive Writing • Comparing and Contrasting

Comparing and Contrasting Two Events Model

Blasting Off!

On July 16, 1969, a rocket carrying three astronauts—Michael Collins, "Buzz" Aldrin, and Neil Armstrong—blasted off from Cape Canaveral on a historic trip to the moon. Twenty-eight years later, on July 4, 1997, the spacecraft *Pathfinder* landed on Mars. These missions had similar goals and were equally important in furthering our understanding of a complex solar system. However, each of these events was also special and unique.

The three astronauts traveled to the moon by rocket and a landing module. In 1969, the world watched in wide-eyed wonder as the Saturn V rocket carrying the *Apollo 11* crew members rose from the launchpad and blasted off into outer space. Several days later, Armstrong and Aldrin climbed into the *Eagle* landing module for their final descent onto the moon's surface. Armstrong piloted the *Eagle* over a field of boulders and carefully settled the landing module down to a flat surface. The *Eagle* had landed.

The images and words broadcast at home brought exciting pictures of the moon to Earth. Armstrong exited the *Eagle*, stepped onto the ladder, and made his way down to the surface. A camera placed near the module broadcast a grainy, ghostly image of Armstrong's descent. He communicated with Mission Control back on Earth by radio, describing the moon's surface as "powdery." Millions of people on Earth watched the event unfold on live television.

The astronauts performed tests on the moon and left mementos before returning to Earth. Armstrong and Aldrin performed a variety of experiments and collected several rock and soil samples. Before they left, they unveiled a plaque commemorating the event that was signed by the three astronauts and then president Richard Nixon. They also planted an American flag beside the plaque. Two-and-a-half days later, the three astronauts returned safely to Earth.

Nearly twenty-eight years later, in 1997, the spacecraft *Pathfinder* approached Mars. It was the second time spacecraft had landed on Mars. Notably, there were no humans aboard this spacecraft, and it landed differently—it used a parachute to slow its descent. Unlike the easy *Eagle* landing, *Pathfinder* hit Mars's surface and bounced 15 times before coming to a stop.

Like the moon landing, the Mars expedition allowed people on Earth to see images of outer space. *Sojourner*, a small rover with wheels, cameras, and other instruments, explored the area around the landing craft like a small, faithful dog sniffing for clues. Obviously the rover could not communicate by radio. Instead *Sojourner* took pictures of the surrounding area and beamed them back to Mission Control. Although the pictures were not live, people were still incredibly excited when they saw the mind-blowing images.

Like the astronauts on the moon, the rover performed experiments to find out if there was life on Mars. In this case, scientists on Earth controlled the rover via remote control. It collected samples, drilled into rock, and continued to explore the area. But unlike *Eagle*, *Pathfinder* and *Sojourner* are still on Mars, beaming back images.

Though they were many years apart, the moon and Mars landings were historical events that remain important today. Each voyage had its own methods of landing and communication, but both provided valuable knowledge. Whether through human contact or remote-controlled spacecraft, people were able to see outer space up close. Both missions performed useful experiments that taught us more about the universe. These great and unforgettable events allowed us to ask ourselves "Where do we go next?"

SECTION 2

Forms of Writing

Try It!

Remember that your compare/contrast essay should be both informative and descriptive. Does the model provide clear information and also create a vivid picture in your mind? What sensory details stand out most to you?

Descriptive Writing • Comparing and Contrasting

Comparing and Contrasting Two Experiences

Comparing and contrasting two experiences is similar to comparing and contrasting two events. The difference is that when comparing and contrasting experiences, it is important to choose subjects you have experienced firsthand. For example, comparing your night at a football game and your night at a basketball game is a good topic because you have personal knowledge of both events. However, writing an essay comparing your experience playing football *for your school* and playing football *professionally* is not the best choice because you probably do not have experience in both!

Again, remember to choose two experiences that are similar. You should not, for example, decide to compare a football game to eating breakfast. Although they are both experiences, there are no obvious points of comparison.

The nice thing about describing your personal experiences is that you do not have to do extra research—everything is in your head. It might be helpful to browse old journals or photographs for ideas and use visualization or quick notes to call to mind some images and memories. Writing about your experiences also allows you to express yourself in a more personal, individual way.

> ### Try It!
> Think of two experiences that mean a lot to you, like visiting an amusement park or going to a museum. What would your points of comparison and contrast be between the two topics?

SECTION 2
Forms of Writing

Organizing Information

Remember that a **Venn diagram** is a graphic organizer that is useful for comparing and contrasting two related subjects. It will help you visualize and organize the similarities and differences between your two experiences.

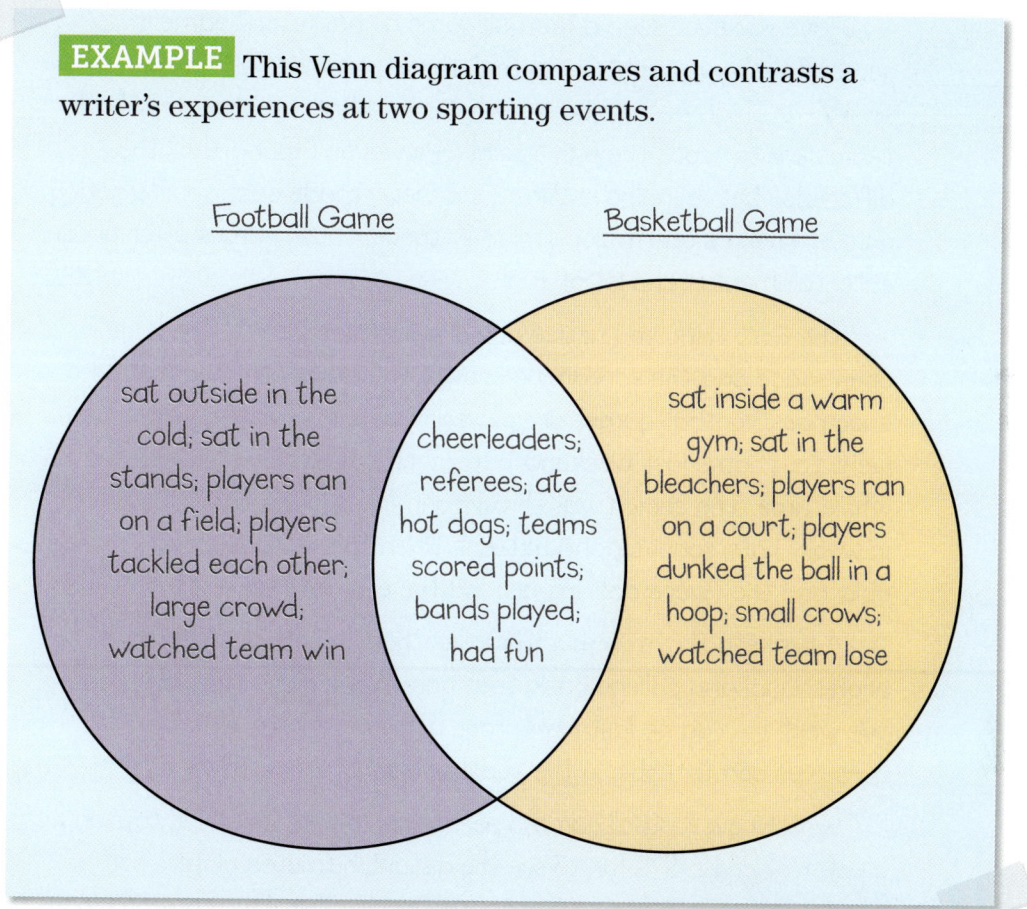

EXAMPLE This Venn diagram compares and contrasts a writer's experiences at two sporting events.

Football Game / Basketball Game

- Football Game: sat outside in the cold; sat in the stands; players ran on a field; players tackled each other; large crowd; watched team win
- Both: cheerleaders; referees; ate hot dogs; teams scored points; bands played; had fun
- Basketball Game: sat inside a warm gym; sat in the bleachers; players ran on a court; players dunked the ball in a hoop; small crows; watched team lose

SECTION 2
Forms of Writing

Use your own Venn diagram to organize and write your essay. Remember to include an introduction, a body that includes the points of comparison and contrast from your diagram, and a conclusion. See the sample essay on the following pages to see how the writer introduced the topic, organized comparisons and contrasts, and concluded the essay.

Descriptive Writing • Comparing and Contrasting

Comparing and Contrasting Two Events Model

Punt the Ball and Dunk It!

Have you ever seen a football game or basketball game in person? Well, you might guess that the experiences are pretty similar—both games use balls, both teams wear uniforms, and both teams try to score the most points. However, I found that the difference between the settings and views made each sports outing unique. There is one major similarity though: both games offer great entertainment and a lot of fun!

The first thing you notice about a football game is the huge open space and the screaming crowd. A football stadium can be enormous. Football games are played in all sorts of weather. When I went to a game last weekend, puffy white flakes of snow fell the whole time. The crowd was shivering in the stands and bundled up in woolly hats, scarves, and mittens. Even the football players looked cold, and they were dashing around the entire time!

A basketball gym is much smaller than a football stadium. All professional and college basketball games are played indoors, too. We went to a game last night, took off our jackets, and made ourselves comfortable in the toasty bleachers.

Watching a football game in person can be like watching toys on a patch of grass. It is fun to see the distant, helmeted players bolt across the green field like little action figures. There was one amazing play where the burly quarterback threw the spinning, brown ball all the way across the field to an open receiver, who ran it in for a touchdown. Even though I was sitting high up in the mountains of the stadium, squinting through the snowflakes, it was still fun to watch.

Watching a basketball game is a little different. Since the gym is smaller than a football stadium, you are usually closer to the action, no matter where you sit. Last night, I was able to see an exciting play from 15 feet away. My favorite player dribbled the ball down the court and dunked the ball. It was amazing!

There is a lot of extra entertainment at sporting events. Part of my experience at the football game included juicy hot dogs and listening to the jaunty marching band play blaring fight songs. I also watched the acrobatic cheerleaders yell and flip and do their best to get the cheering crowd into the game. I laughed at the bumbling mascot during the halftime show. I thought these things were a big part of what make a football game a football game.

But I actually did the exact same things at the basketball game! These sports traditions and silly modes of entertainment made the two experiences feel more alike—the hot dogs even tasted almost exactly the same! While the marching bands, cheerleaders, and mascots wore different colors and chanted different tunes, they were still just as entertaining. This made the smiling basketball fans just as loud and boisterous, too.

The environments at a football stadium and basketball arena are very different, and they make the view of each game special and unique. But the fun and entertainment, as well as the cheers and enthusiasm of the crowd, give both experiences a similar feeling. All in all, I must admit I am a huge fan of both games. The next chance you get, you should check out some football and basketball games yourself. Maybe you will agree with me that both are tremendous fun!

SECTION 2

Forms of Writing

Try It!

Reread the above writing model. What precise words, sensory details, or figurative language does the writer use to bring the two events to life? Notice how the writer's personal voice shows through in the text. Exclamatory sentences and amusing, everyday observations make the topic lively. Can you find some examples?

Descriptive Writing • Comparing and Contrasting

Analyzing the Models

In the compare and contrast essay models, the writers could have chosen a few different ways to organize their main ideas.

Topic by Topic or Part by Part

In each paragraph or section, introduce a **topic**. Describe how the subjects compare and contrast in terms of that topic. Sometimes a writer describes how the first subject reflects the topic in one paragraph and then describes the other subject in the next. If the writer of "Blasting Off!" had organized the essay this way, there would be one section comparing and contrasting the topic of both missions' approach and landing, one comparing and contrasting their images and communication, and one comparing and contrasting both of their experiments and mementos.

Whole Subject by Whole Subject

Describe all the traits of the first subject. Then describe all the traits of the second subject, reminding the reader how it compares and contrasts to the first. In "Blasting Off!" the writer describes the *Apollo 11* event in chronological order and by topic (approach and landing, images and communication, experiments and mementos). The writer then describes the Mars mission in the same order, highlighting important similarities and differences.

Similarities and Differences

In the first half of the body, discuss how the two subjects are similar. In the last half, tell how they are different. For example, first discuss how the moon and Mars missions were alike: both landed on astronomical bodies, both took pictures, both performed experiments. Then discuss how they are different.

Try It!

Look at the organization of "Punt the Ball and Dunk It!" Does the writer organize the essay topic by topic, whole subject by whole subject, or by similarities and differences?

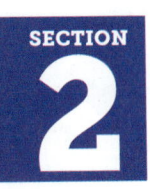

Tips for Writing a Compare and Contrast Essay

STEP 1 Prewriting

- Think of two subjects you would like to compare and contrast. Make sure they are enough alike.
- Use a Venn diagram to note the similarities and differences.
- Choose the best way to organize the information based on your notes.

STEP 2 Drafting

- Follow your organizational plan. Use transition words to highlight similarities and differences.
- Include concrete sensory details that help illustrate the similarities and differences.

STEP 3 Revising

- **Organization** Is your organization clear? Do your topic sentences and supporting details clearly state the points of comparison?
- **Word Choice** Could you add sensory details or precise words to bring the subjects alive?
- **Voice** Do you make your subjects exciting? Could you add some personal observations?

STEP 4 Editing/Proofreading

- **Conventions** Check the spelling of academic vocabulary and capitalization of proper nouns and adjectives.

STEP 5 Publishing

- **Presentation** Type or handwrite a final, clean copy. Add illustrations that reflect your sensory details and help the reader visualize your subjects.

Try It!

Remember to use transition words such as *also, as, in comparison, like, similar to, in the same way, in contrast, unlike, however, instead, yet, on the other hand, whereas,* and so on. What other transition words might you use to compare and contrast?

SECTION 2 Forms of Writing

Opinion Writing

An opinion is the way you think or feel about something. Opinion writing lets the reader know how you think or feel about something. You can write an opinion paragraph to express your opinion. Opinion writing can also encourage readers to think, feel, or act in a certain way. This is called persuasive writing.

Examples of opinion and persuasive writing include the following:

- ▶ Opinion Paragraph
- ▶ Advertisements
- ▶ Persuasive Letter
- ▶ Persuasive Essay

Continue reading this section of the Handbook to see examples and to find out more information about opinion and persuasive writing.

SECTION 2

Forms of Writing

Opinion Paragraph

One way to express your opinion is to write a paragraph that tells the reader the way you think or feel about something. Because an opinion is what YOU think, it can't really be wrong, especially if you have reasons for your opinion. Most opinion paragraphs have three parts: topic sentence, body, and ending sentence.

1. The *topic sentence* tells the reader what the subject of the paragraph is. It also tells the writer's opinion about the subject.
2. The *body* of an opinion paragraph gives the reasons and facts to support the opinion. At least three reasons should be included, and the most important reason is often given last.
3. The *ending sentence* should summarize the paragraph.

Sharing Your Opinion

You should use certain words and phrases to express your opinion. Phrases such as the ones listed below can help you state your opinion.

Opinion Words
- I think . . .
- I feel . . .
- I like . . ./I don't like . . .
- My favorite part is . . .
- This book is so . . .

Try It!

Use one of the above phrases to express your opinion about your favorite animal.

Sharing Your Reasons

You should always include at least three reasons, or facts, to support your opinion. Reasons help the reader understand why you feel or think a certain way. Use linking words such as the ones listed below to connect your opinion and reasons.

Linking Words

- because
- therefore
- since
- for instance
- consequently
- specifically

Organizing Your Ideas

Your opinion paragraph should be organized to make it easy for readers to follow what you are trying to tell them. Graphic organizers are a good way to organize your ideas for your writing. The TREE graphic organizer is an effective way to organize your ideas for your opinion paragraphs.

T	Topic Sentence Tell what you believe.
R	Reasons—3 or more. Why do I believe this? Will my readers believe this?
E	Explanations Say more about each reason.
E	Ending Wrap it up right.

EXAMPLE Liam wants to write an opinion paragraph about the importance of volunteering. Here is his TREE graphic organizer with his ideas.

T	**Topic Sentence** I believe the best way each of us can help improve the world is by volunteering some of our time.
R	**Reason 1:** Volunteers work for free.
E	**Explanation:** Organizations can spend its limited resources on other things.
R	**Reason 2:** Inspire others to volunteer as well.
E	**Explanation:** More help means less work for everyone.
R	**Reason 3:** Make new friends.
E	**Explanation:** Meet new people who could become your friend.
E	**Ending:** When you volunteer, you benefit yourself and others.

Reading Your Writing

Make sure you support your topic with good reasons. The reasons will help you show that your topic makes good sense. Remember to use linking words to connect your opinion and reasons.

Section 2: Forms of Writing

EXAMPLE Liam used his TREE graphic organizer to write his opinion paragraph.

> **Importance of Volunteering**
>
> I believe the best way each of us can help improve the world is by volunteering some of our time. To start with, volunteers work for free. Because volunteers are not paid, charities and other organizations can use more of their money to help people in need. Another reason to volunteer is to inspire others. Your friends or family may see how you are helping others and want to volunteer, too. Consequently, more people will be volunteering, which means more help and less work for everyone. Finally, volunteering is fun and you can make new friends. Because people who volunteer want to help others, you know they are nice people who will make good friends. In the end, volunteering benefits everyone, including you!

Try It!

What is Liam's opinion about volunteering? How many reasons does Liam give in his paragraph? What linking words does Liam use to connect his reasons to his opinion?

Tips for Writing an Opinion Paragraph

STEP 1 **Prewriting**

- What are some things you feel strongly about?
- Make a list.
- List some reasons to support your opinion.
- Put your ideas into a TREE graphic organizer or other web.

STEP 2 **Drafting**

- Write your paragraph. Use your web from prewriting.
- Don't worry about mistakes. You can correct them later.

STEP 3 **Revising**

- **Ideas** Do you have good reasons to support your topic?
- **Organization** Did you write your opinion in the first sentence?
- **Sentence Fluency** Did you use linking words to connect your opinion and reasons?

STEP 4 **Editing/Proofreading**

- **Conventions** Did you check your spelling?
- Did you use capital letters for proper nouns and the beginnings of sentences?

STEP 5 **Publishing**

- **Presentation** Make a neatly typed or written final copy.
- Draw a picture to go with your paragraph.

SECTION 2

Forms of Writing

Persuasive Letter

A **persuasive letter** is a letter written to convince a specific audience to adopt a certain point of view or to take action. The writer can present an opinion and support it with evidence or present a problem and suggest solutions. The details the writer includes should influence the way the reader(s) think, act, or feel about the issue or problem.

When planning a persuasive letter, it is important that you choose an issue you truly care about. Otherwise, it will be hard to develop a strong voice and convince your reader. Unlike some types of expository writing, your opinion on the subject at hand is of central importance, so you should not be afraid to make it known. Using strong details, facts, examples, and expert opinions will help you support your opinion and make it convincing.

Determining Your Audience

When planning your persuasive letter, it is important to first determine the characteristics and needs of your reader. Plan to include arguments and evidence that will specifically appeal to him or her. For example, if you are trying to convince your principal to extend recess, you would not support your argument by saying that class is "not as fun." Instead, you might provide statistics that show students' grades are better at schools that have longer recess periods. It is also important that you use appropriate language for your audience. If you are writing a persuasive letter to a teacher, newspaper, or other adult you do not know, use academic language and avoid contractions and slang. If you are writing to a friend or family member, you can use more conversational language.

Planning Your Letter

Whoever your audience is, decide beforehand what information to include and make sure it will appeal to them. This will ensure that your letter is to the point and convincing. Use a graphic organizer like a topic web or outline to plan your main points and supporting details.

Use the following order to organize your persuasive letter:

- Explain the issue or problem and state your viewpoint.
- Support your opinion with facts, examples, explanations, and/or expert opinions.
- Address the opposing argument.
- Restate your opinion, urge action, and use an emotional appeal.

Format: Use the business letter format on page 74 for your persuasive letter. Remember that a persuasive letter should be short, to the point, and convincing.

Reading Your Writing

Remember that opening with an attention-grabbing lead and providing solid supporting details will help you convince your reader. Also, using persuasive techniques like emotional appeal, repetition, hyperbole, and word choice will make your personal voice evident and your argument more effective.

Try It!

What supporting details or evidence would you provide to convince your principal to extend your recess period? To order more books for the school library? Can you think of a good emotional appeal for one of these topics?

EXAMPLE Zev Harris wrote a persuasive letter to the principal of his middle school suggesting they start a recycling program.

Dear Mrs. Samuels:

Did you know that an aluminum can thrown in the trash will still be an aluminum can 500 years from now? Or that the amount of wood and paper people throw away each year is enough to heat 50 million homes for 20 years? We cannot allow our school to contribute to this problem. I am writing to you about the great need for a recycling program at our school.

Some believe a recycling program would be too much work, but recycling is easy. All we need to do is set aside containers for cans and paper. Volunteers can empty them at the recycling center down the street. This will also create a sense of cooperation and community among the students.

Also, the cafeteria throws away tons of food scraps each day. We can use the food scraps as compost for a school garden. In this way, recycling is good for the environment and healthful too! I am sure you could not deny us such a great opportunity to improve our environment, sense of community, and eating habits.

Yours truly,
Zev Harris

What makes Zev's opening strong and effective? Can you identify the supporting details he provides? Where does he use persuasive techniques? Do you think his letter would have convinced the principal?

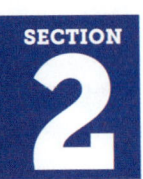

Tips for Writing a Persuasive Letter

STEP 1 Prewriting

- Select an issue you care about.
- Decide on your audience and the tone you will use.
- Use an outline or a graphic organizer to plan your main points and evidence.

STEP 2 Drafting

- Provide facts, examples, explanations, and expert opinions to support your point.
- Add the heading, inside address, salutation, closing, and signature.

STEP 3 Revising

- **Organization** Is your letter organized in a logical sequence?
- **Organization** Do you restate your opinion or offer a solution in the conclusion?
- **Voice** Does the opening grab your reader's attention? Do you use convincing persuasive techniques? Did you use academic language appropriate for your audience?

STEP 4 Editing/Proofreading

- **Conventions** Proofread your letter to check for spelling mistakes.
- **Conventions** Check to make sure the proper names are capitalized. Check all punctuation.
- **Conventions** Did you use the correct business letter format from page 74?

STEP 5 Publishing

- **Presentation** Neatly type your final copy, place it in an envelope, and mail it.

SECTION 2 Forms of Writing

Persuasive Essay

Write a persuasive essay to change the thinking, feeling, or action of your readers about a specific issue. A persuasive essay sometimes requires the research, planning, and formatting of a research report. Other times, you can rely on your own knowledge and experience to support your points. In a persuasive essay, you use your knowledge and research to influence your audience.

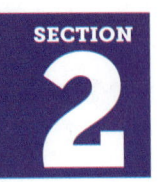

Choose Your Topic

Choose a topic that you care about and want others to care about as well. Make sure it isn't so broad that you would have too much to cover.

> The environment is suffering because people abuse it.

On the other hand, a topic that is too narrow may make finding information difficult.

> The U.S. should stop exporting a chemical that poisons the Swainson's hawk of Argentina.

Begin the Research

Use any of the following resources to research your topic: almanacs, encyclopedias, dictionaries, nonfiction books, magazines, brochures, DVDs, video and audio clips, the Internet, and experts such as a relative or someone in your community.

Decide How to Use the Information

As you take notes, focus on things that will support your view.

Facts and reasons: Look for the facts and reasons that you believe will persuade your audience.

Examples: Find examples in your research or from personal experience that strengthen your position.

Expert opinions: You may interview community members or find opinions in outside resources. Opinions are most persuasive when they come from an expert.

Write to Your Audience

The approach you use will depend on your audience. Select the information and approach that you believe will best persuade your readers by appealing to their interests and experiences. You may choose one or any combination of the approaches below, but make sure the technique also provides organization and structure.

Select a Technique

Organize your essay in one or more of the following ways:

- State a viewpoint and use **facts and reasons** to support it.
- State a viewpoint and provide **examples**.
- State a viewpoint supported by **expert opinions**.
- State a **problem** and describe one or more **solutions**.

SECTION 2 Forms of Writing

EXAMPLE See how these topics vary in audience and choice of technique.

- You think that it's important to wear helmets and safety pads when bike riding, so you write a persuasive essay giving reasons that your class should wear safety gear while riding. Your class is the audience.
- You believe sharks are disappearing, so you write an essay to explain the problem to a general audience and provide a combination of facts and reasons to arrive at some possible conclusions. (See the model on pages 237–238.)

Opening and Concluding Paragraphs

Be sure to include opening and concluding paragraphs in your persuasive essay. The opening paragraph(s) should introduce readers to the purpose of your essay and capture their attention. The closing paragraph(s) should summarize the reasons or solutions and restate the purpose.

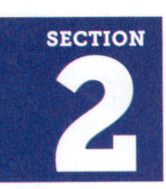

Use a Graphic Organizer

For help with choosing the key points, use a graphic organizer. The TREE graphic organizer helped the writer decide which solutions, facts, or opinions to include in an essay about disappearing sharks.

T	**Topic Sentence** Many species of sharks are disappearing.
R	**Reason 1:** Educate people
E	**Explanation:** People would care more if they knew more.
R	**Reason 2:** Limit shark fishing worldwide
E	**Explanation:** Sharks can't reproduce fast enough.
R	**Reason 3:** Boycott shark products
E	**Explanation:** Not needed for human survival
E	**Ending:** We need to do something now so sharks will be around later.

Reading Your Writing

A persuasive essay is written to change a reader's thinking on an issue. A graphic organizer can help you put your research and ideas in order.

Here's the essay written using the TREE graphic organizer.

Attack of the Shark Killers

Many species of sharks are starting to disappear. The demand for shark meat and products increases every year. As human numbers grow, the number of sharks shrinks. Four hundred species may be threatened beyond recovery. There are several ways to solve this problem.

One solution to the problem would be to educate people about sharks. People would care more about sharks if they knew more about them. Sharks rarely kill people. Although they kill humans once in a while, many more people die from lightning and bee stings. Great white sharks sometimes mistake humans for sea lions, but humans are not their natural prey. Most shark species are completely harmless. If people did not see sharks as threats, they might care about protecting them.

Sharks have an important role at the top of the ocean food chain. They help keep nature in balance. Biologists observe that when sharks disappear, their prey—seals and walruses—multiply to the point of becoming an unhealthy burden on their own environment. If people understood the importance of sharks, they might care about what is happening to them.

Another way to solve this problem would be to limit shark fishing in all countries. The United States is one of the few countries that controls shark fishing, but that doesn't help the many sharks that travel long distances during their lives. A shark may spend its early years off the coast of California only to be killed later in the South Pacific. Sharks replace themselves very slowly. Many don't give birth until they are ten years old. Scientists believe that sharks in eastern U.S. coastal waters have been killed off twice as fast as they can reproduce. Until we know what species are stable, shark fishing should be strictly limited worldwide.

Perhaps the best way to solve the problem would be to boycott, or stop buying, all shark products. Even though shark fishing is sometimes controlled, most products made from sharks are not. Shark fins bring a high price, so some fishermen illegally slice the fins off living sharks and throw the sharks back into the ocean to die. In addition to reducing demand, a worldwide boycott would send a message to those in the business of slaughtering sharks. It would tell them to figure out a way to make their products so that they are not harmful to the environment.

Shark products are not needed for human survival. Shark meat is high in protein, but there are many other ways to get protein. There is also shark-tooth jewelry and some lubricants and cosmetics that contain shark liver. We can do without these products. If we did, the demand for shark products would stop.

Sharks are disappearing. To solve this problem, people should learn that sharks do not pose a threat to their safety and that shark products are not necessary for their survival. Further, shark fishing everywhere should be strictly limited. In addition, if people increased their awareness of sharks' role in the environment, they might be motivated to protect them. Finally, a worldwide boycott would decrease the demand for shark products. It is important to take action now to help preserve the shark population for the future.

Try It!

Answer these questions about the persuasive essay about sharks.
   Did the way the solutions were presented help you organize the ideas as you read? How else could the essay have been organized?

Tips for Writing a Persuasive Essay

STEP 1 Prewriting

- Research with your audience in mind. As you take notes, write down the information that will most influence them.
- Use a graphic organizer to organize your reasons and ideas and to plan your draft.

STEP 2 Drafting

- State the problem and write about the solutions. You could also give your viewpoint and provide facts, reasons, and examples to support it.
- Put the ideas you get from other sources in your own words.

STEP 3 Revising

- **Organization** Is your paper organized logically and persuasively? Is the strongest solution or point saved for last?
- **Organization** Do ideas connect? Does your introduction grab the audience's attention and state the problem or issue? Does your conclusion restate the problem or issue and summarize reasons or solutions?
- **Voice** Does your writing show that you know your audience?

STEP 4 Editing/Proofreading

- **Conventions** Proofread your essay to check for spelling and punctuation mistakes and make sure that all proper names are capitalized.

STEP 5 Publishing

- **Presentation** Neatly type or write the final copy.

SECTION 2 Forms of Writing

Poetry

SECTION 2
Forms of Writing

Poetry is very different from other forms of writing. For one thing, it looks different. Think of some poems you have read. They look very different from stories or articles. The capitalization and punctuation are different. The familiar patterns of sentences and paragraphs are not present in poetry.

There is something else about poetry. It can describe things in a way that you may never have considered. Poetry often contains thoughts and feelings of the writer. It also contains images, or word pictures, that can make a deep impression on readers. The following lessons will give you a chance to explore some different kinds of poetry.

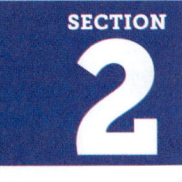

Examples of poetry include the following"

- ▶ Rhyming Poetry
- ▶ Nonrhyming Poetry
- ▶ Pattern Poetry

> ## Reading Your Writing
>
> An important part of writing poetry is being willing to experiment with words and arrange them in the order that best suits the meaning of your poem. Whether the pattern you choose is rhyming or nonrhyming, be sure to select one that adds to the reader's understanding and enjoyment of your poem.

Continue reading this section of the Handbook to see examples and to find out more information about poetry.

Rhyming Poetry

Up until now, all of the writing in this book has been prose. Prose is defined as all types of writing that are not considered poetry. *Poetry* combines the sounds and meanings of words to create ideas and feelings. What are some differences between prose and poetry?

PROSE
- complete sentences
- capitalization necessary
- punctuation necessary
- nonrhyming
- paragraph
- rhythm *sometimes* matters
- sound patterns *sometimes* matter
- images *sometimes* present

POETRY
- fragments allowed
- capitalization optional
- punctuation optional
- rhyming and nonrhyming
- stanzas (groups of lines)
- rhythm *usually* matters
- sound patterns *always* matter
- images *usually* present

Try It!

Think about how poetry and prose look. How would you explain the differences to someone?

Common Forms of Rhyming Poetry

Let's take a look at some of the more common forms of rhyming poetry.

Couplet

A couplet is a two-line poem or a two-line verse of a longer poem. Both lines usually rhyme, are of equal length and meter, or rhythm, and express one thought.

> **EXAMPLE**
>
> On a branch the birdie sat,
> Or, oh my gosh, is that a bat?
>
> Down and down and down and down
> Escalator underground.

Triplet

A triplet is a three-line poem or three-line verse of a longer poem. All three lines usually rhyme and are of equal length and meter, or rhythm. They all express one thought.

> **EXAMPLE**
>
> My heart skips a beat as you tell me the news
> Of your moving away and the path that you choose.
> As for me it is clear I'm the one who will lose.

SECTION 2

Forms of Writing

Quatrain

A quatrain is a four-line poem or a stanza of a longer poem. It expresses one thought and has a variety of rhyming patterns. In one pattern, the first two lines and the last two lines may rhyme. In another pattern, the first and third lines and the second and fourth lines could rhyme. A third pattern could have only the second and fourth lines rhyme.

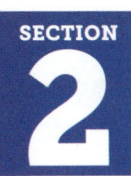

SECTION 2 — Forms of Writing

EXAMPLE

▸ First two lines rhyme; last two lines rhyme:

Everyone remembers old Rodeo Bill,
How he roped his steer with cunning skill.
But now he just sits in the bleachers and grins
While the feisty crowd cheers and the show begins.

▸ First and third lines rhyme; second and fourth lines rhyme:

Coaster rolling on the track,
Climbing to its height
Reach the top, we all lean back
Ready for the fright.

▸ Only the second and fourth lines rhyme:

Cold winds blow and snowflakes fly;
Branches mourn their fallen leaves.
An icy chill crawls up the oak
As Old Man Winter puffs and breathes.

Lyric

A lyric is a type of poem that expresses strong personal emotions, often using details of the five senses.

Over, under, round, and through
These woods fill me with such delight,
Whether wading through the winding creek
Or gazing at a star-filled night.

I uncover treasures of rubies and gold,
Defend fortresses high and mighty,
Slay towering dragons—a sight to behold!
A new adventure waits at every turn.

SECTION 2

Forms of Writing

Try It!

Try writing a rhyming poem. First think of an idea that includes vivid images. Then choose a poetry form and a rhyming pattern. You can use a rhyming dictionary to help you create a list of rhyming words for your poem.

Reading Your Writing

There are many different forms of rhyming poetry. Most of the forms have a specific rhyme and rhythm pattern. When you write your own poems, make sure you follow the pattern for the form you have chosen.

Nonrhyming Poetry

Nonrhyming poetry doesn't have rhyming patterns, but it may have other kinds of patterns. For example, *cinquain poems* always have the same kinds of words and number of words. *Free verse* has not patterns at all.

Common Forms of Nonrhyming Poetry

Here's a sampling of some of the forms of nonrhyming poetry.

Diamante

A diamante is a seven-line poem that has specific information in each line and an exact number of words. This form can also appear in various patterns.

Line 1	one word	subject, noun
Line 2	two words	adjectives
Line 3	three words	participles
Line 4	four words	nouns
Line 5	three words	participles
Line 6	two words	adjectives
Line 7	two words	nouns

EXAMPLE

Scooters
Speedy, smooth
Careening, turning, braking
Taxi, rickshaw, soapbox, bike
Transporting, energizing, relaxing
Funny, fantastic
Travel, plans

SECTION 2 — Forms of Writing

Cinquain

A cinquain is a five-line poem that has specific information in each line. This form of poetry has an exact number of words or syllables per line and can appear in a variety of patterns.

Line 1	one word	title
Line 2	two words	describing title
Line 3	three words	an action
Line 4	four words	a feeling
Line 5	one word	refers to title

EXAMPLE

Planets
Heavenly bodies
Rotating, revolving, renewing
Others are out there
Magnificent

SECTION 2

Forms of Writing

Free Verse

Free verse is just what it sounds like—poetry without rhyme or rhythm (meter). Rather than emphasizing the matching sounds of words, free verse *frees* you to concentrate on ideas and images.

Free verse has no specific form and can be any length. It does not always rhyme, because the ideas and image it expresses are most important. This form of poetry can be used to create different line shapes with word and line placement.

SECTION 2 — Forms of Writing

EXAMPLE

Inky
Hanging.   Dangling.
By   a   thread.
Creeping   Weaving
Leaving   its   web.
And then ………whoosh!
The end.

Reading Your Writing

Many forms of nonrhyming poetry have a specific structure. Make sure that your poem follows the correct format.

Haiku

A haiku is a three-line poem about nature. There is an exact number of syllables for each line. The first line has five syllables, the second has seven, and the third has five.

EXAMPLE

> Wind whips my window,
> Pounding hail pelts my rooftop,
> Skies clear for rainbows.

FUN fact

Haiku originated from Japan. Japanese haiku are usually written in a single vertical line.

Try It!

Try writing a nonrhyming poem. Choose an idea with vivid images. Don't worry about rhyming or rhythm patterns. Instead, concentrate on creating visual patterns with your word and line placement.

Pattern Poetry

Pattern poetry is created from an existing form, often a familiar song. Do you remember this one?

I've been working on the railroad	(8 syllables)
All the live long day.	(5)
I've been working on the railroad	(8)
Just to pass the time away.	(7)
Can't you hear the whistle blowing,	(8)
Rise up so early in the morn?	(8)
Can't you hear the captain shouting,	(8)
"Dinah blow your horn!"	(5)

EXAMPLE Suppose your class needed a field-day spirit song and you were chosen to give this tune new lyrics. You might write something like the lyrics below. Sing it to the tune of "I've Been Working on the Railroad." Notice the matching patterns of rhyme and syllables.

We're the Jaguars of Ms. Smith's class	(8 syllables)
Ready for the race	(5)
We are fast and strong and agile	(8)
And we'll put you to the pace	(7)
Try to understand our message	(8)
We are the best class in the school	(8)
Don't forget our simple motto	(8)
We are smart and cool.	(5)

Let's try another one. Remember this song?

Yankee Doodle went to town	(7 syllables)
A – ridin' on a pony.	(7)
He stuck a feather in his hat	(8)
And called it macaroni.	(7)
Yankee Doodle keep it up,	(7)
Yankee Doodle Dandy,	(6)
Mind the music and the steps	(7)
And with the girls be handy.	(7)

SECTION 2

Forms of Writing

EXAMPLE Using the same melody, here's a student government campaign song.

Amy Edwards came to school	(7 syllables)
To help improve conditions.	(7)
She'll try to get some uniforms	(8)
For all the band's musicians.	(7)
Amy Edwards gets our vote,	(7)
Amy Edwards "Do it!"	(6)
Vote for her this Tuesday morn	(7)
There's really nothing to it!	(7)

Try It!

Make up a song of your own using one of the patterns in this lesson.

Reading Your Writing

Pattern poetry often uses the melody of a favorite song as a format. When writing this type of poetry, choose a melody that you are sure your readers will recognize.

Timed Writing

Sometimes you are asked to write something in a limited amount of time. Often, the reason is a classroom, district, or statewide test. Tests are a big part of your life at school because they are a way to show what you know.

In "timed writing" situations, you are presented with a prompt and asked to write your response in a test booklet. Depending on the test and expectations, the time you are allotted could vary from fifteen minutes to more than an hour. The kind of writing prompt can also vary—you might have to summarize a text, develop a response to literature, create a short story, or write a persuasive letter. Although these high-pressure tests can seem scary, you do not have to crack under the pressure. You can succeed!

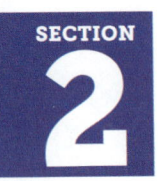

SECTION 2
Forms of Writing

Examples of timed writing include the following:
- Timed Writing Strategies
- Quick Write
- Summary Writing
- Responding to Literature
- Narrative Writing
- Persuasive Writing

The following pages will provide you with strategies to help you prepare for Timed Writing tests and tasks.

SECTION 2

Forms of Writing

Timed Writing Strategies

When have you had to take a timed writing test? Whether it was yesterday, last week, last month, or last year, it is certain that you will have to do this again. That is why it is important for you to know some basics about timed-writing prompts, expectations, and strategies.

SECTION 2 — Forms of Writing

Planning for Timed Writing

Practice

Because serious timed written tests occur infrequently, it is important to **plan ahead**. Remember, planning will help you succeed. One way to plan for writing on demand is to *practice*. The first time you tried to ride a bike, you probably did not do so well, but after practicing you felt more confident and able. Similarly, you would not want to walk into a high-stakes testing scenario feeling nervous and unprepared.

Your teacher will help you prepare by giving you opportunities to respond to the kinds of prompts you might see on a test. Try not to feel overwhelmed by these timed exercises, but take them seriously—they are a chance to drastically improve your test-taking skills, confidence, and performance.

Prewriting

"Planning" for timed writing tests can also refer to *prewriting* during the actual test period. When you have to write an essay for class, you devote time to prewriting so you can organize ideas. Otherwise, your draft would be rambling and unfocused. However, people often skip this important step on timed tests because of time constraints. Keep in mind that if you devote a few minutes to planning and note making, your response will be easier to write and more focused. This is why many test booklets have a "planning page" with a suggested amount of time for prewriting. Rather than cutting into your time, it is a time-management strategy.

Here are some tips that will help you prepare for and manage your time in a timed writing situation.

Timed Writing Strategies

1. Read the entire writing prompt. Circle the directions, and underline each item you are asked to write about. Look for key words and phrases such as *compare and contrast, analyze, summarize,* or *describe* that give specific instructions on *how* and *what* you should write.
2. Take a few minutes to make notes about what you will write. Make notes for each item required by the prompt to remind you as you work. Outline the main points you intend to make in your response. If many items are listed in the prompt, allot yourself enough time to address each one.
3. Write your response to the prompt. Use your notes to organize your draft.
4. Check your response. Did you respond to each requirement in the prompt? Did you stay on topic?
5. Revise and edit as needed. Take a few minutes to correct spelling, grammar, capitalization, and punctuation. Be sure your writing is as neat as possible.

▶ Written tests usually provide specific **directions** for how to respond. For example, a prompt may specify that you should *give examples and cite evidence from the text*. They also often provide specifics about **scoring**. Pay close attention to every item required by the prompt, and allot space in your plan to fulfill each requirement.

▶ Use academic language. Your response is not expected to be perfect, but spend as much time as you can proofreading and making your writing legible. Never turn in a written test early when there is always room to improve!

Quick Write

Although standardized tests account for most of the times that you will have to write on demand, there are other occasions when you have limited time for a written response. A **quick write** is another kind of fast-paced writing assignment in which the writer responds to a prompt. You will usually have from five to fifteen minutes to think about, plan, and write your response to a question or prompt. Teachers often assign quick writes to help students

- generate ideas for prewriting.
- show how well they comprehended a reading selection.
- recall what they know about a specific topic.
- summarize what they have learned from their reading or class discussions.
- organize their thoughts and compose personal responses.

Here are some examples of quick write assignments:

- Think about what we learned about energy conservation, and list three possible topics for your essay.
- Do you agree with the author's position on this topic? Why, or why not?
- Explain the theme of the story in your words.

Write Quickly

The goal of a quick write is to express thoughts or knowledge about a topic very quickly. Therefore, you should write whatever comes to mind and force words onto the page, even if you feel stuck. By continuously writing, one idea might lead to a second idea, which might lead to a third idea, and so on.

Do Not Stop

Treat a quick write like a first draft. Do not be overly concerned about making mistakes, but do your best to follow the grammar, spelling, and punctuation rules you have learned. If you have time remaining, reread and edit your writing.

Testing Connection

Quick writes are less formal than written tests, but they are still great practice for timed writing situations. During a quick write, you can practice using the Timed Writing Strategies from page 255. You should fully and adequately respond to the prompt. The more practice you have responding to prompts, the more comfortable writing quickly and expressing your ideas under pressure will become. Although quick writes are not expected to be perfectly organized or revised, they will still help you develop the skills and confidence you need to make all your timed responses more focused and purposeful.

SECTION 2

Forms of Writing

EXAMPLE Here is a quick write on the following prompt: What role do you think energy plays in our daily lives?

> I think energy can be helpful and dangerous. We use energy every day. My alarm clock relies on electricity. I need electricity to turn on my computer. I know that gasoline and oil are forms of energy. The school bus needs gas to run, so we wouldn't be able to get to school without energy. My mom and dad wouldn't be able to go to work without gas and oil.
>
> Energy is dangerous, too. Some kinds pollute. I've heard on the news that we need to find alternative forms of energy. We need to conserve so our resources don't run out.
>
> There are other forms of energy that are dangerous, too, like lightning and tornadoes. We had a lightning storm a few weeks ago. A lightning bolt hit one of the power lines, and we lost power for a few days. That was scary.

Summary

How many summaries have you written? By now, you probably know what it means to *summarize*. A summary identifies the main ideas and most important details of a text. One type of prompt you might see on a timed written test asks you to write a summary of a nonfiction article (the article is provided in the test booklet). When you are asked to write a summary on a written test, don't panic! You can apply what you already know about summarizing to do well.

Another tool that will help you is the Timed Writing Strategies on page 255. You can use these strategies on any timed writing test. It is especially important that you remember to read the entire writing prompt carefully and make note of all requirements mentioned in the *directions* and *scoring* sections. Otherwise, you will not know what to do.

A summary prompt will often ask you to:
- state the main ideas of the article.
- identify the most important details that support the main ideas.
- use your own words.
- use correct grammar, spelling, punctuation, and capitalization.

Try It!

When responding to any prompt, always remember what you know about the genre, and use those tools to help you write. For a summary prompt, you know you will include the main ideas and most important details. What would you make sure to include if a prompt asked you to write a short story? A persuasive letter?

Remember that most test directions say you will have time to plan, write, and proofread. For a summary, it may also allow you to make notes on the article and reread or return to the article at any time.

The directions for a summary task will ask you to read the article first. The prompt will be provided after the article. Below is a summary prompt from a standardized test and the response a student wrote.

SECTION 2 — Forms of Writing

EXAMPLE Write a summary of the informative text "John Muir: America's Naturalist." Remember that your writing will be scored on how well you:

- state the main ideas of the article.
- use your own words.
- identify the most important details.
- use correct grammar, spelling, punctuation, and capitalization.

> John Muir, a preservationist, was passionate about the environment, and his work still benefits Americans today. Muir's writings led to the creation of many national parks, including Yosemite, Sequoia, Glacier, and Rainier. In fact, he is often called the "Father" of the National Park Service.
>
> Another important contribution by Muir was the formation of the Sierra Club. Artists, lawyers, professors, and scientists came together to preserve the forests of the Sierra Nevadas. However, according to Muir, the main purpose of the club was to "do something for the wilderness and make the mountains glad." Today, the Sierra Club has over one million members and it is the oldest "grassroots" environmental agency.
>
> Millions of people every year visit places, such as Muir Glacier in Alaska and Muir Woods in California, which are named after Muir. John Muir's work has helped millions of people get closer to nature.

Responding to Literature

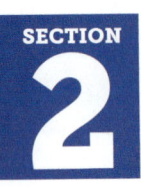

SECTION 2
Forms of Writing

What do you do when you respond to literature? You might *analyze* the characters, plot, setting, theme, or literary devices in a story. Or you might answer a specific question about a story. One kind of prompt you might see on a timed written test asks you to write a response to a short story provided in the test booklet. The prompt is presented after the story so you know what narrative elements you are expected to analyze. When you are asked to respond to literature on a written test, don't panic! You can apply what you already know about analyzing narratives as you write. Turn to pages 108–127 for more ideas about responding to literature.

Another tool that will help you is the Timed Writing Strategies on page 255. You can use these strategies on any timed writing test. Remember to carefully read the entire writing prompt and make note of all requirements mentioned in the *directions* and *scoring* sections before you read and write. Otherwise, you will not know what to do.

> A responding to literature prompt will often ask you to:
> ▶ show your understanding of the story.
> ▶ organize around several clear main ideas.
> ▶ give examples and cite evidence from the story.
> ▶ use correct grammar, spelling, and mechanics.

Test Tip Do not be afraid to underline, circle, or make notes on the story provided in the test booklet as you read. These notes may help you as you plan and write your response. You might want to read the prompt before you read the story so you know what to look for.

Responding to literature prompts often ask you to analyze a character. Below is an example of a standardized test prompt about a character and the response a fifth grader wrote.

EXAMPLE In "Just 17 Syllables!" Danny Flores goes through several struggles and changes. Use details from the narrative to explain how he adjusts to his changes.

    The main character in "Just 17 Syllables!" is Danny Flores. Danny Flores is from Ohio, but his family has recently moved to Tokyo. Danny learns a valuable lesson about adjusting to change. At the beginning of the story, Danny is sad, misses his friends from Ohio, and is disinterested in what the class is doing at the Rikugien Gardens in Tokyo. While in the Gardens, Danny does not pay attention to the teacher, but instead, is interested in his cell phone and thinks about all of the things he left behind in Ohio. Danny almost cries just thinking about the hockey rink and his friends from Ohio.

    Although Danny is sad, he shows respect when he bows to Professor Nakano and when he turns off his cell phone after his teacher glances at him. After Danny puts his cell phone away, he begins to pay attention to the professor's presentation on haiku, and even becomes interested in some of the facts he is learning about haiku and Basho.

    As Danny and his classmates are writing their own haikus, Danny is nervous and unsure if he can write one. However, Danny thinks of himself as a samurai haiku writer, and becomes inspired and starts typing. Danny is proud of his haiku and enjoys when the professor reads his poem aloud. Danny ends up enjoying his day at the Gardens.

    Danny is a typical boy who is afraid of change and is unsure of his new home. However, as Danny begins to learn more about his new home, he starts to accept the changes and even begins to like it.

SECTION 2

Forms of Writing

Narrative

Do you like to write stories? Have you ever had to write one for a test? One kind of prompt you might see on a timed written test will ask you to write a fictional narrative. The test booklet will provide you with *directions* and information about *scoring*, as well as the narrative *prompt*. If you are asked to write a fictional narrative for a written test, don't panic! You can apply what you already know about story writing as you work.

Another tool that will help you is the Timed Writing Strategies on page 255. Remember to carefully read all requirements mentioned in the directions and scoring sections before you write. Otherwise, you will not know what to do.

Narrative prompts give you an imaginative scenario to write about. Below is a prompt and the response a student wrote.

> **EXAMPLE** Imagine that you have arrived on a distant planet to help start an American space colony. The next morning you decide to explore. Write a story about what happens next. Remember to:
> - develop a plot with beginning, middle, and end.
> - use narrative strategies like dialogue, suspense, or naming of narrative action.
> - develop a setting and characters.
> - use correct grammar, spelling, and mechanics.

Space Nation 1 is a swampy planet in a distant galaxy. The three suns shed only a dim light through the gray fog and mist. I arrived yesterday with a youth coalition to help scout the land. The few edible roots we've found are not nutritious. The adults at camp are hopeless and worried.

I was worried too before I met Lucinda and Thomas. Lucinda is tall, loud, and sarcastic and has a robot chihuahua named Tango. Thomas is shy, like me, and he knows a lot about biotechnology. Today, we went exploring in voice-controlled hovercraft. As we zipped over a muddy marsh, Tango wouldn't stop barking. Then, Thomas stopped his craft. My eyes followed his gaze to the swamp's edge. We all saw it—a silhouette beckoning us. Was it alien life? We raced after it, over the swamp, through the trees, twisting through messy vines and thickets. Tango was panting and barking like mad.

Suddenly we arrived on the other side. The suns shone down on a blue river and grassy valley. It reminded me of home. The figure was a slender boy, strangely human, and about my age. "Hello" he said gently. "I am Caron." Giggles came from the trees as more children approached, some hesitant and some skipping joyfully.

"Wh-wh-what are you?" I asked.

"We are the Singshees of Temutec," Caron said. "We have plentiful food and resources, if you come in peace."

"Yes, of course . . ." I said. "Th-th-thank you." Tango stopped barking and was licking Caron's hand affectionately.

Lucinda, Thomas, and I grinned widely as we rode away. "Wait till the adults hear about this . . ."

SECTION 2

Forms of Writing

Persuasive Writing

One kind of prompt you might see on a timed written test will ask you to write a persuasive essay or letter on a given topic. Persuasive writing prompts assign you a topic but allow you to choose your own opinion. The test booklet will provide you with specific *directions* and information about *scoring* in addition to the prompt. If you are asked to write a persuasive piece for a written test, don't panic! You can apply what you already know about persuasion as you work. Turn to pages 230–239 for ideas about organizing your persuasive writing and making it convincing.

Another tool that will help you is the Time Writing Strategies on page 255. Remember to carefully read the entire writing prompt and make note of all requirements mentioned in the *directions* and *scoring* sections before you read and write. Take a look at this persuasive prompt and a student's response.

SECTION 2
Forms of Writing

> **EXAMPLE** Imagine that your principal is considering changing the dress code to uniforms. Your school does not currently have uniforms, and the final decision will be announced in one week. Think about your opinion. Then write a letter to convince your principal of your position. Remember to:
>
> ▸ state your position on the topic.
> ▸ address opposing reader concerns and arguments.
> ▸ support your position with examples and evidence.
> ▸ use correct grammar, spelling, capitalization, and punctuation.

Dear Principal Mane:

    Would you like your power of self-expression to be taken away? Changing the dress code to uniforms threatens students' individuality, freedom, and success.

    In our school, individual accomplishment, not conformity, is encouraged. Our Spelling Bee champ and star basketball player, individuals loved by all, both strongly oppose uniforms. Also, part of our curriculum is celebrating diversity. We even have a "Diversity Day." How can we celebrate individuality and diversity while we are wearing the same thing?

    Some argue that uniforms will make students focus more on studies and less on fashion. However, it is important to note that our school already receives above-average ranking on statewide tests. In a survey of 100 students, only six thought uniforms would improve their grades. In addition, uniforms are impractical and uncomfortable, making them a distraction during class.

    Before deciding to change our dress code, remember that your students have always been responsible and dedicated. Please do not take away the freedom we have earned!

                           Sincerely,
                             Lupita Ruiz

SECTION 2

Forms of Writing

Test Tip Always use your planning page to organize your ideas. Remember to use persuasive techniques to convince your audience. For a persuasive letter, however, do not worry about the correct letter format. You will not be scored on that.

SECTION 3

Writing Strategies

Sentence Fluency 268

Ideas 292

Organization 306

Word Choice 326

Voice 334

Conventions 346

Presentation 356

We don't have to guess what features contribute to great writing. Through the years, language experts have discovered certain traits, or qualities, that are common in excellent writing. In the following section you'll get an in-depth look at each of these characteristics of great writing and find ways to apply them to the writing you do every day.

Sentence Fluency

Good writing is like good music. It sounds good! What makes it sound good? The answer is sentence fluency.

Sentence fluency means the way you arrange your sentences so that they read smoothly. When your writing reads smoothly, one sentence flows into the next. Smooth writing is easier to read. It is more interesting to read too!

SECTION 3

Writing Strategies

Examples of sentence fluency that can make your writing clearer and more interesting include the following:

- ▸ Writing Sentences
- ▸ Combining and Expanding Sentences
- ▸ Sentence Problems
- ▸ Paragraphs
- ▸ Types of Paragraphs
- ▸ Variety in Writing

EXAMPLE Sentences that all begin the same way sound boring! Read this paragraph. How would you change some of the sentences to make the paragraph more interesting?

Lin went to the zoo with her aunt. Lin saw lions and elephants at the zoo. Lin also saw monkeys. Lin liked the elephants best.

Continue reading this section of the Handbook to see additional examples and to find out more information about sentence fluency.

SECTION 3

Writing Strategies

Writing Sentences

Sentences are the building blocks of writing. Learning how to construct good sentences is part of becoming a good writer. There are different kinds of sentences, but they all have some things in common.

It is difficult to precisely define a **sentence.** One definition is that a sentence is a group of words that has a subject and predicate and expresses a complete thought. The **subject** tells who or what the sentence is about, and the **predicate** tells more, including what the subject is or does. Every sentence begins with a capital letter and ends with a punctuation mark.

In the sentences below, the subject is in **bold** and the predicate is in *italics*.

> **The first telescope** *was a refracting telescope.*
> **Isaac Newton** *built a reflecting telescope.*

Kinds of Sentences

Different kinds of sentences give different kinds of information to readers. The four kinds of sentences are declarative, interrogative, imperative, and exclamatory.

A **declarative sentence** makes a statement. Declarative sentences end with a period.

> Germs cause many kinds of illnesses.
> Sneezing sprays germs into the air.

An **interrogative sentence** asks a question. Interrogative sentences end with a question mark.

> Do you have a cold?
>
> Would you like this cough drop?

An **imperative** sentence gives a command or makes a request. An imperative sentence ends with either an exclamation point or a period. If the sentence expresses a strong emotion, it ends with an exclamation point. All other imperative sentences end with a period.

Note that the subject of an imperative sentence is not stated. Instead, the subject is understood to be the pronoun *you*.

> Cover your mouth!
>
> Get plenty of rest.

An **exclamatory sentence** expresses strong emotion, such as surprise, fear, or excitement. Exclamatory sentences end with an exclamation point.

> I used a whole box of tissues!
>
> This virus won't go away!

Try It!

What kind of punctuation should be used at the end of this sentence?

> Please fix me some soup

SECTION 3
Writing Strategies

Combining Sentences

When two sentences contain many of the same words or ideas, you can combine them. You might combine parts of sentences or whole sentences to make your writing more interesting and easier to read.

Combining Subjects, Objects, Verbs, and Modifiers

You can combine parts of two shorter sentences to make one sentence that reads more smoothly. Use the conjunctions *and, but,* and *or* to make compound subjects, objects, and verbs.

> Rectangles are polygons. Hexagons are polygons.
> **Rectangles and hexagons** are polygons.
> (compound subject)

> Did Jasmine draw a bar graph? Did Jasmine draw a line graph?
> Did Jasmine draw a **bar graph or a line graph?**
> (compound object)

> Claudio checked his answer. Claudio erased his answer.
> Claudio **checked and erased** his answer.
> (compound verb)

A **modifier** is a word or group of words that adds information to a sentence. A word that modifies a noun is an adjective. A word that modifies a verb is an adverb. Use a comma or a conjunction to combine modifiers from different sentences.

> I drew a large triangle. I drew a right triangle.
> I drew a **large, right** triangle.

> Solve the problems quickly. Solve the problems carefully.
> Solve the problems **quickly but carefully.**

Combining Phrases

Phrases from separate sentences can be combined to improve the flow of your writing. You might even be able to combine phrases from several sentences to avoid repeating words.

> The key is under the mat. The mat is on the porch.
>
> The key is **under the mat on the porch.**

> Sam found the key. Sam unlocked the door.
>
> Sam **found the key and unlocked the door.**

> The dog ran up the stairs. It ran to the front door. Then it jumped on Sam.
>
> The dog ran **up the stairs to the front door and jumped on Sam.**

When you combine words or phrases from different sentences, be sure the new sentence makes sense. Otherwise, you might confuse your readers.

▸ Sam threw a ball to the dog. Sam threw a ball high in the air.

▸ Sam threw a ball to the dog high in the air. (This sentence is confusing. The dog isn't high in the air.)

▸ Sam threw a ball high in the air to the dog. (This sentence correctly combines the two original sentences.)

SECTION 3

Writing Strategies

Creating Compound Sentences

Two simple sentences that are related can be combined to form a **compound sentence.** Both parts of a compound sentence express a complete thought. Use a conjunction such as *and, but,* or *or* between the two simple sentences, and place a comma before the conjunction.

> Mariah loves to swim. She wants to be a lifeguard.
>
> Mariah loves to swim, **and** she wants to be a lifeguard.

> You can wear your swimsuit. You can change at the beach.
>
> You can wear your swimsuit, **or** you can change at the beach.

Creating Complex Sentences

Another way to combine sentences is by creating complex sentences. A **complex sentence** is made of an independent clause and one or more dependent clauses. A **clause** is a group of words that has a subject and a verb. An **independent clause** can stand alone as a sentence, but a **dependent clause** cannot. A dependent clause begins with a subordinating conjunction such as *after, although, because,* or *when* or with a relative pronoun such as *that, which,* or *who.* To combine two sentences into a complex sentence, make the idea from one of the sentences into a dependent clause. Note that a comma is not always used between the independent and dependent clauses.

> Mariah joined the swim team. She became the captain.
>
> **After Mariah joined the swim team,** she became the captain.

> These are Mariah's lucky goggles. She wears them at every meet.
>
> These are the lucky goggles **that Mariah wears at every meet.**

Varying Sentence Beginnings

Beginning your sentences in different ways helps add variety to your writing. This not only keeps your readers interested but it also makes writing more fun.

The natural order of a sentence is for the subject to come first, followed by the predicate.

The roller coaster climbed toward the peak.

You can organize your sentences in many different ways, such as moving part of the predicate to the beginning of the sentence.

EXAMPLE

Before: I checked the strap on my seat **nervously.**
After: **Nervously,** I checked the strap on my seat.

Before: I closed my eyes and screamed **at the top of the hill.**
After: **At the top of the hill,** I closed my eyes and screamed.

Before: My legs were shaking **when I got off the ride.**
After: **When I got off the ride,** my legs were shaking.

SECTION 3

Writing Strategies

Try It!

Rewrite the following sentence using a different beginning.
I got in line because I wanted to ride again.

Reading Your Writing

A sentence expresses a complete thought as a statement, a question, a command, or an exclamation. You can combine sentences or parts of sentences to avoid repeating words and to make your writing read more smoothly. Sentences can begin in many different ways. Use variety in your sentences to keep readers interested.

Sentence Fluency • Writing Sentences

Combining and Expanding Sentences

Sometimes several sentences share information. For example, they have the same subject or verb. By combining these sentences, you can avoid repeating words. These ideas from shorter sentences can be combined into one sentence by using a series of words.

> In the tidal pool we saw starfish. We also saw sea horses. We also saw sea urchins.
>
> **Better:** In the tidal pool, we saw starfish, sea horses, and sea urchins.

In the first set of sentences, several words are repeated. Each sentence has the same subject and verb. In the improved sentence, the repeated words are left out. A series of words is used to combine the three sentences into one. The meaning is the same, and sentence fluency is improved.

> We swam. We snorkeled. We explored the beach.
>
> **Better:** We swam, snorkeled, and explored the beach.

In the first series of sentences, each one has the same subject. In the improved sentence, the repeated words are left out. A series of words is used to combine the three sentences into one.

> The water sparkled in every direction. The water was clear and calm.
>
> **Better:** The clear, calm water sparkled in every direction.

In the first series of sentences, each one has the same subject. The sentences are combined by adding the adjectives *clear* and *calm* to the first sentence.

Combining Sentences with Appositives

An **appositive** is a word or group of words that rename another word in the same sentence. An **appositive phrase** is a group of words that includes an appositive and other words that modify it. Use appositives and appositive phrases in your writing to cut down on the need for short explanatory sentences. They give you yet another way to produce writing that is varied and smooth.

> **EXAMPLE** Before using an appositive:
>
> > My oldest sister is a marine biologist. Her name is Francesca León.
>
> After using an appositive to combine sentences:
>
> > My oldest sister, **Francesca León,** is a marine biologist.
>
> Before using an appositive phrase:
>
> > The spinner dolphin is a type of dolphin that rotates in the air. Spinner dolphins jump high out of the water and spin up to 14 times before landing.
>
> After using an appositive phrase to combine sentences:
>
> > The spinner dolphin, **a type of dolphin that rotates in the air,** jumps high out of the water and spins up to 14 times before landing.

Do you see how the appositives smoothly provide and combine information? Appositives are especially helpful when you are trying to produce varied, interesting sentences in small amounts of space.

Expanding Sentences

Another good way to vary sentences is to expand them. When you expand a sentence, you add details, phrases, or clauses that lengthen the sentence and add variety to your writing. Usually, these additions make your writing more informative, vivid, or interesting. You might ask yourself the following questions to expand a sentence: When? Who? Why? How? What kind? How often? How many? Which one?

Expanding with Phrases

Participial and prepositional phrases may be combined to vary sentence length. Participial phrases are phrases that begin with a participle and act as adjectives modifying nouns. **Prepositional phrases** are phrases that begin with a preposition and end with a noun or pronoun. They modify nouns, adjectives, adverbs, or verbs.

Notice how the writer took more specific information about dolphins and converted it into **participial phrases** to attach to the sentence. In the expanded sentence, the original short sentence is the main clause.

> **EXAMPLE**
>
> Original Sentence: Dolphins do a range of spectacular jumps in the wild.
>
> Expanded Sentence: **Leaping high above the waves, spinning in the air, and somersaulting overhead,** dolphins do a range of spectacular jumps in the wild.

Prepositional phrases can also be added to expand sentences. Look at the next example. The original sentence is now the main clause in the expanded sentence.

> **EXAMPLE**
>
> Original Sentence: The gulls searched for food.
>
> Expanded Sentence: **On a hot summer day,** the gulls searched for food **at the beach**.

Expanding with Clauses

Another good way to expand sentences is to add clauses to your writing. Adding clauses allows you to provide interesting or necessary information and avoid short, choppy sentences.

> **EXAMPLE**
>
> Original Sentence: Ted and Jeremy made a large sandcastle.
>
> Expanded Sentence: Ted and Jeremy, **who are identical twins,** made a large sandcastle.

In the example sentences above, new information is added as a dependent clause in the expanded sentence. The dependent clause modifies *Ted and Jeremy*. When a dependent clause that modifies a noun or pronoun provides information that is not essential to the meaning of the sentence, it is set off by commas. When the dependent clause provides essential information, it is not set off by commas.

More about Expanding with Clauses

Sometimes, you might need to add details to provide important information about the action that is happening in a sentence. Using a dependent clause, you might add details that explain how, where, or why something happened.

> **EXAMPLE**
>
> Original Sentence: Tony paddled out to the waves breaking on the second sandbar.
>
> Expanded Sentence: Tony paddled out to the waves breaking on the second sandbar **because he wanted to get away from all the other swimmers**.

In the example sentences above, the second sentence explains why Tony paddled out to the waves breaking on the second sandbar. The dependent clause provides information the reader might need to know. It modifies the verb *paddled*.

SECTION 3
Writing Strategies

Sentence Problems

A good writer recognizes problem sentences and knows how to correct them. Sentence fragments, run-on sentences, and rambling sentences are three common mistakes to watch for in your writing.

Fragments

A **fragment** is a group of words that does not express a complete thought. A fragment is missing a subject, a predicate, or both.

> Meets in the cafeteria. (missing a subject)
> The doctors and nurses. (missing a predicate)
> Just in time. (missing a subject and a predicate)

These fragments confuse the reader with incomplete information. Adding the missing parts makes the messages clear.

> The student council meets in the cafeteria.
> The doctors and nurses prepared for surgery.
> Lucy arrived just in time.

Try It!

Correct the following fragment to make a sentence.
    All the way home

Run-On Sentences

A **run-on sentence** contains more than one complete thought. To correct a run-on sentence, add a comma and a conjunction, or rewrite it as two separate sentences.

Run-on: J. K. Rowling is my favorite author she wrote the books about Harry Potter.

Correct: J. K. Rowling is my favorite author. She wrote the books about Harry Potter.

Run-on: I own two of the books I borrowed the others from the library.

Correct: I own two of the books, but I borrowed the others from the library.

Rambling Sentences

A **rambling sentence** contains too many thoughts connected by conjunctions. This problem can be corrected by writing a separate sentence for each thought. Some parts of a rambling sentence might really belong together. In this case, just add a comma before the conjunction.

Rambling: My family went to California last summer and there were so many things I wanted to see and we did drive across the Golden Gate Bridge and go to Disneyland but I didn't see the giant redwood trees and my parents said we will go back someday.

Correct: My family went to California last summer. There were so many things I wanted to see. We did drive across the Golden Gate Bridge and go to Disneyland, but I didn't see the giant redwood trees. My parents said we will go back someday.

SECTION 3
Writing Strategies

Reading Your Writing

The most common sentence problems are fragments, run-on sentences, and rambling sentences. Learn to recognize and correct these mistakes so that your message will be clear to readers.

Sentence Fluency • Sentence Problems

Paragraphs

A **paragraph** is made of two or more sentences about one idea or topic. Many paragraphs include a topic sentence, supporting sentences, and a closing sentence. All of these parts help make an organized and coherent paragraph.

A **topic sentence** states the paragraph's main idea. The first sentence of a paragraph is often the topic sentence; however, you might find it later in the paragraph, even at the end. Most paragraphs that inform or persuade have topic sentences. Most narrative paragraphs do not include a topic sentence.

Supporting sentences tell more about the paragraph's main idea. Sentences that do not support the main idea do not belong in the paragraph. Supporting sentences should be arranged in a logical order. For example, you might present information by order of time, location, or importance.

Many paragraphs have a **closing sentence.** A closing sentence provides a final thought about the main idea, a summary of the paragraph, or a smooth transition to the next paragraph.

EXAMPLE Here is an example of an informative paragraph taken from "John Muir: America's Naturalist." Note that the first line of a paragraph is indented. Look for the topic sentence, supporting details, and closing sentence.

> Today, Muir is also remembered by places that bear his name. Muir Glacier in Alaska and Muir Woods in California are two examples. Every year, millions of people visit these and other parks and preserves to get closer to nature. That is what John Muir would have wanted.

Staying on Topic

All of the sentences in a paragraph should relate to the main idea. If a writer includes information about a different topic, it is confusing to readers. The student who wrote the paragraph below realized that one of the sentences does not stay on topic.

EXAMPLE

> A legend is a type of story that is passed down from one generation to the next. Legends are often repeated because they are important to a certain group of people. ~~Examples of culture can be found in people's behavior and beliefs.~~ Members of that group tell the legends again and again to help keep their culture alive. Many Native American people tell legends about their ancestors' beliefs and way of life. These stories can teach as well as entertain listeners.

A sentence that doesn't stay on topic in one paragraph might be a good main idea or supporting sentence in another paragraph. Try to include all of your interesting information in an organized way.

Try It!

Does the following sentence belong in the sample paragraph above?
There are many different kinds of legends.

SECTION 3

Writing Strategies

Sentence Fluency • Paragraphs

Supporting the Main Idea

Writers use different kinds of evidence to support their ideas. Use examples, facts, and expert opinions to help you make your point.

Examples: In the sample paragraph on page 282, the writer used examples to support his main idea. The examples make it clear that several places bear John Muir's name.

Facts: Writers may also support a main idea with facts. Using facts and scientific data helps make your writing more believable.

Expert Opinions: Sometimes, a writer uses an expert's opinion as support for a main idea. This happens most often in persuasive writing, such as a letter to the editor. A writer might express an opinion, then use this type of evidence to convince readers that the opinion is reasonable.

Starting a New Paragraph

Paragraphs give order to your writing. Knowing when to start a new paragraph is important for helping your readers stay focused.

Start a new paragraph when

- you start writing about a new idea or subtopic.
- you start writing about a new location.
- you start writing about a different time.
- a new character is speaking.

EXAMPLE In the following narrative paragraph from "A Year on the Bowie Farm," the author organized the paragraph based on time.

> A few weeks later, the veterinarian arrived early to check on the calves. It was 7:00 a.m., and the dairy operation was in full swing. Mr. Meredith poked his head into the milking parlor and shouted over the noise of the milking machines. "Sara?"

Reading Your Writing

Most opinion and informative paragraphs include a topic sentence, supporting sentences, and a closing sentence. Supporting sentences can include examples, facts, or evidence to support the main idea. Remember to start a new paragraph when you start a new idea. This will give order to your writing and help your readers stay focused.

SECTION 3

Writing Strategies

Sentence Fluency • Paragraphs

Types of Paragraphs

You can use different types of writing for different purposes.

Narrative

Narrative writing is used for telling stories. When writing narrative paragraphs, use chronological order to show when events happen. Use signal words such as *then*, *next*, and *when* to show changes in time.

Keep in mind that most narrative paragraphs do not include topic sentences. Instead, they rely on dialogue and description to move the action along.

EXAMPLE The following narrative paragraphs are from "A Year on the Bowie Farm." Notice the signal words, dialogue, and description.

> Sunday dinner was a sit-down meal for the Bowies, always. It was the one time of the week that everyone was in the same place at the same time. There was always a lot to talk about, from the week gone by to upcoming plans.
>
> "So I've been thinking..." Elijah said to no one in particular as he spooned green beans onto his plate.
>
> His father raised one eyebrow and passed the platter of roast chicken to Victoria. "Oh? What have you been thinking about?"

Descriptive

In descriptive paragraphs, writers use vivid words to create an image or experience for the reader. Good descriptions include words that appeal to the readers' five senses: sight, hearing, taste, touch, and smell.

Descriptive writing is often used within other types of writing. For example, you may use it in stories, informative reports, and letters. You might also use it in an observational report.

When writing a descriptive paragraph, organize by order. This can be front to back, left to right, top to bottom, or any other way that will make sense to the reader.

EXAMPLE Read this paragraph and note how the writer organized the description from top to bottom.

> We stopped in our tracks when we saw the gigantic moose. Its enormous antlers looked as if they could easily weigh 40 pounds. Its huge, bulging eyes seemed to bore right into us as we tried to stand perfectly still. The moose's body was wet from the lake it was wading through, and its legs disappeared into the murky green water.

Try It!

Write two descriptive sentences about an animal. Remember to appeal to the readers' senses.

Informative

Informative writing is used for giving information or explaining. Most newspaper and magazine articles are informative. Textbooks and biographies are also informative. When you write to give information, remember to think about your audience. Ask yourself what they might already know and what they might want or need to know.

Informative paragraphs usually begin with a topic sentence that clearly states what will be discussed. Informative paragraphs can be developed by facts, reasons, examples, or a combination of these.

EXAMPLE In this informative paragraph, the writer uses examples to support the main idea, which is explained in the topic sentence.

> Minerals are in many things that we use every day. For example, quartz is a mineral used to make clocks and watches. The quartz helps them keep accurate time. You may not know it, but you even write with minerals. The mineral graphite is used to make pencils, and chalk is made from a mineral called gypsum. There are probably at least three minerals in your bathroom at home. Powder is made from a mineral called talc, and mirrors are made from the minerals silica and silver. Minerals start out deep in the ground, but they end up all around us.

Reading Your Writing

Different kinds of writing are used to tell a story, describe, explain, or persuade. No matter what your purpose is for writing, it is important to include all the parts of a paragraph and to think about your audience. Write about something that will interest your readers and that they will understand.

Persuasive

In a persuasive paragraph, a writer tries to get readers to think, feel, or act a certain way. Knowing your audience is very important in persuasive writing. This will help you choose the best strategy for presenting your argument. For example, you might present your opinion as a problem, then suggest a solution. Providing evidence to support your point of view is another effective way to persuade. You might also present the points of your argument in order of their importance. This leaves readers with your most convincing point fresh in their minds.

EXAMPLE Brandon wrote the following persuasive paragraph. What strategy did Brandon use in his paragraph?

> The legal voting age ought to be lowered from 18 to 10. By age 10, most people can read well enough to understand the ballots. Voting would also teach us to be responsible, which is something adults tell us is important. Many issues on the ballots relate to schools, so the people who go to school ought to have a vote. Voting decides what will happen in the future, and kids are affected by those decisions. If we are the future, then we should get to help create it by having the right to vote.

FUN fact

Persuade comes from a Latin word meaning "thoroughly advise." When you write a persuasive paragraph, you "thoroughly advise" readers of your point of view!

SECTION 3
Writing Strategies

Variety in Writing

Variety in writing refers to using sentences and words so they are interesting and not repetitious for readers. You can add variety by using synonyms. You can also include sentences of different lengths and build sentences in different ways. Readers enjoy reading writing that's varied in the way it is put together.

Use Synonyms

Synonyms are words that mean the same or almost the same as another word. They can help you avoid using the same words over and over. The first example below uses the word *saw* repeatedly. Notice how the second example uses synonyms to improve the revised paragraph.

Example 1

We **saw** the parade go down Main Street. We **saw** the mayor in a convertible followed by an old-fashioned car carrying the school board president. Next we **saw** a lot more old-fashioned cars. In one of the cars I **saw** a chimpanzee sitting next to the driver. When the chimp **saw** people throwing peanuts, he excitedly pounded his hands on the dashboard.

Example 2

We **watched** the parade go down Main Street. We **saw** the mayor in a convertible followed by an old-fashioned car carrying the school board president. Then a lot more lot more old-fashioned cars **appeared**. In one of the cars I **spied** a chimpanzee sitting next to the driver. When he **spotted** people throwing peanuts, he excitedly pounded his hands on the dashboard.

Change the Length of Sentences

Using sentences of different lengths will improve the rhythm and flow of your writing. Paragraphs with lots of short, same-length sentences can be stiff and boring. Read both paragraphs below. Notice the varied sentence length in the second paragraph.

Example 1

Native Americans of the plains used all buffalo parts. Buffalo horns were used as cooking tools. They were also used to carry hot coals to campgrounds. Hooves made glue. Buffalo fat supplied soap. Bones were made into tools. Backbones with ribs became toboggans.

Example 2

Native Americans of the plains used every part of the buffalo. Buffalo horns were used as cooking tools and to carry hot coals from one campground to the next. Buffalo hooves could be made into glue, while buffalo fat became soap. On the northern plains, backbones with ribs became toboggans for children.

Vary Sentence Beginnings

Another way to create variety in your writing is to vary the beginnings of sentences. When you don't, your writing may sound dull like the paragraph below that uses *we* to begin every sentence. Read both examples below. The second example uses a dependent clause to begin the first sentence and a different subject for the last.

Example 1

We ran out of things to do in our car. **We** forgot to take the things that would entertain us. **We** left books, travel checkers, and electronic games at home.

Example 2

As we traveled in our car, we ran out of things to do. **We** had forgotten to take enough things to entertain us. **Books, travel checkers, and electronic games** had all been left behind at home.

SECTION 3

Writing Strategies

Sentence Fluency • Variety in Writing

SECTION 3

Writing Strategies

Ideas

Ideas are the basis of all great writing. When writing is clear and focused, ideas are communicated. When writing is dull and confusing, ideas remain locked away, never reaching the intended audience. Use the lessons in this unit to help you visualize your ideas even before your pen touches the page. Once you begin, never be afraid to write and rewrite until you are sharing your ideas exactly as you had intended!

Examples of ideas that can make your writing clearer and more interesting include the following:

▶ Developing Narrative Stories
▶ Developing Informative Texts
▶ Research and Organizational Text Features

EXAMPLE Read the following paragraph. What words does the writer use to create a vivid setting for the story?

> One morning long ago, in a forest behind the king's great castle, a beautiful young princess went out to play. The princess breathed in the scent of spring flowers as she skipped toward a pond at the center of the forest. In her delicate hands she held a smooth, glistening, golden ball that was her most precious possession. When she reached the peaceful pond, still covered with morning mist, the ball slipped from her hands and into the cool water.

Continue reading to see examples and to find out more information about ideas for your writing.

SECTION 3
Writing Strategies

Developing Narrative Stories

Story Elements

Narrative stories have four major ingredients: **character, plot, setting,** and **point of view.** Carefully develop these components in your narrative writing to create interesting stories that seem real even if they could not possibly happen.

Character

Characters are the people in a story. Create characters with personality who seem as if they could be real. Show, don't tell, readers about the different aspects of a character's personality. Use these five techniques to create lifelike characters.

▶ Show what a character says, and how she or he says it.
"The pitcher's throwing really well, and I'm up next," he said excitedly to his teammate.

▶ Show the way the character acts.
Tom sat alertly in the dugout watching the pitcher.

▶ Show what a character is thinking.
It was the ninth inning and the score was tied. Tom realized that if he could get a base hit, his team could score a run.

▶ Show how a character feels.
Tom was feeling nervous but hopeful. He had already hit two pitches thrown by this pitcher.

▶ Show how other characters respond to or think about the character.
"I'm glad you're up next, Tom," said the coach. "I know you can get a base hit."

Keep this in mind: The goal in creating characters is to make them seem real. Real characters are **well-developed** characters. Characters such as those in *James and the Giant Peach* are not even human, but they seem real because they have interesting personalities that remind us of humans we know.

SECTION 3
Writing Strategies

Plot

The **plot** is what happens in a story. It is the chain of events in which there is both a **conflict** and a **resolution.** The conflict and its resolution may involve a struggle that characters must go through before the conclusion. Follow these steps:

Introduce a conflict, or problem, at the beginning

In **James and the Giant Peach** by Roald Dahl, James, the main character, is sad and lonely. He wants to meet and play with other kids. His aunts mistreat him and don't allow him to leave the garden. James wishes he could go out and explore the world.

In the middle of the story, show how characters deal with the conflicts.

James gets part of his wish, to explore the world, when he goes on a perilous journey on a giant peach. When the peach floats in the ocean, James must figure out how to protect it from attacking sharks. As it floats in the air, he struggles to protect himself and his fellow travelers from angry Cloud-Men. When they finally approach New York, James must figure out how to land.

Most stories have a climax or highest point of interest that takes place just before the problem is solved.

When an airplane suddenly cuts the strings that carry the peach, James and his friends believe they are finished as they fall to Earth. In a final surprise they are saved when the peach is spiked on the pinnacle of the Empire State Building.

The resolution happens after the climax, when the problem is solved.

James becomes a hero in New York. The peach stone becomes his new home. He is no longer lonely because both his insect friends and hundreds of kids come to visit and play with him.

SECTION 3

Writing Strategies

Setting

The setting is the **time and place** in which story events take place. If your story has more than one setting, you will need to include descriptions for each one. When you write about a setting, use interesting sensory details to make the scene come alive for readers. Include how the setting looks, smells, sounds, and feels.

Time *When* your story takes place is part of setting. Stories may be set in the past, present, or future. For example, a story occurring in a major city in 1900 might tell about horses and buggies in the streets. A story set 300 years in the future might describe transportation that is entirely different. A setting's time can either be general, such as the recent past when most of *James and the Giant Peach* happens or more specific, such as the day the giant peach grows—*a blazing hot day in the middle of summer*.

Place *Where* your story takes place is the other half of setting. It can be general such as "the south of England" where the book begins or specific such as James's peach stone house in Central Park, New York City. Roald Dahl's more detailed descriptions show how setting may relate to the plot. He describes the garden of James's aunts' house as "large and desolate." It covers the whole top of the hill and has only one tree. The setting shows why James is lonely.

> There was no swing, no seesaw, no sand pit, and no other children were ever invited to come up the hill and play with poor James.

Describe each setting in your story with vivid detail to make it real and interesting for readers. Use descriptions that appeal to sight, smell, touch, and sound to give readers the feeling that they are there. Focus on the features of your setting that relate to the plot and, as the action moves, describe each new setting.

SECTION 3
Writing Strategies

Point of View

Point of view is the position from which a story is told. It is *where* the storyteller or narrator is in relation to the story. When you write a story, be consistent with the point of view you choose.

First-Person Point of View

The narrator is one of the characters, often the main character, in the story. The narrator, or main speaker, uses the first person pronouns *I, me, my, we, us,* and *our* to describe what he or she says, does, and thinks. Although the actions and words of other characters are described, only the thoughts of the narrator may be. Use the first person "I" in your writing when you want your readers to feel close to and identify with the narrating character.

Third-Person Point of View

The story is told from a point of view outside the action of the story. The narrator is not a character in the story but is instead an outside observer.

Third-person pronouns *he, she, they, him, her,* and *them* describe what characters say, do, and sometimes think. When you write a story in the third person, you may tell the thoughts and emotions of one character, many characters, or none.

Reading Your Writing

In your writing, take the time to develop your characters, plot, and setting, as well as a single, consistent point of view so readers feel like they've entered a world that's complete.

SECTION 3
Writing Strategies

Ideas • Developing Narrative Stories

Developing Informative Texts

Informative text is nonfiction writing that informs readers about a topic. You can find informative text in nonfiction books, encyclopedias, newspapers, and magazines and on websites that explain or tell "how to." Informative writing sometimes uses headings, diagrams, charts, and maps to help readers understand information. Informative writing may tell about real people and events, provide steps on how to do something, or supply readers with facts and reasons.

Organizing Informative Writing

How you choose to organize your informative writing will be determined by your purpose. Why are you writing? Do you want to compare and contrast two things? Do you want to describe the causes and effects of an event? Do you want to ask a question and present information that helps answer it? Do you want to inform readers about a problem and its possible solutions, or do you want to explain a process? You may be able to think of other ways to organize your writing, but whichever one you choose, keep in mind that your purpose is to give readers information. Knowing what you want to achieve will guide you as you organize the information in a way that is easy for readers to understand.

SECTION 3
Writing Strategies

Try It!

For which of these would you use informative writing?
- ▶ You want to tell a funny story about the time you tried to cook dinner.
- ▶ You want to explain how chocolate is made from cocoa beans.
- ▶ You want to tell how skateboard and in-line skate tricks are alike and different.

Compare and Contrast

Informative text that compares and contrasts describes the similarities and differences between things. When you compare two things, you tell how they are alike. When you contrast, you explain how they are different. If you write an essay or report that includes a section that compares and contrasts, you will want to explain to readers at the beginning *what* you are doing so they know the purpose of the text. Knowing your own purpose will also help you organize your ideas as you write.

Before You Write Brainstorm the important information about your subjects and create separate lists for each.

Sort it Out Look over the details you've listed and sort them by similarities and differences.

Organize and Write When you describe the similarities and differences of a subject, you can do it in one of two ways. 1) Describe your first subject and then discuss the similarities and differences of the second subject. 2) List the similarities and differences of subjects feature by feature as in the following example.

EXAMPLE This is how my cat Felicity acts. She likes to lie around during the day, but at night she prowls around the yard. Whenever Felicity is awake, whether it is day or evening, she can be found purring. Although she acts differently during the day than she does at night, she seems happy both times.

Felicity's eyes are very different from day to evening. During the day when she is in bright sunlight, her eyes become thin slits to keep out light. At night when she is outdoors, the pupils of her eyes open wide to let in light. My vet told me cats see almost as well at night as they do during daytime.

SECTION 3

Writing Strategies

Ideas • Developing Informative Texts

Cause and Effect

When informative text is organized by cause and effect, it describes a **cause**—a condition or event—and also the **effect**— what happens as a direct result of the condition or event. When you write about cause and effect, you explain why one or more things happen.

Organizing Your Writing You may choose to describe the causes first or the effects first. With either approach, make sure the cause-and- effect relationship is clear. Use transition words such as *because, if, then, since, so, therefore,* and *as a result* to guide readers and emphasize the relationships between causes and effects.

EXAMPLE This paragraph from a report on tornadoes discusses the cause first and then the effect.

> The air before a violent thunderstorm is unstable. That means it changes direction and moves up and down, mixing with the air above and below it. It moves around **because** two different types of air come into contact with each other. When warm, moist air bumps up against cold, dry air, it rises. As it rises, it cools, sinks, warms up, and rises again. All this moving around of air **results** in strong, vertical wind currents. **If** the currents are big and powerful enough, and **if** the air begins to turn, the **result** is the formation of a violent tornado.

Do you see how the paragraph first describes what causes tornadoes? The cause is unstable, moving air which in turn has its own cause—the collision of warm and cold air. One cause leads to another. Do you see how the transition words emphasize the connections between causes and effects?

SECTION 3

Writing Strategies

Question and Answers

Another way to approach a subject for informative writing involves asking a question and attempting to answer it. The attempt to answer some questions may involve stating theories. You could also do research and answer other questions by presenting facts and reasons. Your subject and the type of questions you ask will determine your approach.

Take the Reader with You For example, you could write a piece that begins by asking why people mow their lawns. After capturing your reader's attention with a question, you could come up with your own reasons for why people mow lawns. Walk the reader through your thought process as you give the reasons why you believe people mow lawns. To organize your reasons, use transition words that show order of importance such as *first, second, third, finally,* and *most important.*

> **EXAMPLE** Why do people mow their lawns? **First** most people think short, mowed grass looks better. They like how it makes their yard appear neat and under control. **Second** a mowed lawn is a better surface for playing outdoor games like touch football. It's harder to run in long grass. **Third** and **most important,** people mow their lawns because their neighbors do. It's what people expect of them. They don't want to be the ones who stand out with a messy lawn.

Do you see how the example gives reasons in order of importance and uses transition words to signal readers when reasons are presented? Although the example asks just one question and gives three reasons, you may wish to ask more than one question and give any number of reasons when you use the questions/answers approach. Just be sure your writing is organized and clear.

SECTION 3

Writing Strategies

Problems and Solutions

Another way to approach informative writing is to point out a problem and offer one or more solutions. This approach takes a problem and carefully describes it so readers understand why it is a problem. Then it explains how one or more solutions can solve the problem.

Before You Write Begin by asking yourself about the size of the problem. Is it a far-reaching problem or a smaller one? Ask what causes the problem and how many people it affects. Plan to write about things that are as important to your readers.

Gather Your Information and Write Will you need facts and reasons to explain the causes and solutions? Do research in the library or online. Does the topic require observation? Take time to observe, interview others, and take notes. As you write, describe solutions in detail and tell how each will work. If your solutions don't completely solve the problem, let readers know.

The example below relies on personal observation to explain the problem and the solution. It tells about just one solution in detail, but longer expository pieces normally describe more than one solution.

> **EXAMPLE** There is a lot of litter at Chadick Park, and the problem seems to be getting worse. Everywhere you look, there is trash. The picnic area is littered with cans and paper. The playing fields don't look much better. Even the walking trails have trash on them. The trash cans that are available are always overflowing.
>
> One way to solve the problem would be to put more trash and recycling bins at the park. I have seen only one recycling bin, and it is off in one corner of the park. Most people won't take the time to go all the way across the park to throw away their cans and bottles. Adding more trash bins and placing them conveniently will encourage people to dispose of their trash properly.

Explain a Process

Informative text that tells readers how something happens or how to do something step-by-step explains a process. To describe the process, be clear about your purpose and use words that your readers will understand.

To organize, use transition words that show time order such as *first, second, third, then, after, next,* and *last* to list the steps of the process. Clearly defining the steps and listing them in the order they occur will help readers understand and remember what you are trying to explain.

EXAMPLE My mom makes great beans and rice. This is how she does it. First, she soaks the beans overnight. Then she cooks onions and garlic in a heavy pan. After those are ready, she adds some chicken broth. Next, she adds the beans and lets it simmer until the whole house smells delicious. Last, she cooks the rice and serves the beans over the rice in a hot bowl for me.

Do you see how the example uses transition words to order each step of the process? In informative writing, steps should be listed in the order they should be done and events should be listed in the order they occur.

Reading Your Writing

Informative text tells about real people and events, provides factual information about a topic, or describes a process. Depending on your purpose, you can organize your informative writing in many different ways. The important thing is to organize the information in a straightforward way so readers can understand it.

Research and Organizational Text Features

Do you sometimes have to research to find ideas and information for writing assignments, projects, and presentations? How do you find the specific information you need? **Organizational text features** will aid you in locating and understanding information. These features are found mostly in nonfiction texts like reference books, textbooks, and biographies, but they can also be found in narrative fiction and other genres.

Types of Organizational Text Features

Footnote/Endnote

A **footnote** is a note placed at the bottom of a page that relates to a number placed after a passage in the text. The footnote cites the reference that the information for that passage came from. An **endnote** is similar to a footnote, but it appears in the back of a book instead of at the bottom of a page. Sometimes footnotes or endnotes are used to provide extra information that may not have been important enough to include in the text.

Bibliography

A **bibliography** is an alphabetized list of sources that a writer used to create a text. The sources can be books, magazines, Web sites, audiovisual materials, interviews, and other informational resources. Bibliographies are normally listed at the back of a book.

Heading

A **heading** is the title that appears at the top of the page or at the beginning of a section or chapter. The heading tells the reader what he or she is about to read or that the topic is changing. A **subheading** is more specific than a heading. It might be above a certain paragraph or passage.

Caption

A **caption** is a brief summary or description of a visual, like a photo, graph, or diagram. A caption states important information such as who is in a picture or what a graph or diagram shows.

Index

An **index** is a detailed list of topics that is arranged alphabetically at the back of a book. The index tells the reader the page numbers where he or she can find information in the book.

Table of Contents

A **table of contents** is a list of a book's chapters, articles, or sections and the pages on which they start. The table of contents is located at the beginning of a book so readers can reference it and skip ahead to the pages they need.

Try It!

- Page through this book and find examples of a heading, subheading, table of contents, and index. How did they help you locate relevant information?
- Think of three ways you could use organizational text features to enhance your own writing. Which text features would you use for a fictional story, a magazine article, and a research report?

SECTION 3

Writing Strategies

Organization

Have you ever seen the framework of a new building before the walls are put up? Even though the foundation and framework might not be as beautiful as the outside, they are essential for the building to remain standing. The organization of a piece of writing is like the framework of a building upon which everything else is hung or attached. It may not be lyrical or graceful, but it is absolutely necessary for the writing to be a success.

SECTION 3

Writing Strategies

Examples of way to organize your writing include the following:
- Ordering Information
- Using Outlines
- Using Graphic Organizers
- Creating Effective Beginnings and Endings

Try It!

Here are four writing topics. Continue reading to find out which type of graphic organizer should be used for each topic.
- describe a puppy
- compare and contrast oranges and bananas
- write your opinion about school uniforms
- write a character analysis

Continue reading to see additional examples and to find out more information about how to organize your writing.

SECTION 3

Writing Strategies

Organization

Ordering Information

To communicate clearly, you must present your ideas in a logical order. There are a variety of ways to organize your ideas. Which one you choose depends upon your purpose for writing.

Organizing by Time

One way to organize your writing is chronologically, or in time order. When organizing by time, you place events in the order in which they happened. You may want to describe events from least to most recent or the other way around. Use transition words that indicate time such as *yesterday, this morning, tomorrow,* and *tomorrow evening* to tell when each event occurred or will occur. This kind of order is almost always used in biographies and autobiographies. It may also be used in writing stories.

SECTION 3
Writing Strategies

> **EXAMPLE** *Two days ago I rode my bicycle to school, but yesterday it rained so my mother drove me. Today my friend and I had enough time to walk to school. We hope to walk again tomorrow.*
>
> Notice what happens when this same information is not organized by time and does not use transition words.
>
> *It rained so my mother drove me to school. I hope we can walk. Another day I rode my bicycle, and another day a friend and I walked.*

Do you see how much clearer the first paragraph is than the second? The mixed-up order and lack of transition words that indicate time make it difficult to figure out when things happened and how they are related. The first paragraph not only lets the reader know exactly when each event occurred, it also shows how the events are connected.

Organizing by Order

Another way to present information is to organize your events by the order in which they occur. When you organize by order, you don't tell the exact time, but you tell when events happened in relationship to one another. Use transition words that indicate order such as *before, first, next, then,* and *later* to show order.

> **EXAMPLE** *__Before__ the squirrel jumped onto our deck, it climbed the large holly tree. __Next__ it scrambled out onto the end of a long branch and made a bold leap to the railing. __Then__ it jumped onto a tomato plant, took one bite out of a ripe tomato and landed squarely on the deck. __Last__ it stared into the window at us and swished its tail in a short, jerking motion.*

Try It!

Try reading the paragraph above without transition words. Do you see how ordering the events with transition words not only places the events in order but also makes the paragraph easier to read? When you don't take the time to order information, readers will be unsure about the relationship of events or descriptions, and they will have to struggle through choppy writing to figure out what you are trying to tell them.

SECTION 3

Writing Strategies

Organizing by Order of Importance

A good way to organize ideas is to write about them in order of their importance. Persuasive writing orders ideas from the least important reason to the most important. Newspaper stories order ideas the opposite way—from most to least important. Writing that informs or explains may order ideas either way, beginning with the most important or least important. Use transition words such as these—*first, second, third, most important,* and *finally*—to show order of importance.

> **EXAMPLE** We should be allowed to have a school newspaper. **First,** a newspaper would keep students informed about what is happening in the school. It could have a section for each grade and a calendar of events. **Second,** a newspaper would give students a chance to be involved in a different kind of school activity. Some kids would like to participate in something besides sports or the other clubs we have at school. **Finally,** and **most important**, working to put a newspaper together would help kids learn about responsibility and cooperation. The students putting the paper together would have to work as a team to make sure the deadline for publishing was met.

Did you see how this persuasive paragraph ordered its points from least to most important? Below, the paragraph from a news story opens with the most important information and follows with information that is less important.

> Fishermen have caught what may be the largest squid on record. The Colossal squid measures 33 feet in length and weighs approximately 990 pounds. The squid was caught in the Ross Sea near Antarctica. The Colossal squid is a marine mollusk. Little is known about these large but elusive creatures.

SECTION 3
Writing Strategies

Organizing by Location: Top to Bottom and Left to Right

Another way to organize information involves describing where things are located. When you write to explain or write to describe, you may find it useful to order details from **top to bottom** or from **left to right.** To cue your reader, use transition words such as *on top of, under, to the right of,* and *to the left of.* Take care not to jump around, but order your details in a way that is easy to read and easy for your reader to picture what you are describing.

EXAMPLE The first description below moves from top to bottom. The next description moves from left to right.

> The set for the play *The Jungle Book* amazed us. Large trees formed a rain forest canopy. **Above** the canopy was the ceiling, painted to look like a bright blue sky. **On top** of the canopy, puppetlike birds flitted from tree to tree. **Beneath** the canopy were lots of hanging vines and **under** that were thick clumps of moss and ferns.

> We looked over the obstacle course. Ten large tires formed a path on **the far left. To the right** of the tires we saw a shallow pool filled with thick mud. **Next to** that was a sandbox filled with sawdust. **To the right** of the sandbox was a climbing wall and to the **far right** a large pile of shredded foam.

SECTION 3

Writing Strategies

Reading Your Writing

Be sure to order your information in the way that makes the most sense for what is presented. Ordered writing is easier for readers to follow. If you do not order your long descriptions and explanations, readers will have a difficult time understanding your ideas.

Using Outlines

An **outline** is a good way to organize information for a nonfiction report. Let's say that you have found many facts for a report on the topic of emperor penguins. The following steps will help you organize those facts into an outline. Then you can use your outline to write the report.

1. Read over your note cards and sort them into three or more groups of facts, depending on how many subtopics you need to cover. For this report, one group of cards tells what a penguin weighs, how tall it is, and so on. You might call that group "Physical Description." Another group of cards describes what these penguins eat, so you could call it "Diet." The names of the groups are your **subtopics.**
2. Decide which subtopic to discuss first in your report. Arrange the other subtopics in a logical order.
3. Start your outline. Label each subtopic with a Roman numeral. Leave space between each subtopic for the main points that support them.
4. Read all note cards in each subtopic. Pick out the main ideas or **main points.** You will list them in your outline under the subtopic that they relate to. Label the main points with a capital letter. List any **supporting details** under the appropriate main points. Label the details with a number.

For example:
    I. Subtopic
        A. Main Point
           1. Detail
           2. Detail
        B. Main Point

If you have any smaller details, facts, examples, or explanations that relate to your supporting details, you may list them below the appropriate detail and label them with a lowercase letter.

The next two pages show note cards with facts about emperor penguins. The third page shows the facts organized into an outline. Notice how the writer organized the information from the notes.

SECTION 3
Writing Strategies

The emperor penguin is the largest of 17 kinds of penguins. "Emperor Penguins—Fun Facts." National Geographic Kids. November 19, 2006.

www.nationalgeographic.com/kids/creature_feature/0101/penguins2.html

Penguins really do sing to attract mates. Their call or song also helps their chicks find them in the huge colonies where they live. "Penguin Love Songs—The Science Behind the Movie *Happy Feet*." National Geographic Kids. November 20, 2006.

www.nationalgeographic.com/ngkids/0611/1.html

Emperor penguins can dive 1,300 feet or deeper into the sea. Scientists don't yet know how they can find food in that dark water. Stonehouse, Bernard. *Penguins*. New York: Facts on File, 2000.

All penguins live in the Southern Hemisphere (South Pole, New Zealand, Australia, South Africa, South America). "Penguins." Zoobooks – The Encyclopedia of Animals. November 19, 2006. www.zoobooks.com/newFrontPage/animals/animalFacts/sniglet_pp.html

When the mother penguins head for the sea to eat, they waddle as far as 90 miles but travel less than one mile an hour. Guiberson, Brenda. *The Emperor Lays an Egg*. New York: Henry Holt, 2001.

Emperor penguins have a black cap, blue-gray neck, orange patches on their ears and bills, and yellow breasts. "The Emperor Penguin: Aptenodytes forsteri." Australian Antarctic Division, Australian Government. November 19, 2006.

www.emperor-penguin.com/emperor.html

SECTION 3

Writing Strategies

Organization • Using Outlines

Females lay one egg and then leave. They travel 50 miles or more across the ice to find food in the sea. "Emperor Penguins—Fun Facts." National Geographic Kids. November 19, 2006.
www.nationalgeographic.com/kids/creature_feature/0101/penguins2.html

Only thousands of father penguins stay behind during winter in the Antarctic. All other living things go someplace warmer. The sun hardly shines at all during these long, cold, windy months. Guiberson, Brenda. *The Emperor Lays an Egg*. New York: Henry Holt, 2001.

The male carries the egg on his feet, covered with a very warm layer of feathered skin. For about 65 days, he keeps the egg warm—and eats nothing. Finally, the egg hatches. "Emperor Penguins—Fun Facts." National Geographic Kids. November 19, 2006.
www.nationalgeographic.com/kids/creature_feature/0101/penguins2.html

When the mother comes back, the father leaves to find food. After he returns, the mother and father take turns caring for the chick. Stonehouse, Bernard. *Penguins*. New York: Facts on File, 2000.

To stay warm, the fathers, holding their eggs on their feet, huddle together in huge groups. As the temperature dips to –60o F, they take turns standing in the middle of the huddle. Guiberson, Brenda. *The Emperor Lays an Egg*. New York: Henry Holt, 2001.

Emperor penguins have a big head and short, thick neck. Their wings are tiny, like flippers. Males and females look alike. "Penguins." Antarctic Connection. November 19, 2006.
www.antarcticconnection.com/antarctic/wildlife/penguins/emperor.shtml

SECTION 3
Writing Strategies

Here is an outline for a report about emperor penguins.

I. Physical appearance
   A. Largest of 17 kinds of penguins
      1. Grow 40–45 in. tall
      2. Weigh 44–99 lbs.
   B. Have a black cap, blue-gray neck, orange patches on their ears and bills, and yellow breasts
   C. Males and females look alike.

II. Habitat and diet
   A. Live only in Southern Hemisphere
   B. Eat squid, fish, and crustaceans

III. Roles of males and females
   A. Females lay one egg a year.
      1. Then they leave for two months to find food.
      2. They return to take care of the hatched chicks.
   B. Males care for the egg for 65 days.
      1. They do not eat during this time.
      2. They hold the egg carefully on their feet.
      3. They cover the eggs with a warm, feathered layer.
      4. There is no nest.
      5. As soon as the egg hatches and the female comes back, the male begins a long walk to find food.
   C. Males and females keep the same partners each year.

IV. Adaptations to survive
   A. Lay only one egg at a time
   B. Can dive 1,300 feet deep to find food
   C. Eggs incubate during winter so new chicks will be born in spring, when they can find food
   D. Fathers huddle together for protection against wind, cold

Margin notes:
- Every A should have a B. Every 1 should have a 2.
- These two main topics have few details, so they were combined.
- Use a period after each Roman numeral, letter, and number.
- Use a capital letter for the first word of each subtopic, main point, and detail. You do not have to write in complete sentences.

SECTION 3

Writing Strategies

Organization • Using Outlines

Graphic Organizers

Graphic organizers are planning tools that writers can use to collect and organize information. There are many different kinds of graphic organizers. Choose one that works with the kind of writing you will be doing.

Topic Web

A topic web can be used for many purposes. For example, you might use a web to list characteristics of a person or thing, to show how story characters are related, or to identify subtopics related to a main topic. The web below lists characteristics of the American barn owl.

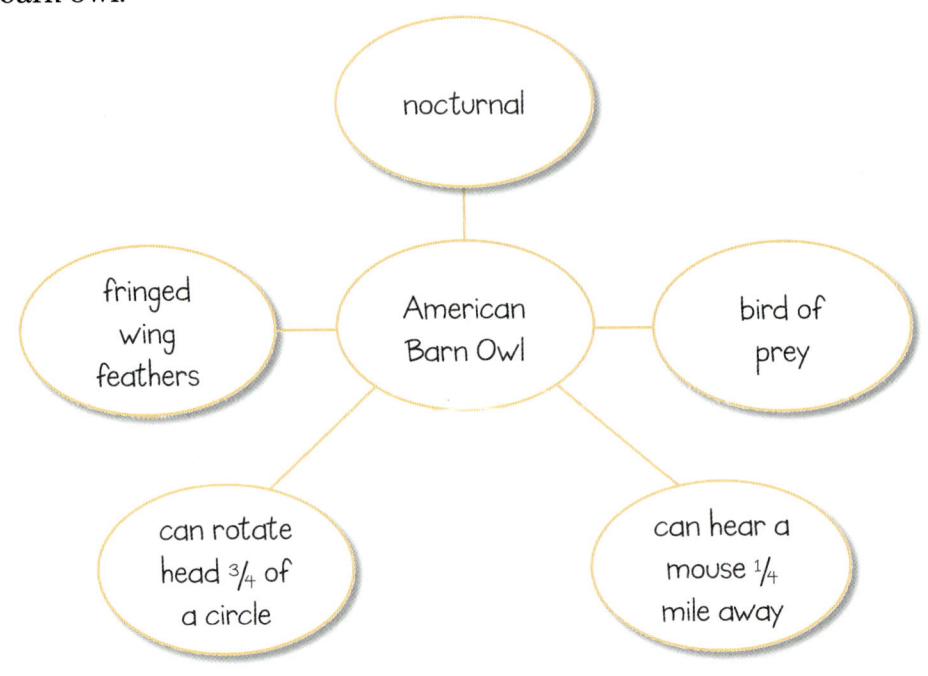

- American Barn Owl
  - nocturnal
  - fringed wing feathers
  - bird of prey
  - can rotate head 3/4 of a circle
  - can hear a mouse 1/4 mile away

SECTION 3
Writing Strategies

Story Map

A story map is used to outline the events of a story, either fiction or nonfiction. You can also include information about the story's characters and setting. Below is a story map from "Alejandro's Gift" by Richard E. Albert. Notice how the story map includes major events but excludes minor details.

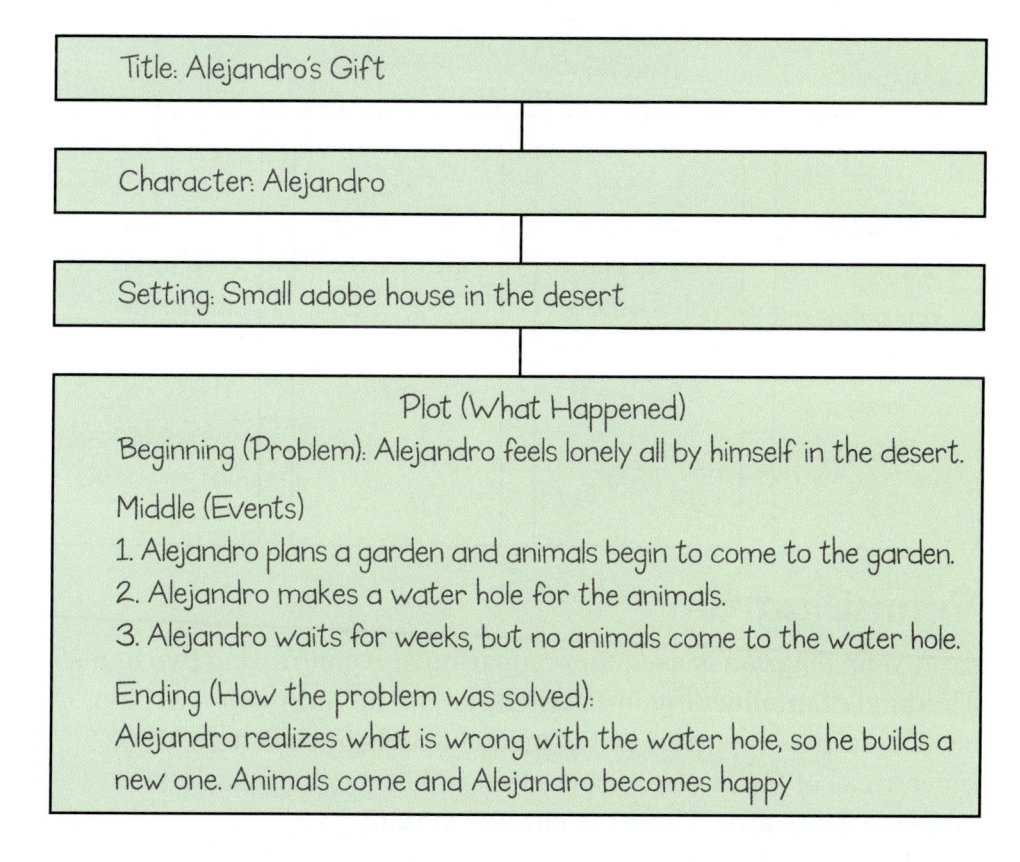

Title: Alejandro's Gift

Character: Alejandro

Setting: Small adobe house in the desert

Plot (What Happened)

Beginning (Problem): Alejandro feels lonely all by himself in the desert.

Middle (Events)
1. Alejandro plans a garden and animals begin to come to the garden.
2. Alejandro makes a water hole for the animals.
3. Alejandro waits for weeks, but no animals come to the water hole.

Ending (How the problem was solved):
Alejandro realizes what is wrong with the water hole, so he builds a new one. Animals come and Alejandro becomes happy

---

SECTION 3

Writing Strategies

Time Line

A time line is used to show a sequence of events. In addition to showing the order in which events occurred, a time line can show relationships among events. This kind of graphic organizer is especially useful if you are writing about people (a biography or autobiography) or historical events.

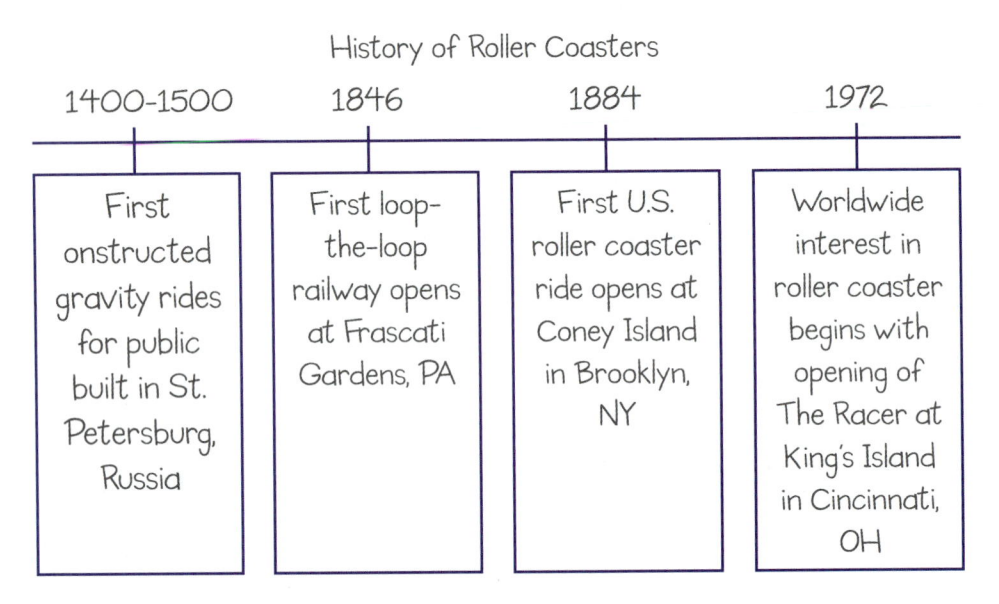

History of Roller Coasters

1400-1500	1846	1884	1972
First onstructed gravity rides for public built in St. Petersburg, Russia	First loop-the-loop railway opens at Frascati Gardens, PA	First U.S. roller coaster ride opens at Coney Island in Brooklyn, NY	Worldwide interest in roller coaster begins with opening of The Racer at King's Island in Cincinnati, OH

Venn Diagram

A Venn diagram is used for comparing and contrasting two items. This kind of graphic organizer can be useful in informative writing, such as science reports. List the unique details of each item in the outer areas of the circles. List the things that the items have in common in the area where the circles overlap.

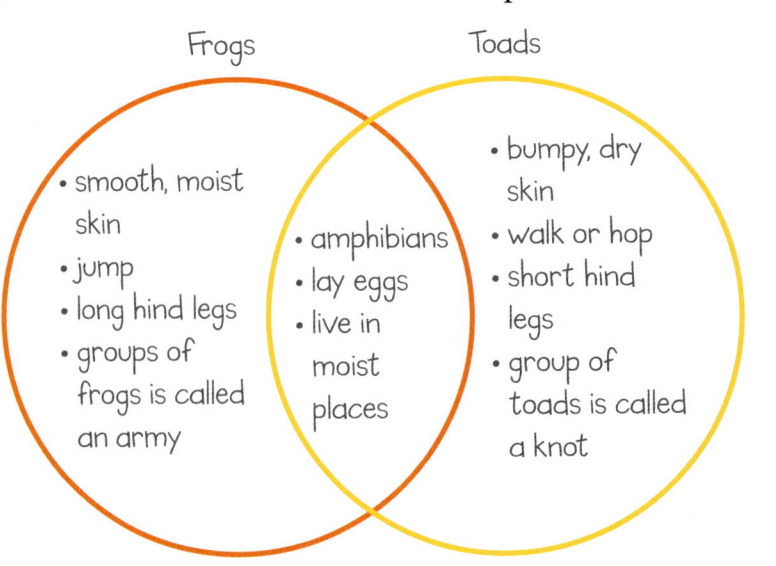

Frogs
- smooth, moist skin
- jump
- long hind legs
- groups of frogs is called an army

(both)
- amphibians
- lay eggs
- live in moist places

Toads
- bumpy, dry skin
- walk or hop
- short hind legs
- group of toads is called a knot

Organization • Graphic Organizers

TIDE Graphic Organizer

If you are writing to give information, it is helpful to organize your ideas into main topics and subtopics. Doing this during the prewriting phase will make both researching and writing easier.

The TIDE graphic organizer is one way to plan and organize the main topic and subtopics for a piece of informative writing. This sort of organizer also helps you discover whether you need to do more research.

T	**Topic** Tips for Parakeet Owners
ID	**Important Detail** The Birdcage -should have two perches and a swing -use plastic seed guards -decorate with bells and colorful toys
ID	**Important Detail** Care and Feedings -give quality seed and fresh water daily -change paper towel at bottom of cage every 3 days -give "seed tree" treat occasionally
ID	**Important Detail** Training -avoid sudden movements -training to talk -finger training
E	**Ending** With proper care and training, parakeets can be very nice pets.

SECTION 3

Writing Strategies

TREE Graphic Organizer

A TREE graphic organizer can help you organize your reasons and explanations for an opinion paragraph. You should include at least three reasons and explanations that support your opinion. A TREE graphic organizer will help you see if you have included enough reasons.

T	**Topic Sentence** I think that everyone should learn how to swim.
R	**Reason 1:** important for safety
E	**Explanation:** in case you fall in water
R	**Reason 2:** swimming is fun
E	**Explanation:** play with friends in the water
R	**Reason 3:** good exercise
E	**Explanation:** use muscles in arms and legs
E	**Ending** Learning how to swim is a good idea, so sign up for swimming lessons today.

Cause-and-Effect Chart

Cause-and-effect relationships are important in many different kinds of writing. Science reports and papers about historical events might focus on cause-and-effect connections. You might also write a story in which several events cause a certain effect on a character or characters. Note that one cause might have several effects, or many causes could result in one effect.

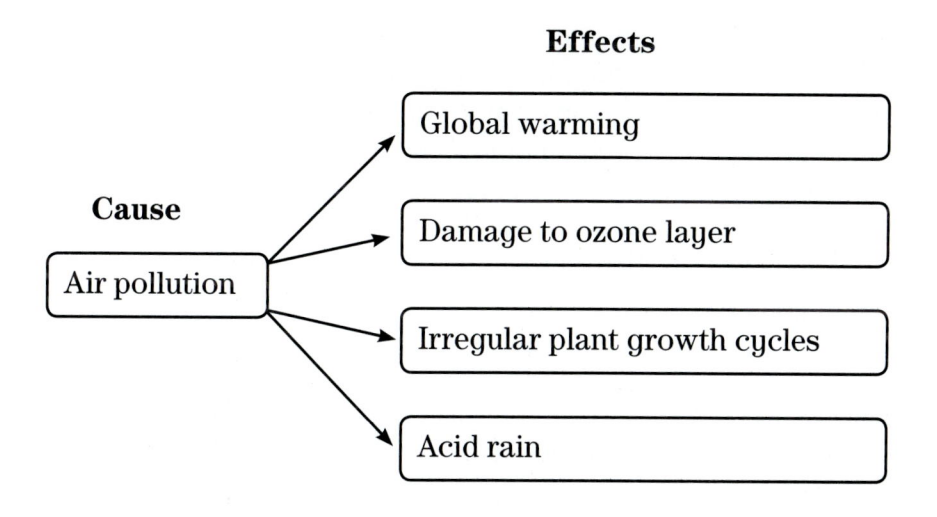

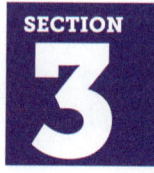

Effects

Cause

Air pollution →
- Global warming
- Damage to ozone layer
- Irregular plant growth cycles
- Acid rain

SECTION 3

Writing Strategies

Reading Your Writing

Writers can choose from many different graphic organizers to help them gather information and organize their ideas. Your stories and reports will be more organized and easier to read if you get your thoughts and facts in order before you start writing.

Effective Beginnings and Endings

A good beginning to your story or report makes your readers want to keep reading. A good ending helps them remember what you wrote.

Writing Effective Beginnings

A good beginning grabs the reader's attention with an effective lead. The type of beginning you use will depend on whether you are writing fiction or nonfiction. In both types of writing, however, the beginning should make them interested in your topic or story. Below are a few of the ways to begin your writing.

Tell about a Problem

Write a lead about a problem in the opening paragraph to encourage your audience to think actively about your topic.

> Many of us are just too busy. We record our favorite show so we won't miss it when we go out. We eat our dinner and listen to the radio while we finish our homework. All of the "important" things we do leave little time to spend with family and friends.

Ask a Question

Begin with one or more questions to get readers thinking about your topic.

> When was the last time you were really nervous? Can you remember how you felt? I remember it well. I was a beginning debater. I sat across from the best debater in school. She looked calm and relaxed while I just couldn't stop sweating or keep my hands from shaking.

Tell an Interesting Fact

There is nothing like an interesting fact to capture a reader's attention. When readers see an interesting fact in the lead, they are likely to want to read more.

> There were once billions of beautiful passenger pigeons in the United States and Canada. There were so many pigeons that when they flew they darkened the skies, completely shutting out the sunlight. Today, not a single passenger pigeon lives.

Describe an Experience

Start by writing about something that happened to you or another person. This is a great way to encourage readers to identify from the start with the person about whom you are writing. In writing fiction, you may wish to start with dialogue to describe your personal experience.

> "Look what I found," my friend Lenny called to me as he stooped to pick something up from the street. "It's a five dollar bill. Isn't this great!"
>
> "Yes, but you should ask around to see if someone lost it," I answered. "If you can't find out who lost it, we can split it."
>
> "What do you mean split it?" asked Lenny. "It's mine!"

SECTION 3

Writing Strategies

Writing Effective Endings

Your ending is your conclusion. An effective ending consists of a single sentence or paragraph that does any of the following:

- ▶ It may summarize your key points or the main idea.
- ▶ It may bring the action or events to an end.
- ▶ It may provide a reflection on how the topic affects the world or life in general.
- ▶ It may provide a reflection on how the topic influences the individual reader.
- ▶ It may provide an interesting or unique way of thinking about what you have written.

Take care not to introduce new ideas in the closing paragraph or sentence. Instead, make sure that the final paragraph or sentence clearly signals the end to what you have written.

Summarizing

When you write an ending that summarizes, you can end with a statement that restates the main idea. A nonfiction report about how the game of basketball has changed in the last one hundred years ends with a statement that reminds the reader of the article's general purpose.

> To sum up, I found out that the game of basketball has changed in many ways. The baskets, the ball, the court, the shots, and especially the rules have all changed since the game was invented one hundred years ago.

Ending with a Reflective Paragraph

Another way to end is by concluding with a paragraph in which you reflect on or think about what you have written. A final reflection might encourage readers to think about how the information influences the world or them personally or urge them to see it in a different light. Read the example below. Do you see how the paragraph begins with the plants and animals inside the rain forest and moves outward toward readers and the rest of the world?

> Once a rain forest is gone, it is gone forever. Plants that live there disappear, and the animals that live there lose their homes and food. For people, that means fewer of the scents, flavors, and valuable medicines we get from the rain forest. Vanishing rain forests affect the world's atmosphere as well. We should take it seriously when we hear of another rain forest being destroyed. When a rain forest disappears, so does a vital part of our planet.

Ending for Stories

When writing an ending for your stories, try to increase the tension in the story by using action, dialogue, and details to make the character's struggle more exciting for the reader. Once you have done that, remember to show the reader the climax and how the character solves the conflict in the story. Be certain to "tie up the loose ends" in the resolution by making sure the reader gets all necessary questions about the story answered.

Word Choice

Language is the core of communication, so choosing the right word for the situation is important. Nine synonyms might exist for the word *happy*, but only one will be the perfect choice in a particular sentence. Choosing the right word for the right situation will often give strength to your writing and draw the reader in through your original, memorable, and striking use of words. Be a wordsmith, and choose your words carefully for maximum effect on your reader.

SECTION 3

Writing Strategies

Examples of ways to use different word choices in your writing include the following:

- Using a Thesaurus
- Academic Language
- Figurative Language

EXAMPLE By choosing verbs that have certain feelings associated with them, you can relay these feelings to your reader. Read each sentence below. What feeling is associated with the verb in each sentence?

- Sam smirked at the politician's comments.
- Sam smiled at the politician's comments.
- Sam snickered at the politician's comments.
- Sam beamed at the politician's comments.

Continue reading to see additional examples and to find out more information about making good word choices in your writing.

SECTION 3

Writing Strategies

Using a Thesaurus

A **thesaurus** offers synonyms, words with the same or nearly the same meanings. A thesaurus can help add variety to your writing. It can keep you from repeating the same words over and over.

A thesaurus can be organized in two ways. In one kind of thesaurus, you use the index to look up the word you want to replace. Here is the listing for the word *walk* from the index of one thesaurus:

walk

nouns path 281.4; arena 281.7

verbs go slow 198.4; travel 319.2

walk off with 894.2

walk on air 345.8

Now you can use those numbers to look up *walk* as a noun or a verb. You can also find the meaning of idioms, such as *walk on air*. Right now, you want a synonym for *go slow*. The pages that come before the index have guide numbers at the top, like the guide words in a dictionary. To find synonyms for *go slow,* you look for 198.4. It's on the page with the guide numbers 197.3-198.9. Here is what you find:

198.4. go slow, plod, drag, creep, crawl, trudge, poke along

The second kind of thesaurus is organized like a dictionary. The definition and synonyms follow the word.

walk

Verb. 1. to move at a moderate pace by taking steps. Synonyms: step, trudge, stroll, march, amble, hike, roam. 2. (informal) to go on strike or quit one's job. Synonyms: quit, strike.

Using Academic Language

Do you speak the same when you are at home watching movies with your friends and when you are giving an oral report in front of your principal? It's hard to imagine using the same tone, word choices, and sentence flow in all the places you go and with all the people you talk to. Similarly, when you write, you need to use language that is *appropriate* for your audience and purpose. You should use **academic language** for most written and oral projects in school and other formal settings.

- Use the **grammar** and **conventions** of academic English instead of the dialect you speak at home. For example, you might write *I want a ticket, but there are none left* rather than *I wanna ticket, but there ain't none left*.
- Avoid using slang terms, abbreviations, and contractions such as *didn't* and *can't*.
- Use **academic vocabulary** when appropriate. Academic vocabulary includes words that are specifically related to a subject area. For example, the words *carnivore* and *herbivore* are academic vocabulary words related to science. These words help your audience understand information you provide.

SECTION 3
Writing Strategies

Use academic language for the following:
- business letters and formal communications
- oral presentations
- reports and other expository or persuasive writing
- standardized tests

You can use nonacademic language or your home dialect for writing and presentations with an informal tone, such as e-mails, journals, poetry, dialogue in narratives, and skits.

A **dialect** is a variety of language that is shared by a group of speakers. Everyone speaks a dialect or dialects, and all dialects have grammar rules. Academic English is the dialect, or variety, of English that you learn in school. Your home dialect is probably different. You switch back and forth between them depending on which is appropriate for your setting.

Figurative Language

Figurative language refers to words or groups of words that stand for more than their literal meaning. Writers use figurative language, sometimes called **figures of speech,** to create vivid pictures in readers' minds. Figures of speech frequently make comparisons that rely on the experience of the audience.

Simile

A **simile** is a figure of speech that compares two things that are not alike by using the word *like* or *as*.

> The rug was as soft as a bed of moss.
>
> The motorcycle rumbled like thunder in the distance.

How does the second example work? Readers are familiar with the sound of thunder. By comparing the sound of the motorcycle to rumbling thunder, the simile creates a connection to a well-known sound in the reader's mind.

Now look at the simile below. Does it work?

> Diego's whistle sounded like that of the crested flycatcher.

Most readers are not familiar with the crested flycatcher bird or its whistle, so they would have no idea how Diego's whistle sounded. Similes are great for creating fresh, clear images, but be sure to base them on your audience's experience.

Try It!

To what could you compare each of these two things in order to create a simile that your friends would understand?
- The heat of a summer day
- The screeching brakes of a car

Metaphor

A **metaphor** is a figure of speech that compares two unlike things without using the words *like* or *as*. A metaphor sometimes uses context or the surrounding information to make a comparison. Metaphors also rely on the experience of the audience.

> The air-conditioned waiting room was a refrigerator.
>
> The trip was a nightmare.

The first example assumes that readers will know from experience and context that the waiting room was not an actual refrigerator but that its temperature was like one. The second example assumes that the audience has experienced a bad dream and can then understand that the trip was not a pleasant experience. When you use metaphors, be sure that the context and the experience of your audience support the image.

Personification

Personification is a figure of speech in which an object or idea is given human qualities. As with other types of figurative language, personification involves making a comparison. Personification relies on context and the ability of readers to relate human qualities to the thing described.

> The old house creaked and complained about its worn and aching joints.
>
> The friendly harbor welcomed us with outstretched arms.

The first example gives something that is not human—a house—the qualities of a person complaining about worn and aching joints. The second example compares a harbor to a friendly person. The comparison works if readers imagine a U-shaped harbor with arms of land, like the hugging arms of a person.

SECTION 3

Writing Strategies

Exaggeration

Exaggeration in writing means stretching the truth to make a strong statement or to add humor. Use exaggeration to add interest to your writing with the understanding that readers are not to take your descriptions literally.

Exaggeration is a great way to capture and hold your reader's attention. Through overstatement, exaggeration can add emphasis to your descriptions and ideas. Readers should understand from their own experience and through context that the description isn't meant to be taken word-for-word. Think of using exaggeration to make readers smile.

> I was so tired I collapsed on the bottom bunk.
>
> My feet were killing me.
>
> The morning sunlight blinded me as it came through the window.

Hyperbole

Hyperbole is a type of extreme exaggeration often used for humorous effect. It is sometimes used in writing to describe the quality of one thing by comparing it to a more extreme quality in another.

> He was so hungry that he ate everything but the table.
>
> My backpack felt as if it had ten bowling balls inside it.

The first example uses hyperbole by making a simple, yet extreme, statement. The second example uses hyperbole by comparing the first item, the weight of a backpack, to that of something far heavier—ten bowling balls. The comparison is so exaggerated that it becomes humorous.

Use exaggeration and hyperbole only at key moments in your writing. If you use it too often, readers may tire of the technique and it will lose its impact.

Idiom

An **idiom** is a word or group of words that cannot be understood by knowing only the literal meaning. People learn idioms or expressions as they learn their language. Idioms can add personality and a natural feel to your writing, although they are not normally used for formal writing. Sometimes idioms say exactly what you want to communicate—just be sure your audience knows what they mean from context and experience.

Read each of the sentences below. The idiom is in bold type. Its meaning is in parentheses.

- Our teacher **went out on a limb** for us when she asked the principal if we could have class outside today. (to take a risk)
- Nadine had **cold feet** at her piano recital. (to be very nervous)
- It never **dawned** on me to try the red button. (to understand)
- Could you show Terry **the ropes?** He's never worked at the refreshment stand. (to explain how something is done)

Do you see how idioms make writing sound natural, almost like the way people talk?

As you get older, you will understand the meanings of more and more idioms. Younger people and people who have recently learned English have some trouble understanding them. When you use idioms in your writing, use them correctly and in a context that helps make their meaning clear.

Reading Your Writing

Figurative language makes your writing interesting. Similes, metaphors, and personification bring fresh images to the reader's mind. Exaggeration can capture and hold your reader's interest, while using idioms helps make your writing sound natural. When using any of these, be aware of how they match with the experience of your audience and place them in a context that will make their meanings clear.

SECTION 3

Writing Strategies

Voice

Voice is the trait that makes writing your very own. It's what separates your writing from someone else's writing. A writing voice full of enthusiasm and purpose will energize your reader from the very first sentence.

The voice you use will change depending on what you are writing. If you are writing a story, you may want to use a voice that appeals to readers' emotions. Your goal may be to make them laugh or cry or have some other emotional response. If you're writing a report, you may want to use a voice that gives just the facts and which appeals to a reader's sense of reason. You may want to convince the reader that you are presenting a reasonable point of view.

You might change your voice for the following reasons:

- Writing for Different Audiences and Purposes
- Developing Persuasive Writing
- Adding Sensory Details
- Creating the Sound of Language

Reading Your Writing

Take time to decide on your audience and purpose before you begin writing. You will be more successful in communicating with your reader.

Continue reading to see examples and to find out more information about using voice in your writing.

SECTION 3

Writing Strategies

Audience and Purpose

The goal of writing is to communicate with others. Your audience and purpose should guide how and what you write.

Audience

Audience refers to your readers, the people who will read what you write. Think about who they are. Are they old or young? Will certain information interest them more than other information? How and what you write should be influenced by what you know about your audience. Look at the following examples.

Audience: eight-year-olds

Before you get a pet, think about how it will fit into your house. If you live in an apartment, you may want to think about smaller animals. Gerbils, hamsters, and goldfish do not need a lot of room. Dogs and cats make great pets but need more room.

Audience: working adults

People should consider where they live and how much time they have before choosing a pet. Gerbils, hamsters, and goldfish take up little space and require less care than dogs and cats. Dogs, especially, require a greater time commitment.

Audience: people who live alone

Pets are wonderful companions. They add life to a quiet house or apartment and may ease loneliness. Before getting a pet, consider the amount of space you have and your ability to care for it. Gerbils, hamsters, and goldfish take up little space and require less care than cats and dogs. Larger dogs require more space.

Analyzing the Examples

Do you see how the author chose simpler words such as *think* and *need* for the eight-year-olds and more difficult words such as *consider* and *require* for the working adults and older people? Your word choice will depend on the age and reading level of your audience.

What do you notice about the information in each example? The paragraph for working people discusses time commitment and the fact that the owners may be away during the day. The piece for eight-year-olds focuses on what size of pet is appropriate for where they live. Notice how the writing voice changes each time to show that the writer cares about each audience and wishes to make a connection. The things about which the author writes are also aimed at what is important to each audience.

Purpose

Your **purpose** is your reason for writing. Whenever you write, you should be aware of *why* you are writing. Are you writing to inform? Are you writing to explain? Are you writing to entertain? Are you writing to persuade? Being aware of your purpose will help you stay clear and focused as you write.

Write to Inform

When you write a school report or an article, you are writing to inform and sometimes explain. For example, if you want to tell readers about a volcano that erupted in Mexico, you write to inform. You will want to include information such as time, exact location, how many people it affected, and other details.

SECTION 3
Writing Strategies

Write to Explain

If you want to describe to readers why a volcano erupts and what leads to an eruption, you write to explain. It's like writing to inform, but it goes a step further by telling *how* something happens. Other reasons for writing to explain include giving directions or telling how to do something.

When writing to explain, it is especially important to present the ideas in an organized way. To tell about how and why a volcano erupts, you can use transition words (such as *first, second, third*) for each event that leads to the eruption so readers can easily follow the process.

Write to Entertain

When you write to entertain, you want to capture your readers' attention so they enjoy what they are reading. You could, for example, write an adventure story about a family who escapes from an erupting volcano. Instead of giving all the scientific reasons for eruptions, you would use descriptive language that appeals to your audience.

The purpose of most fiction is to entertain, but other types of writing can entertain as well. Knowing your purpose while you write will guide you and help you make what you are writing funnier, scarier, or more entertaining in another way.

> **Try It!**
>
> See if you can come up with a purpose and audience for each of these topics.
> - All pet goldfish should live in aquariums with air pumps.
> - A story about two goldfish who become friends.
> - Step-by step instructions on how to clean your tank while you are away.

Write to Persuade

When you write to persuade, you write with the purpose of getting your readers to change their minds about something or take some action. Think about the information that would most likely influence them. For example, if you want to persuade people to get more exercise, you could include one or more of the following: an emotional appeal for living longer and feeling better, facts about possible results of not exercising, the opinions from doctors and fitness experts who study the benefits of exercise, or examples of people who have improved their health through exercise. When you write persuasively, you should be clear about what you expect from your readers, whether it is help with a solution or simply a change in thinking.

Try It!

Is your purpose to **inform, explain, entertain,** or **persuade** in each item below?
- You need to give a friend directions to get to your house.
- You want to tell a story about the time you ate turkey for breakfast.
- You want to convince your parents to let you sleep over at a friend's house.
- You need to write a report on dolphins.

Reading Your Writing

Knowing your purpose and audience guides you as you write by helping with word choice, writing voice, and the ideas you choose to emphasize.

SECTION 3

Writing Strategies

Voice • Audience and Purpose

Developing Persuasive Writing

Persuasive writing is written for the purpose of influencing its readers to take action. It sometimes has the added purpose of changing the way readers think or feel about a topic. It often does both.

You can use one of two techniques to get readers to think and/or act differently: 1) State an opinion and support that opinion with facts, examples, and reasons. 2) State an opinion and appeal to the audience's interests and emotions.

EXAMPLE This paragraph shows persuasive writing that uses facts and reasons.

> The fifth-graders at Stetson Elementary School should have a longer lunch break. We are supposed to get twenty-five minutes to eat our lunches. However, since we are the last group to go to the cafeteria, we get less time. The other groups run late and take up extra time. By the time the younger grades finally clear out, and by the time we file in, stand in the food line, and actually sit down, we have only fifteen minutes left to eat. We don't have enough time to finish our food. Just a few more minutes would make a big difference. It might also improve how we do in our afternoon classes.

When you write persuasively, you may need to research your facts by visiting the library, searching online, or by interviewing others. You can also use examples from personal experience or expert opinions such as can be obtained through interviews and research. Use the facts, examples, and expert opinions that will have the most weight with your audience.

Use the second technique when you think your audience will be most influenced by an appeal to their interests or emotions. The example on the next page shows how to support a similar viewpoint by appealing to emotion.

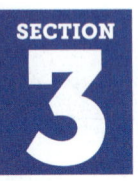

SECTION 3
Writing Strategies

> **EXAMPLE**
>
> The fifth-graders at Stetson Elementary School should have an earlier and longer lunch break. Have you ever felt so weak from hunger that you couldn't concentrate? What if you then had to wolf down your food in a short amount of time? This is what the fifth graders have to do. We have to wait until all the other groups have eaten their lunches to go to the cafeteria. Then we have to eat in a hurry before the next bell rings. We feel rushed and less important than the other grades. Please, would those who plan the schedule figure out a way to give the fifth graders an earlier or longer lunch break?

Do you see how this example appeals to the emotions? Instead of listing facts, like *fifteen minutes* or the reasons why lunch is too short, it tells how the fifth-graders feel and encourages the reader to identify with them. The last line shows how some persuasive writing asks for action on an issue.

Audience and Purpose

Knowing who your audience is and what their interests are will also help you shape your persuasive writing. For example, if your topic is one to which you know your audience feels connected emotionally, you could appeal to their emotions. Knowing how the interests of your audience relate to the topic will also help. For example, if you are writing to persuade the parents of the Home and School Association to donate new gymnastic mats, you could emphasize safety. When writing to persuade, use the approach and language that will influence your audience.

You should also think about the purpose, or reason, you are writing. Do you want to influence the thinking of your audience on a topic? Do you want to get people to act on something? Do you want to point out a problem? Knowing your purpose will guide you and help you organize as you select facts, reasons, or emotional descriptions to influence your readers.

Organizing Your Persuasive Writing: Ask and Answer Questions

One useful way to organize your persuasive writing is to ask and answer a question. When you ask a question, you involve readers and get them immediately thinking about your topic in an active way. The answer or answers you give can be the facts and reasons you use to get your readers to see your point of view and accept it as reasonable. The example shown below tries to persuade the audience to believe that the writer will be old enough to baby-sit in sixth grade.

> **EXAMPLE**
>
> How old does someone need to be in order to baby-sit? It depends on how mature and well-trained the person is. I think I will be mature enough and have the training to baby-sit when I start sixth grade next year. These are my reasons. First, people tell me that I'm mature for my age. Second, this summer I will be taking the baby-sitting course offered at the YMCA. I'll learn what baby-sitters should and shouldn't do as well as what to do in case of an emergency. Third, I have lots of experience taking care of my younger cousins when my aunt comes over to visit. If a person has both maturity and training and is in at least sixth grade (as I will be next year), she should be allowed to baby-sit.

Do you see the question in the opening sentence? When it asks how old a person should be in order to baby-sit, it states the topic of the persuasive paragraph. The reader expects the information that follows to answer the question. The writer answers the question in the third sentence, mentioning maturity, skills, and being in sixth grade as traits that are generally required. The three reasons that follow answer with specific examples showing why the writer has the maturity and training required. The concluding sentence summarizes the answers/reasons and uses the persuasive word *should* to recommend that he or she should be allowed to baby-sit, restating the paragraph's purpose.

SECTION 3
Writing Strategies

Organizing Your Persuasive Writing: Order Your Reasons

Another way to organize your persuasive writing is to first state your opinion or goal and follow it with the supporting reasons in order of importance. List your reasons—which may be facts or examples—in order of importance from least to most important.

EXAMPLE

Buckwalter Farm should not be turned into a golf course. It should remain public open space for the following reasons. First, another golf course isn't needed. According to the tourist bureau, we have 175 golf courses in the tri-county area. Second, most golf courses are not environmentally friendly. They use large amounts of water and chemicals to keep their greens in shape. Their artificial landscape is far more harmful to native plants and animals than that of Buckwalter Farm where chemicals are no longer used. Third, people have been going to Buckwalter Farm for years, to fish in the pond, to pick apples in the orchard, and to explore nature by the stream. The farm means a lot to people of all ages in the community—far more than any golf course ever would. Sign the petition to keep Buckwalter Farm from being turned into a golf course.

SECTION 3
Writing Strategies

Reading Your Writing

Use persuasive writing to influence readers to think and act differently by giving them facts and reasons or by appealing to their emotions. Write with a specific purpose and with your audience in mind. Organize persuasive writing by asking and answering a question and by discussing reasons in order of importance.

Adding Sensory Details

One way to help readers better understand what you write is to use visualization. Let your readers *visualize*, or *see*, what it is that you are describing.

To do this, close your eyes and imagine the scene or subject you are describing. Concentrate on the sights, sounds, smells, tastes, and textures. Use words and concrete sensory details that appeal to the reader's five senses—details that are specific and vivid that paint a picture in the reader's mind.

Take a look at the following two passages:

Passage 1

I got up in the morning. I looked outside and saw the sun. It was shining in my window. There were a few clouds in the sky. I stretched and yawned and went downstairs.

I could smell pancakes and bacon. I was hungry. I sat down in the dining room.

Passage 2

I opened my eyes to find sunlight streaming through my window. A few puffy clouds floated in the blue morning sky. I slowly stretched, reaching towards the ceiling. Then I yawned a big yawn and padded down the stairs to begin my day.

The smell of juicy bacon and blueberry pancakes filled the dining room. I felt my stomach rumble as I scooted into my chair.

Use Specific Details and Descriptive Words

In the first passage, the writer uses very general words and very few specific details. It is hard for readers to form a clear picture in their minds of the setting and action. Readers will probably lose interest and not care about the characters or events.

In the second passage, the writer uses concrete sensory details and descriptive, vivid words to describe the action and setting. Verbs such as "streaming" and "floated" are very specific and bring to mind certain images. Adjectives such as "puffy," "fuzzy," and "bright" also help the reader to visualize what is being described.

Creating the Sound of Language

Writers, especially when they're writing poetry, choose words not just for what they mean but also for how they sound. To tune your ear to the sound of language, pay attention to how the words that you read and write create sounds and effects. This lesson includes some special writing devices you can use.

Alliteration

Alliteration is the repetition of the consonant sounds at the beginning of words. You may have seen alliteration used in advertising or for movie and book titles such as **Ch*arlie and the* Ch*ocolate Factory*.

Alliteration is most often used in poetry, but it can also be used in fiction. Use alliteration when your goal is to have readers be entertained by what you have written. *The snake slithered across the sidewalk* is an example of alliteration that repeats the *s* sound and makes the snake's movements seem to come to life.

Assonance

When you use assonance in your writing, you repeat the sounds of vowels. Assonance can add a pleasing sound to your writing and may be used in poetry, and in stories, when you want readers to enjoy the sound of what you've written. *D*a*n fl*a*shed a set of br*a*ss keys* is an example of assonance that repeats the short *a* sound.

Onomatopoeia

When you use onomatopoeia, you use a word that imitates the sound made by or connected with the thing to which you refer. As with other methods that highlight sound, you will want to use onomatopoeic words most often in writing that entertains. Use onomatopoeia to make sounds come alive for your readers. In the sentence *"We heard the **pitter-patter** of rain on the tin roof,"* **pitter-patter** mimics the sound that rain makes as it falls on a tin roof.

SECTION 3

Writing Strategies

Conventions

Is it easy to read someone's writing when it is full of usage errors and punctuation mistakes? You know that it is important to edit and proofread your writing and that you should apply what you know about grammar, usage, and mechanics in the editing stage. You want your finished piece of writing to be correct and free of errors when you present it to your audience.

Conventions are the mechanics of writing, and they include spelling, grammar, punctuation, capitalization, and indentation. These are what you should check when you edit and proofread your writing. Correctly using conventions makes your writing easier for your audience to understand and more enjoyable to read. Without writing conventions, people would have an awful time reading anything. Imagine if there were no capital letters or periods in the sentences in this paragraph. You would not be able to tell where one sentence ended and the next began. You can see why it is important to know about writing conventions.

SECTION 3

Writing Strategies

As you edit and proofread, remember to check for the following conventions:

- end marks
- conventions in dialogue
- capitalization
- commas, colons, and apostrophes
- subject/verb agreement and other grammatical errors
- correct spelling

Continue reading this section of the Handbook to find some tips for improving this aspect of your writing.

SECTION 3

Writing Strategies

Editing

Inside the Writing Process: Editing

Editing your work will make your revised writing clearer, cleaner, and more accurate. It addresses *conventions*, one of the traits of good writing. In the editing step, you evaluate the correctness and clarity of each sentence in your writing.

Many writers prefer to check for one type of error at a time. An editing checklist can help you make sure that you do not forget to check for a specific type of error in your writing. A good habit to get into is to keep a list of the common errors you make in writing. What words do you frequently misspell? Do you tend to misuse commas in your writing? These are the kinds of items you should note on your personal editing checklist.

Using Proofreading Marks

Whenever you edit your own or someone else's writing, use proofreading marks to indicate exactly where a change needs to be made in a draft. Do you recall the proofreading marks below?

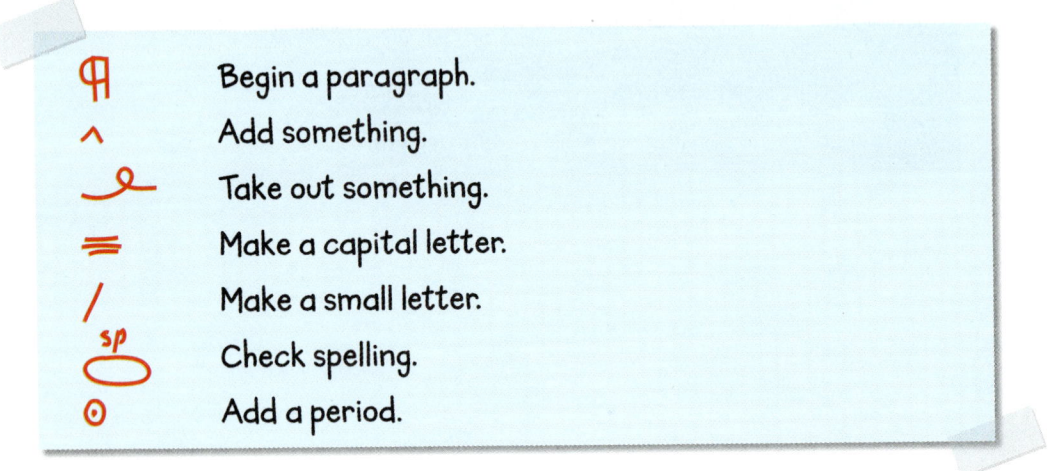

Mark	Meaning
¶	Begin a paragraph.
∧	Add something.
Ꜿ	Take out something.
≡	Make a capital letter.
/	Make a small letter.
sp	Check spelling.
⊙	Add a period.

SECTION 3
Writing Strategies

Since Marcie has memorized the proofreading symbols, she was able to quickly and easily make the following corrections to her paragraph.

EXAMPLE

The Longest ~~Nite~~ Night

One day, a hurricane was in the ocean not far from us. First, my mom and I put the lawn furniture in the ~~garage~~ garage. dad ~~borded~~ boarded up the windows, then we went to the store to ~~by~~ buy water, candles, ~~bateries~~ batteries, and ~~flashlites~~ flashlights. The wind was blowing so hard the trees bent over the ground! by morning the storm was over. I was glad no one in my family got hurt.

Reading Your Writing

If you don't edit/proofread your work, mistakes might keep the reader from understanding your ideas. You should use a checklist to help you correct your work.

SECTION 3

Writing Strategies

Other Editing Techniques

In addition to using proofreading marks, there are a few other techniques you can use to effectively edit your writing. First, make sure a dictionary is available to you so you can check the spelling or the definition of a word. Second, you can read your writing out loud so you can hear the problems in addition to seeing them on the page. Finally, try pointing to each word as you read it out loud. That will ensure that you locate any missing words or letters, as well as any extra or repeated words.

Editing on a Computer

The word-processing program on your computer should include features for editing and proofreading. Although these features are helpful, keep in mind that this software may suggest corrections that don't make sense in certain sections of your work.

When you write on a computer, it is best to handwrite your corrections on a printed copy of your revised writing. After editing your work, you can enter the changes on the computer. Save any changes you make on the computer, and make sure you keep your edited hard copy so you have a record of the changes that have been entered.

Some software programs can check your document for spelling errors as you go. These programs may automatically correct some misspelled words, like changing *teh* to *the*.

Grammar check detects incorrect subject-verb agreement and some commonly confused words. It is important to check your work after using the computer to be safe.

Editing Checklist

Use this checklist as a guide for editing and proofreading your written work.

- ▶ Have I read over my writing carefully, pointing to each word?
- ▶ Have I used appropriate proofreading marks for my corrections?
- ▶ Are there any missing or repeated words in my sentences?
- ▶ Are all of my sentences complete, or do I have fragments?
- ▶ Have I checked for all other sentence problems, including run-ons, awkward sentences, and misplaced modifiers?
- ▶ Have I used punctuation marks correctly—including commas, colons, semicolons, quotation marks, parentheses, dashes, and hyphens?
- ▶ Is my usage correct? Do the subjects and verbs in each of my sentences agree?
- ▶ Have I followed the rules of capitalization?
- ▶ Have I used a dictionary to check the spelling and definitions of words?
- ▶ Are my paragraphs the appropriate length?
- ▶ Are my paragraphs indented?

Important Note: A number of reference materials can help you edit your work. Dictionaries, handbooks or style guides, and thesauruses are good references to have available.

Try It!

Read each sentence out loud and point to each word. Can you find the errors?
- ▶ I enjoy going the pool on hot summer days.
- ▶ It's impossible to know if if a tornado will strike a certain location.

Conventions · Editing

End Marks

The Period (.)

The **period** is the most frequently used end punctuation mark. Use a period to end a sentence that makes a statement (declarative) or one that makes a command or polite request (imperative).

Anjuli invented a new way to tie-dye T-shirts. (statement)

Please buy five yellow T-shirts. (request)

Put the new T-shirts on that shelf. (command)

Periods in Outlines

Use a period after every Roman numeral that labels a main topic and after every letter or Arabic numeral that labels a subtopic or subdivision.

I. Main topic
    A. Subtopic
        1. Subtopic division
            a. Subdivision of a subtopic
            b. Subdivision of a subtopic

Periods as Decimals Points

Use a period as a decimal point, between the whole number and fractional figure.

8.5 kilometers   **75.5 percent**   **$5.50**

The Question Mark (?)

A **question mark** ends a sentence that asks a question (interrogative). Use a question mark only at the end of a sentence that asks a direct question.

When will we ever tie-dye our T-shirts?

May I sit next to Kailey?

Do not use a question mark after an indirect question. Indirect questions are usually reworded statements (declarative sentences) or commands (imperative statements).

She asked to borrow some rubber bands.

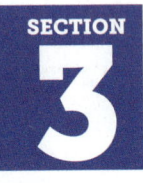

The Exclamation Point (!)

Use an **exclamation point** after a word, short phrase, or sentence to show strong feeling. The word or short phrase that an exclamation point follows may be an interjection, expressing strong emotion.

Good Grief! Wow! Ouch!

Used with a sentence, an exclamation point may express strong feeling or make a command.

Get down from there right now!

Try It!

Add the correct end punctuation to each of these sentences.
- We sold our tie-dyed T-shirts at the fund-raiser
- Did you hear what happened
- Wow
- We sold them all in 15 minutes

Reading Your Writing

Knowing when *not* to use punctuation is just as important as knowing when to use it. That may make all the difference between strong, clear writing and writing that exhausts its readers. For instance, overused exclamation points leave readers gasping for breath. For greater impact, use them only when they are absolutely needed.

Conventions in Dialogue

Dialogue is the written conversation between characters in stories. Showing characters talking is a great way to make them and the events in your stories come to life. However, you must carefully follow certain conventions when you use dialogue.

Here's what dialogue can do for your writing.

- Dialogue makes the characters seem real by showing what they think and feel.

"That show about eagles last night was great," said Angie.

- Dialogue helps keep readers interested.

"That guy in the show will be speaking here next week," announced Jake.

- Dialogue moves the action of the story along.

Angie exclaimed, "Oh, good, let's go hear him!"

Punctuating Dialogue

- Dialogue should be enclosed in quotation marks.

"He's the best," said Jamie. "He's the best there is."

- Commas, periods, question marks, and exclamation points always go inside the quotation marks.

"Just a minute," said Mr. Sanchez quickly. "Are there any other nominations?"

- Use speaker tags such as *said Mr. Sanchez, he asked,* and *said Jamie* to let your readers know who is speaking.

SECTION 3
Writing Strategies

354 **Conventions** • Conventions in Dialogue

Placing Dialogue in Your Story

To make clear who says what, be sure to begin a new paragraph every time the speaker changes. Also, speaker tags are sometimes omitted when one or just a few words at a time are spoken.

> **EXAMPLE**
>
> Notice the use of speaker tags and paragraphs in this dialogue.
>
> "Susie, thanks for coming over," said Jess.
>
> "Hey," Susie said cheerfully, "what are friends for?"
>
> They stared at the book lying on the table.
>
> "Who would have thought this thing could cause so much trouble?" she sighed.
>
> "What are you going to do?" asked Susie. "Try to find out who it really belongs to, I guess," Jess replied.
>
> "Good luck on that."
>
> "I know," said Jess. "But I have a few ideas. Let's get started."

Do you see how the dialogue involves the reader and moves the action of the story along? Does it tell you anything about the characters? Does the writing sound natural, like the way people talk?

Reading Your Writing

Use dialogue to keep readers interested, to provide information about characters' moods and personalities, and also to move the action of your story. Write dialogue so that it sounds natural, and be sure to use punctuation, speaker tags, and paragraphing so your readers are clear on who says what.

Presentation

Presentation is the last big step in the writing process. You have worked very hard to make your writing sound good, to have good sentences, to make sense, and to be correct with facts and information. Now it is time to make it *look* good! Make sure your final draft is neatly written or typed. Add pictures or other illustrations. Think about publishing your writing in the school paper. When you present your writing in a pleasing way, people will want to read it.

SECTION 3

Writing Strategies

You should keep the following ideas and concepts in mind when you present your writing:

▶ Using Multimedia Sources to Enhance and Publish a Paper
▶ Creating Oral Presentations
▶ Evaluating Growth

Try It!

Your papers and reports will be much more interesting—and communicate better—if you make them multimedia. What types of multimedia elements could be added to the following types of writing?

▶ an informative report on snakes
▶ directions to the library
▶ a play about a wicked queen
▶ a newspaper article about school lunches

Continue reading to this section of the Handbook to find out more information about presenting your writing.

SECTION 3

Writing Strategies

Using Multimedia Sources to Enhance a Paper

The term *multimedia* means "using more than one medium." Used this way, *medium* means "a way of communicating." (The plural is *media*.) Anything that uses two or more ways of communicating is multimedia. For example, a report that includes pictures is multimedia. (Pictures and words are two ways of communicating.) A movie in French with captions in English is multimedia. (You watch the action while you read the words.) Maybe you served egg rolls during your talk about the Chinese culture. That made your report multimedia. The sight, smell, and taste of egg rolls are a welcome way of communicating.

Your papers and reports will be much more interesting—and communicate better—if you make them multimedia. Below are some ideas to consider. The first few are low-tech. However, some of those on the next page require special skills and equipment.

- In a report on another country, include a map or a drawing of its flag. Find photographs of its people and the houses, villages, and cities where they live. Show that nation's forests, shorelines, deserts, or mountains.
- If you can, borrow traditional clothing from that country and wear or display it. You might dress a doll in traditional clothing.
- Display a traditional craft from that nation. If possible, demonstrate how to do the craft, such as weaving a blanket.
- When you report on a famous person, dress like him or her. Or make and display a "wanted" poster for the famous villain you are describing in your report.
- Add a graph, spreadsheet, time line, or diagram to your paper. Graphics can organize a lot of information so that readers can quickly understand it. If you are explaining a process or giving instructions, you probably need to include a diagram.
- Show slides as you give your report. The slides might be scanned pictures, digital photos, or your own drawings. You can also use special software to prepare charts and colorful graphics. A chart of your main points will help your audience remember them. Or you might display photos of a volcano before and after it erupted. You could show how your town looked a century ago and how it looks today. Or you might display photos of extinct or endangered species.

SECTION 3
Writing Strategies

Using Multimedia Sources to Publish a Paper

Now you know that *multimedia* means "using more than one medium," or way of communicating. You can use a combination of different media to publish or share your paper, too. Using several media can make your paper more interesting. It can also make your points clearer.

- Videotape your informative presentation. Make it into a documentary. Be sure to include charts, photos, and other visuals so your viewers have something to look at as they listen to you talk. If possible, include several short segments, such as an interview with an expert or comments from a number of people about the topic.
- Videotape your persuasive report, perhaps as a television commercial. You might include appropriate background music and sound effects. Part of your report might be interviews with people affected by the problem you want to solve.
- Use word processing to make your report look like a two-column newspaper article. Include a title, your "byline" as author, and one or two photos.
- Use desktop publishing to turn your report into a short book, complete with photos, illustrations, graphs, or other visuals. Don't forget a title page, table of contents, and perhaps an index and glossary.
- As you present your report, play a recording of appropriate music. For example, if you are describing Russia, play Russian folk tunes. If you are describing the Revolutionary War, play music from that time period, such as *Yankee Doodle Dandy*.
- Create a large illustration or diagram on poster board. Then use paragraph-length captions to explain the parts of a machine or the parts of a living thing. Number the captions so people read them in order. You can explain a process this way, too, such as how cans are recycled.
- Help create a school or classroom website. It can combine printed information, interesting graphics, and sound. Then you can post your reports and stories for classmates to read at school and for friends and family members to read at home.

SECTION 3

Writing Strategies

Creating Oral Presentations

You know that presentation refers to how you share your published writing with your readers. **Oral presentations** are one way for you to actively share your ideas and engage a live audience. When you give a presentation, you are like an actor on a stage. The audience watches your every move and listens to every word you say. That is why it is important to remain calm and confident, use appropriate language, and pronounce words clearly when you give your presentation.

There are many other ways to meet the needs of your audience during a presentation. One way is to speak fluently and use sentence variety. No one wants to listen to someone speak in a repetitive flat tone. By speaking expressively, altering your intonation, and using effective pacing and pauses, you make your presentation more appealing. In addition, gestures, facial expressions, and verbal cues can emphasize key points and phrases and help your audience follow important ideas. Making eye contact and asking questions will also keep the audience focused.

Use the following tips to engage your audience:

- Use a clear **organizational structure**. Develop a solid *focus*, *point of view*, and *plan* before speaking.
- Use **audio/visuals** such as photographs, maps, diagrams, and audio and video clips to illustrate concepts. You can also use skits or dramatic scenes to add interest.
- Use appropriate language for your audience and purpose. For informative presentations, you should use **academic language**. For narrative or dramatic presentations, you have more flexibility.
- Focus on **precise word choice**. Use *academic vocabulary* to make informative presentations more educational. Use *concrete sensory details* to make your narrative presentations more exciting.

Narrative Presentations

A **narrative presentation** tells a story. The story can be true or make-believe. Whatever story you choose to tell, you should use the same **story grammar** and strategies as when you write a narrative.

During your narrative presentation, make sure you do the following:

- ▸ Establish the **point of view**. Who tells the story? Which pronouns should you use?
- ▸ Establish the **setting**. Where did the story take place?
- ▸ Describe the main **characters**.
- ▸ Make sure the **plot** is clear. Describe the conflict, key events, climax, and resolution.

However, a narrative presentation is not simply reading a story aloud. Your retelling should be animated and suspenseful to actively engage the audience. Use descriptive words and phrases. For example, consider these two sentences: "The soldiers went into the desert" "The exhausted soldiers stumbled through the sweltering desert, not knowing if they would make it out." Which is more exciting?

Many presenters fall into the trap of telling, rather than showing, the audience what happens in a story. To fix this problem, make sure the audience experiences the story through the character's actions and words, not just through your descriptions. Do not just tell the audience what happens in a story, but *show* them what happens. You can accomplish this by making your dialogue interesting, acting out each character's speech through inflection and voice modulation, and acting out the plot with dramatic gestures or movements.

SECTION 3

Writing Strategies

Presentation Tip

A good introduction is key to any presentation. Begin your narrative presentation by setting up the mood with a strong introductory sentence, such as "A thick fog rolled slowly across the field" or "I wasn't sure how I was going to get out of this one."

Presentation • Creating Oral Presentations

Informative Presentations

The first step in developing an informative presentation is to frame a **key question** or questions related to your subject. For example, selecting questions such as "How does a television work?" or "Why are the 1970s known as the Golden Age of Film?" will help you figure out the subtopics you want to research and the sources you should use. As you research, you will focus your key question by finding and recording useful supporting details, facts, and examples. Before you give your presentation, you will organize all this information in a plan.

When you give an informative presentation, you should open by establishing a **controlling idea or topic** or the answer to your key question. For example, you might begin by stating "There are many reasons why the 1970s are known as the Golden Age of Film." Then you would support your controlling idea or topic with details, facts, examples, and explanations. One effective way to do this is by focusing on the questions *what, where, who, when, how,* and *why*. For example, you might ask and answer the questions "What films were made in the 1970s?" and "Who wrote some of the important films in the 1970s?" Conclude by summarizing, by offering a thoughtful reflection, or by taking questions from the audience.

Another way to open your presentation is with a question rather than a statement. In fact, you might pose the key questions you framed at the beginning of your research. Asking a question is an engaging way to establish your controlling idea. For example, immediately asking your audience "How does your television work?" will give them a clear idea of what your presentation will be about. After providing facts, examples, and explanations to answer your question, you would conclude by returning to the original question, demonstrating how you answered it, and identifying any new questions.

Presentation Tip

Did you notice that the structure of an informative presentation is similar to that of an informative essay or report? Sometimes, though, information given orally is hard to follow. Remember to use presentation aids like charts, diagrams and audio/visuals and to clearly define academic vocabulary so your audience can follow along.

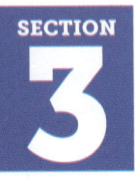

SECTION 3

Writing Strategies

Oral Responses to Literature

An **oral response to literature** is an analysis of a fictional book or story. Like a written response to literature, it shares the presenter's interpretation of a literary work and supports the interpretation with evidence and examples from the text. An oral response to literature could examine one or more of the following: a character or characters, the setting, the plot, the theme or themes, figurative language (similes, metaphors, symbols, personification, imagery, etc.), or the author's techniques for influencing the reader.

Structuring an Oral Response to Literature

- Briefly **summarize** the most significant events and details in an engaging way (stick to the most important characters and key events).
- **State your opinion or interpretation** so the audience knows what aspect of the story you are analyzing. Clearly articulate your understanding of the ideas or images you will focus on.
- Use **examples and textual evidence**, such as references to characters' actions or pivotal events and direct quotes from the text, to support your interpretation.
- **Conclude** by restating the main points of your interpretation and posing a thoughtful reflection or question to the audience.

Be a Good Listener!

Listeners are just as important to a good presentation as the speaker. Remember to do the following:

- Make eye contact with the speaker and listen attentively.
- Interpret the speaker's purpose, message, and perspectives as he or she speaks. You may even keep track of these by taking notes or writing down questions.
- Respond to the speaker by asking questions and sharing any inferences or conclusions about the presentation.

SECTION 3
Writing Strategies

Presentation • Creating Oral Presentations

Evaluating Growth

An important part of the writing process is to evaluate your growth as a writer. In what areas have you improved? What areas do you still need to work on?

To evaluate your growth as a writer, find several pieces of writing that you wrote at different times during the school year. Then evaluate the following aspects of your writing, beginning with your earliest piece of writing, and ending with your latest.

Sentence Fluency

A piece of writing that has sentence fluency flows smoothly from one sentence to the next. Study your writing samples. To evaluate for fluency, look for the following things in each sample:

- Do I use sentences of different lengths to improve the rhythm and flow?
- Do I vary the kinds of sentences I use?
- Do I begin my sentences in different ways?
- Do I use clauses, appositives, and phrases to combine and expand my sentences to create smoothness?
- Do I use transition words?

Did your sentence fluency improve from one piece of writing to the next? How did your sentence fluency improve? How can you improve your sentence fluency in the future?

Word Choice

Study your writing again, this time evaluating for word choice:

- Do I use exact, specific words that appeal to the reader's senses?
- Do I stay away from general, nonspecific words? For example, instead of writing "walked," you could write "strode," "tiptoed," "marched," and so on.
- Do I use words that *show* rather than *tell?* For example, instead of writing "Sam is happy," you could write, "Sam is smiling from ear to ear."
- Do I use words that have the right feeling? For example, what is the difference between "giggle" and "snicker"?
- Do I avoid repeating the same words over and over?

How did your word choice improve from one piece of writing to the next? How can you improve your word choice in the future?

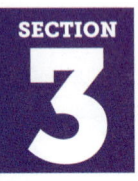

Voice

Voice is a writer's own special way of stating ideas. Study your writing samples again, this time evaluating for voice.

- ▶ Does your voice match the purpose of your writing? For example, if you are writing a serious persuasive essay, your voice shouldn't be light-hearted or funny.
- ▶ Does enthusiasm for what you are writing about show through in your voice?

Did your voice improve from one piece of writing to the next? How did your voice improve? How can you improve your voice in the future?

Organization

It is important to order your ideas in a way that allows readers to easily follow the story line or train of thought in a piece of writing. Study your writing samples to determine how well you organized your ideas.

For Informative Writing:
- ▶ Do you use topic sentences in each paragraph?
- ▶ Does one idea/paragraph logically follow the previous one?
- ▶ Do you use transition words to guide readers from one idea to the next?
- ▶ Does your opening sentence grab the reader's attention and introduce your topic?
- ▶ Does your last paragraph leave readers with something to think about?

For Narrative Writing:
- ▶ Does your story have a clear beginning, middle, and end?
- ▶ Do you include a problem, and a resolution to the problem?
- ▶ Do story events follow logically from one to the next?

Conventions

Now study your writing samples to see if you have improved in the areas of spelling, punctuation, and capitalization. What did you do right? What areas need improvement?

SECTION 3

Writing Strategies

SECTION 4: Vocabulary

Compound Words 368

Antonyms 370

Synonyms 371

Analogies 372

Connotation 374

Homophones 376

Homographs 378

Multiple-Meaning Words 380

Greek and Latin Roots 382

Prefixes 384

Suffixes 386

Context Clues 388

Academic Vocabulary 390

Adjectives and Adverbs 392

Precise Verbs 394

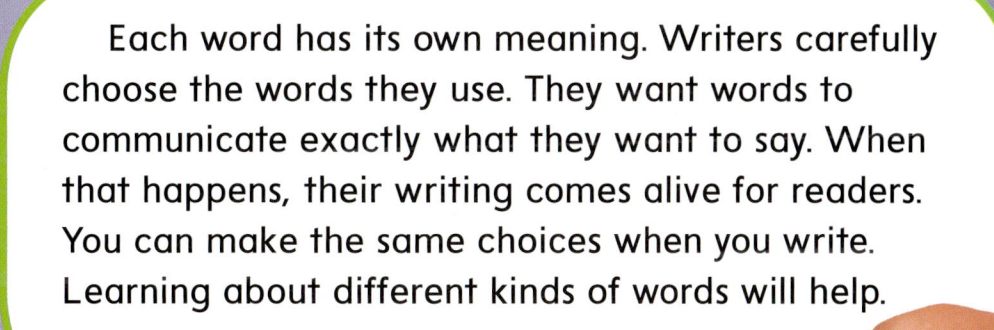

Each word has its own meaning. Writers carefully choose the words they use. They want words to communicate exactly what they want to say. When that happens, their writing comes alive for readers. You can make the same choices when you write. Learning about different kinds of words will help.

Compound Words

A **compound word** is a word that is made by joining two or more smaller words. The words in a compound word may be nouns, a noun and another kind of word, or two words that are not nouns. A compound word may be written in one of three ways: closed, hyphenated, or open. A closed compound has no space between the words. An open compound does. In a hyphenated compound, a hyphen separates the words.

Closed	Open	Hyphenated
barefoot	rain forest	warm-blooded
goldfish	hearing aid	off-season
football	ice storm	play-off

How do you know when a compound should be closed, open, or hyphenated? There are no clear rules, so if you aren't sure, look up the word in the dictionary.

Often, you can tell the meaning of a compound word by studying its smaller words.

At the end of the stream was a **waterfall.**

water + *fall* = place where *water* is *fall*ing over rocks

You can't always figure out a compound word's meaning based on the words that make it up. For example, *headquarters* doesn't mean "the *heads* of *quarters*"; it means "the main center of command or operations."

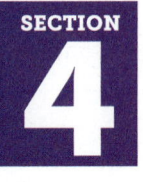

Try It!

Snowdrift is a common compound word. Based on its two smaller words, what is the definition of *snowdrift*?

Writing Connection

Compound words can help make your writing more specific. For example, it is much clearer and easier to write "I put some twigs and leaves in the fireplace" rather than "I put some twigs and leaves in the place inside where we make fires."

SECTION 4

Vocabulary

Vocabulary • Compound Words

Antonyms

Antonyms are words with opposite, or nearly opposite, meanings. The following are pairs of antonyms.

| near, far | fast, slow | odd, even | happy, sad |

Some words have more than one meaning, and therefore they have more than one antonym.

start, stop   fair, cloudy
start, end   fair, unjust

Antonyms are useful for contrasting things or ideas. Notice how antonyms are used in the paragraph below to contrast two dogs.

> The two dogs were different in many ways. Ranger was tall and husky, whereas Muffy was short and dainty. Ranger had short, black fur, whereas Muffy's fur was long and white.

Some words have many synonyms, or words with the same or similar meanings. These words often have many antonyms, too.

brave, courageous, daring   timid, fearful, cowardly

When you choose an antonym in your writing, make sure that it means exactly what you want to express. Often, only one antonym is the best choice for the exact meaning you want to express.

Try It!

Replace the underlined words with antonyms to express the opposite meaning.

The <u>old</u> house was <u>small</u> and <u>shabby</u>.

SECTION 4
Vocabulary

Synonyms

Synonyms are words that have the same, or nearly the same, meanings. For example, *work, labor,* and *toil* are synonyms. Here are more groups of synonyms.

> huge, enormous, gigantic   old, aged, ancient

Even though words are synonyms, they are not always interchangeable. You must decide which words express your thoughts most exactly. For example, some words whose meanings are similar to *unhappy* include *gloomy, sullen,* and *dismal.* However, because these words all have slightly different meanings from *unhappy,* they can't be substituted for one another.

Read the paragraphs below. Notice how the first is different from the second, even though the ideas are basically the same.

> It was a hot day, and the waves were rolling up on the beach. We ran into the ocean and dunked our heads under the cold water. The cold waves felt soothing against our hot skin.

> It was a sweltering day, and the waves were crashing onto the beach. We dashed into the ocean and dunked our heads under the cold water. The cool waves felt refreshing against our sunburned skin.

SECTION 4
Vocabulary

Writing Connection

When you use synonyms, rather than using the same words over and over, your writing is much more interesting.

Analogies

An **analogy** is a comparison of two words based on how the two words are related. Here are some examples of how words can be related.

Synonyms

The relationship between the words in the pairs below is that they are synonyms, or mean the same thing.

neat is to *tidy* as *tiny* is to *small*

Antonyms

The relationship between the words in the pairs below is that they are antonyms, or opposites.

kind is to *cruel* as *noise* is to *quiet*

Part to Whole

The relationship between the words in the pairs below is that the first word names something that is a part of the whole thing named by the second word.

sleeve is to *coat* as *arm* is to *body*

Object to Group

The relationship between the words in the pairs below is that the first word is an object that is part of the larger group named by the second word.

cat is to *animal* as *banana* is to *fruit*

Try It!

What word best completes the following analogy?
Hammer is to *tool* as *sweater* is to _____.

FUN fact

Analogies are often used as word games in puzzle books.

Connotation

Would you rather be called "clever" or "cunning"? You likely would rather be called "clever" because of its connotation. **Connotation** is the feeling a word creates in the reader, or a word's suggested meaning. The words *shack* and *cottage,* for example, both have the general meaning of "a small house." But *cottage* has a positive connotation. *A cottage* suggests a charming little house. *Shack,* on the other hand, has a negative connotation. *A shack* brings to mind an old, run-down little house.

Here are some more words with similar meanings but different connotations.

Positive	Negative
slender	skinny
fragile	weak
confident	conceited
thrifty	stingy
determined	stubborn
brave	reckless

When you write, you often choose a word from among a group of synonyms because of its connotation. For example, the words *small* and *puny* have similar meanings, but you would use the word *puny* only if you wanted to express a negative image.

In the sentence below, depending upon what you mean to say, one word fits better than the other because of the words' connotations.

My friends were (**chatting/gossiping**) about me when I joined them.

Although both *chatting* and *gossiping* have the basic meaning of "talk," *chatting* suggests a light-hearted, friendly conversation. *Gossiping* suggests an unkind and even harmful conversation. You would choose the word that most exactly communicates what you want to say.

Using Connotation in Your Writing

Writers use the connotations of words to produce positive or negative images in readers' minds. For example, if a writer wants readers to like a certain character in a story, the writer will use words with positive connotations to describe that character. If you read that a character is cheerful, kind, and helpful, you probably will like that character.

Here are two paragraphs that present the same basic information. Because some of the words have different connotations, the tone and meaning of each paragraph is different. Which paragraph produces a negative image in your mind? Why?

As I approached the house of the people who live next door, their hound began to growl. It glared fiercely and aggressively at me. Just as the beast lunged at me, the woman shrieked at it to stop.

As I approached my neighbors' house, their dog began to bark. It gazed steadily and confidently at me. Just as the dog approached me, my neighbor commanded it to stay.

Try It!

Read the sentences below. How do the underlined words affect the meaning of the sentences?
- The boy <u>gobbled</u> his sandwich and then <u>slurped</u> his milk.
- The boy <u>ate</u> his sandwich and then <u>drank</u> his milk.

Writing Connection

Knowing the connotations of words helps you choose words that express your ideas exactly. It also helps you create positive or negative images in your readers' minds.

Homophones

What's wrong with the sentence below? If you say it out loud, it seems to be fine. In written form, it doesn't make sense.

Theirs *two* much **reign** *too* play **bawl**.

The italicized words are homophones. Homophones are two or more words that sound the same but that have different meanings and spellings. Because homophones sound the same, it is easy to write one word when you mean another.

Common Homophones

to	I took my little brother <u>to</u> the baseball game.
two	I had <u>two</u> tickets.
too	My sister wanted to come <u>too</u>.
by	I walked <u>by</u> the bakery after school.
buy	I wanted to <u>buy</u> some bagels.
hole	The bagel has a <u>hole</u> in the middle.
whole	I didn't eat the <u>whole</u> bagel.
their	Did the girls forget <u>their</u> books?
they're	<u>They're</u> going to the library.
there	They go <u>there</u> every Thursday.
your	Where is <u>your</u> coat?
you're	<u>You're</u> going to need it today.
its	The dog wagged <u>its</u> tail.
it's	<u>It's</u> time to feed the dog.
hear	Did you <u>hear</u> that noise?
here	I think it came from over <u>here</u>.

SECTION 4

Vocabulary

More Homophones

Even when you know the different meanings of homophones, they can still cause spelling problems because they sound the same. When you proofread your writing, be alert for homophones. More common homophones are listed below. These are a little trickier than the homophones on the previous page because they aren't used as often.

pair	I have a new <u>pair</u> of shoes.
pear	This <u>pear</u> is ripe and juicy.
pare	I will <u>pare</u> the potatoes before I boil them.
rain	The gentle <u>rain</u> fell softly on the grass.
reign	The <u>reign</u> of Queen Victoria lasted for more than fifty years.
rein	The rider tightened the left <u>rein</u> to turn the horse to the left.
whether	Do you know <u>whether</u> rain is expected today?
weather	The <u>weather</u> has been sunny all week.
knight	A <u>knight</u> wore armor for protection.
night	Owls usually hunt at <u>night</u>.

Try It!

Which homophones correctly complete the sentence?
Do you know (weather/whether) you can (buy/by) a new bike?

Writing Connection

Because homophones sound the same, it's easy to make a mistake by writing one homophone when you really mean another. When you proofread your writing, you can make sure that you've used the correct spelling of a word that has homophones.

SECTION 4
Vocabulary

Homographs

Some words are spelled exactly the same way but have different meanings and origins. These words are called **homographs.** For example, the word *arms* has two meanings: "human upper limbs" and "weapons."

Many homographs also are pronounced the same way. Some of these are shown below.

The duck waddled back to the pond. (large, wild bird)
He had to duck his head when he entered the house. (lower suddenly)

What is the date of your birthday? (time at which an event occurs)
A date is similar to a raisin, only larger. (sweet, dark fruit)

The ice is firm enough for us to go ice-skating. (solid; hard)
My mother works for a law firm downtown. (company)

The gardener will prune the rose bushes. (trim)
I had a sandwich, a salad, and a prune for lunch. (a dried plum)

The water in the pool is refreshingly cool. (tank filled with water)
My dad taught me to play pool. (game played with balls on a table)

My mother likes to rest after dinner. (relax)
I will eat the rest of my sandwich later. (remainder)

I like raspberry jam on my toast. (fruit preserve)
Mother tells me not to jam all my clothes together in the closet. (squeeze)

I will clip my younger sister's hair. (cut; trim)
I need to clip these papers together. (attach)

I felt the icy wind stinging my cheeks. (did feel)
A pool table is usually covered with felt. (soft cloth)

I left early for the party. (did leave)
I turned left at the intersection. (direction)

Complete solar eclipses are rare. (uncommon)
Do you like your steak cooked rare? (not cooked much)

I can hardly hear you above that racket coming from the stadium. (noise)
I brought my racket and balls so we can play tennis. (paddle used in tennis)

More Homographs

Some homographs are pronounced differently.

A single <u>tear</u> slid down the baby's cheek. (drop of moisture from the eye)
Did you <u>tear</u> your new coat? (rip)

The girls <u>wound</u> ribbons in their hair. (wrapped)
Did you <u>wound</u> your knee when you fell? (hurt)

Pencils used to be made of <u>lead</u>. (metallic element)
Will you <u>lead</u> the hikers along the trail? (show the way)

The <u>dove</u> flew away to its nest. (bird)
We <u>dove</u> into the cool water. (did dive)

Will you please <u>close</u> the door? (shut)
Make sure no one is standing <u>close</u> to it. (near)

Some homographs that have more than one syllable are pronounced differently because the accent shifts.

I will <u>record</u> the results of my science experiment. (write down)
I played an old <u>record</u> that my dad used to listen to. (music disk)

Our test will cover the <u>content</u> of this science chapter. (all things inside)
I will be <u>content</u> to sit here and enjoy the sunshine. (satisfied)

The Sahara is the world's largest <u>desert</u>. (hot, dry area)
Please don't <u>desert</u> me now! (leave)

SECTION 4

Vocabulary

Try It!

How is the word *wound* pronounced in each use below?
  The nurse wound a bandage around the wound on my arm.

Vocabulary • Homographs

Multiple-Meaning Words

Some words are spelled the same way and have the same origins but different meanings. For example, the word *engage* has two meanings: "to bind oneself to do something," as in engage oneself to be married, and "to arrange for the use or services of," as to engage a gardener to take care of a garden.

Most words that have more than one meaning and the same origin are also pronounced the same way. Some of these types of words are shown below.

The band's music was very loud. (noisy)

The singer wore a loud checkered shirt. (unpleasantly bold or bright in color)

My friends and I are going shopping at the mall. (a group of stores)

The cherry trees were in full bloom all along the mall. (a grassy strip between two roadways)

My brother is big and strong. (having great physical power)

A strong wind shook the leaves from the tree. (moving with great speed or force)

By the time we finished our game, I had built my army to 500 soldiers strong. (having a specified number)

I finally figured out the solution to the math problem. (answer)

I washed the car with a strong cleaning solution. (a liquid in which something has been dissolved)

The patient waited for the physician in the waiting room. (someone who receives medical treatment)

The patient dog waited for the boy to throw the ball. (capable of waiting)

More Multiple-Meaning Words

Many words that have more than one meaning are related to science. These words often have a second meaning that describes a specific scientific concept. Some of these are shown below.

I cannot <u>force</u> my brother to help me. (to make someone do something)

The <u>force</u> of the moon's gravity acts on Earth's oceans. (an influence that produces a change in speed or direction of motion on an object)

My grandmother appreciates the <u>frequency</u> of my visits. (the condition of happening often)

Radio waves have low <u>frequency</u>. (the number of waves that pass a fixed point each second)

The constant barking of our neighbors' dog has caused <u>friction</u> between them and my parents. (disagreement)

The <u>friction</u> of the book against the floor caused the book to stop sliding. (the force that resists motion between two bodies in contact)

The pilot had to <u>circle</u> the plane over the airport. (move around)

We must measure the diameter of the <u>circle</u>. (a closed curve, every point of which is equidistant from the center)

SECTION 4
Vocabulary

Try It!

What are two related but different meanings of the word *lid*?

Writing Connection

Many related words with more than one meaning have very specific definitions for one of their meanings. Learning these meanings will help you express specific concepts in your writing.

Greek and Latin Roots

Many English words have Greek and Latin roots. When you know the meanings of a word's root or roots, you can sometimes figure out the word's general meaning.

Greek Roots

Study the Greek roots and their meanings given below.

Root	Meaning	Sample Words and Definitions
bio	life	**bio**logy: the study of life **bio**logist: a scientist who specializes in biology
geo	earth	**geo**logy: the study of the history of the earth **geo**thermal: heated by Earth
graph	write	auto**graph**: a person's signature tele**graph**: a written message sent a long distance
mech	machine	**mech**anic: a person who works on machines **mech**anism: a tool or device
meter	measure	dia**meter**: the width of a circle baro**meter**: an instrument that measures the pressure of the atmosphere
phon	sound	**phon**ics: the study of sound tele**phon**e: an instrument used for speaking over long distances

In your reading, look for words that have the roots described in this section. Try to figure out the meanings of the words based on their roots.

SECTION 4
Vocabulary

Latin Roots

Study the Latin roots and their meanings given below.

Root	Meaning	Sample Words and Definitions
aqua	water	*aqua*rium: tank in which animals that live in water are kept *aqua*tic: growing or living in water
aud	hear	*aud*itorium: a place where people listen to speakers
dic	speak	*dic*tate: to say something aloud to be recorded *dic*tion: the way in which words are pronounced
form	shape	trans*form*: to change the shape or appearance of re*form*: to change one's habits for the better
ject	throw	e*ject*: to throw out; cause to leave re*ject*: to throw out or discard
ped	foot	*ped*al: a lever worked by the foot *ped*estrian: a person walking
struct	build	*struct*ure: anything that is built con*struct*: build

SECTION 4
Vocabulary

Writing Connection

When you know the meanings of Latin and Greek roots, you can figure out the meanings of many unfamiliar words that have these roots. As you learn new words, you will expand the vocabulary that you use in writing.

Vocabulary • Greek and Latin Roots

Prefixes

A **prefix** is one or more letters added to the beginning of a root or base word that changes the word's meaning. For example, when the prefix *re-* is added to the word *view*, the meaning becomes "view again." When the prefix *pre-* is added to *view*, the meaning becomes "view before."

Some prefixes have the same or similar meanings. Knowing the meanings of prefixes will help you figure out the meanings of unfamiliar words. Look at the list of prefixes below. Notice how each prefix changes the meaning of the base word.

Prefix	Meaning(s)	Sample Words
anti-	against	antibacterial, antifreeze
bi-	two	bicycle, bipartisan
dis-	not; opposite	disagree, disapprove
im-	not	impractical, impossible
in-	not	inactive, inexact
inter-	among; between	interweave, interstate
mis-	not; wrong	miscalculate, misbehave
non-	not	nonpoisonous, nonstop
over-	too much	overdo, overworked
pre-	before	preheat, predate
re-	again	redo, repaint
semi-	half	semicircle, semimonthly
tri-	three	triplet, tricycle
un-	not; opposite of	unwise, unhappy

Prefixes Change the Meaning of Words

Below are some words with prefixes used in sentences. Notice how each prefix changes the meaning of the word.

> The coach <u>approved</u> of his players' behavior.
> The coach <u>disapproved</u> of his players' behavior.

> The child was <u>impatient</u> and <u>unhappy</u>.
> The child was <u>patient</u> and <u>happy</u>.

Keep in mind that you can't add all prefixes to all words. For example, although you might want to combine the prefix *un-* with the word *appear, unappear* is not a word. The word that correctly expresses this meaning is *disappear.* If you are unsure about adding a prefix to a word, check the dictionary.

Even when you know the meaning of a prefix, you might not be able to figure out a word's meaning. This sometimes happens because the base word also has an ending. Other times, you may not know the meaning of the base word. You must then look up the meaning of the base word with its prefix in the dictionary.

Look at the words below. Which meanings could you figure out if you separated the base word from its ending?

Word	Meaning	Prefix	Base Word
illegible	not readable	*il-*	legible
overprotected	too much protected	*over-*	protected

Writing Connection

By learning the meanings of prefixes, you will understand how they change the meanings of words, which will increase your vocabulary.

Suffixes

A **suffix** is one or more letters added to the end of a root or base word that changes the word's meaning. A suffix can also change the part of speech of a word. For example, adding *-ful* to the noun *hope* makes the word *hopeful*, an adjective.

Knowing the meanings of suffixes will help you figure out the meanings of unfamiliar words. Look at the chart below and notice how each suffix changes the meaning of the base word.

Suffix	Meaning	Sample Words
-able/-ible	is, able to	workable, sensible
-er/or	one who	singer, actor
-ful	full of	careful, graceful
-ish	relating to	selfish, childish
-ist	one who performs or practices	guitarist, geologist
-less	without	helpless, tireless
-ly	like; resembling	motherly, slowly
-ment	state or condition of	enjoyment, contentment
-ness	state; condition; quality of	goodness, fairness
-ure	action; process	enclosure, procedure
-y	being or having	sticky, funny

Try It!

How does the suffix change the meaning of the word?
  I spent a restful night at the hotel.
  I spent a restless night at the hotel.

Rules for Adding Suffixes

When you add suffixes to base words, follow the rules below.

> If a suffix begins with a vowel and the base word ends with a silent *e,* drop the *e* before adding the suffix:
>
> desire + able = desirable
>
> blue + ish = bluish
>
> expose + ure = exposure
>
> If a base word ends with a *y,* change the *y* to *i* before adding the suffix—unless the suffix begins with an *i:*
>
> beauty + ful = beautiful
>
> rely + able = reliable
>
> geology + ist = geologist
>
> fury + ous = furious

Keep in mind that you can't add all suffixes to all words. For example, although you might want to add the suffix *-ful* to the base word *friend, friendful* is not a word. If you are unsure about adding a suffix to a word, look it up in the dictionary.

Even if you know the meaning of a word's suffix, you might not be able to figure out the word's meaning because you don't know the meaning of the base word. For example, you may come across the word *perishable*. Even though you know that the suffix *-able* means "is" or "able to," if you don't know that *perish* means "spoil" or "die," you won't be able to define the word. In this case, you must look up the meaning of the base word or the word with its suffix in the dictionary.

SECTION 4

Vocabulary

Writing Connection

By learning the meanings of suffixes, you will understand how they change the meanings of words. As you learn these new meanings, you will increase your vocabulary. The more words you know, the better you will be able to express yourself in writing.

Context Clues

What do you do when you come across an unfamiliar word in your reading? Before you reach for a dictionary, you probably try to figure out the meaning of the word by looking at the context. The **context** is the words and sentences that surround the unfamiliar word. The context usually gives you clues about the meaning of the unfamiliar word.

There are different kinds of context clues. In this lesson, you will learn some tips for finding and using context clues to figure out the meanings of unfamiliar words.

Tips for Using Context Clues

Some writers give a *definition*. They list the meaning of the word within the sentence or surrounding sentences. Look for clue words such as *or, that is,* and *in other words.* These all point to a definition.

> Frogs are *amphibians*, or animals that live both on land and in the water.

Some writers *compare* or *contrast* the unfamiliar word with another word. Look for comparison and contrast words, such as *also, like, too, but, unlike,* and *on the other hand.*

> Like many other *predatory* birds, owls hunt.

Cause-and-effect relationships may also be used to explain an unfamiliar word. Look for words such as *because, as a result,* and *therefore.*

> Because owls are *nocturnal*, their eyes are well adapted to darkness.

More Tips for Using Context Clues

Often an unfamiliar word appears in a *series*. Sometimes you can figure out the meaning of the word based on the other words in the series.

> The crown was made of diamonds, rubies, emeralds, and *amethysts*.

Sometimes you have to use the general context to figure out the meaning of a word because there are no specific clues available.

> Our cancelled flight put us in a difficult *predicament*.

Another example is the word *pound*. It has several different meanings, including "a unit of weight," "to hit again and again," "to drive into," as to *pound* a stake into the ground, and "pen or fenced area." How can you tell which meaning fits this sentence?

> We chose our pet from among the dogs at the pound.

First you can tell that *pound* is used as noun. From this context clue, you know that *pound* in this sentence does not mean "to hit again and again" or "to drive into." By further studying the word's context, you can tell that the meaning "a unit of measure" doesn't make sense. Thus, you can determine that the meaning of *pound* in the sentence above is "a pen or fenced area."

Try It!

Use the context clues in the sentence below to figure out the meaning of *legumes* in the sentence below.
   I like peas, beans, and other *legumes*.

Academic Vocabulary

In school you use vocabulary words that are specific to each subject that you study. In this lesson you will learn some words commonly used in math, science, social studies, and health.

Math

combine: add together

denominator: the part of a fraction written below the line

division: the mathematical operation of finding out how many times one number is contained in another number

equivalent: equal

minimum: the least amount

maximum: the greatest amount

numerator: the part of a fraction written above the line

percent: one part of 100

sequence: an ordered set of numbers

Science

carnivore: an animal that eats other animals

constellation: a group of stars

habitat: a place where an animal or plant naturally lives

herbivore: an animal that eats only plants

iceberg: a large floating mass of ice detached from a glacier

mammal: a warm-blooded animal that nurses its young

omnivore: an animal that eats both plants and other animals

parasite: an organism that lives off another organism

reptile: a cold-blooded animal

Social Studies
candidate: a person running for office
civil rights: the individual rights of citizens guaranteed by the U.S. Constitution
Congress: the chief law-making body of the United States made of the Senate and House of Representatives
currency: money
export: to sell or carry goods to other countries
import: to buy or bring goods into a country
frontier: the imaginary line that marks division between settled and unexplored territory
government: the laws and customs of a political unit and the people who enforce them
urban: relating to a city
veto: to refuse to approve a bill

Health
bacteria: tiny organisms that can cause disease
cardiovascular: related to the heart and blood vessels
contagious: easily spread from one person to another
carcinogen: something that causes cancer
diagnosis: the act of identifying a disease based on symptoms
digestion: the process of converting food into simpler forms
epidermis: the outer layer of skin
molar: large tooth located in the rear of mouth
symptom: a change in normal body functions that indicates disease

FUN fact

A majority of science, math, health, and social studies words have Greek or Latin origins.

Try It!

Choose a word from each of the lists in this lesson. Define the words using your own words.

Adjectives and Adverbs

Adjectives and adverbs describe, or modify, other words. Adjectives modify nouns. Adverbs modify verbs, adjectives, and other adverbs. When adjectives and adverbs appeal to the senses, writing is more specific, vivid, and interesting.

Adjectives and adverbs limit the meanings of the words they describe. In other words, they make the meanings of the words they describe more specific. Read these sentences.

> The rain fell onto the soil.
>
> The light rain fell silently onto the parched soil.

In the first sentence, the noun *rain* could mean any kind of rain—heavy rain, steady rain, light rain, damaging rain, and so on. Also, the verb *fell* could mean fell in any way—continuously, loudly, and so on. The same is true of the general word *soil*. Because *rain*, *fell*, and *soil* are so general, the reader comes away with a fuzzy picture after reading this sentence.

In the second sentence, the meaning of the general noun *rain* is now limited to mean only rain that is light and gentle. The general verb *fell* is now limited by the adverb *silently*. Also, the general noun *soil* is now limited to soil that is parched. These modifiers appeal to the senses. They give the reader a much clearer and more vivid image of the scene.

Choose adjectives and adverbs in your writing that will give specific information to your readers. What exactly do you want your readers to visualize?

The noun and verb in the group of sentences below are the same, but the adjectives and adverbs are different. Notice how the different adjectives and adverbs communicate different ideas.

> The rider stopped his bike.
>
> The *nervous* rider stopped his bike *shakily* and *suddenly*
>
> The *experienced* rider stopped his bike *smoothly* and *easily*.

Words to Avoid

Try not to use adjectives and adverbs that are overused, especially those that don't appeal to the senses. Adjectives such as *nice, good, pretty,* and *bad* are used so much that they don't have much meaning. They aren't specific, so they don't give the reader a clear image. The same is true of overused adverbs such as *very, really,* and *quite.*

Connotation

Sometimes you choose between two modifiers that are similar in meaning based on what *feeling* is connected with each. This feeling is called the word's **connotation**. (See pages 374–375 for more on connotation.) By choosing words that express certain feelings, you relay these feelings to your reader. For example, although *stingy* and *thrifty* both have the general meaning of "frugal," *stingy* has a negative connotation, while *thrifty* has a positive connotation. You would choose one word over the other based on whether you wanted to express a positive image or a negative image.

Try It!

What adjectives and adverbs could you add to the sentence below to express a positive image?

The girl sang a song.

Writing Connection

When you use precise adjectives and adverbs in your writing, you give your readers clear images. You can convey positive or negative images of things or actions simply by choosing accurate words to describe them. Vivid, specific adjectives and adverbs also make your writing more enjoyable for your readers.

Precise Verbs

Most verbs express action. They tell what is going on. The verb is therefore the word in the sentence that usually communicates the most meaning. This is why you should be especially careful in choosing verbs.

When you choose a verb, think about exactly what kind of information you want to give your readers. What exactly do you want your readers to visualize?

Study the verbs below. Notice how each group of verbs has a slightly different meaning. Visualize each action as you read.

As a writer, you know exactly what you want to communicate. Choosing precise verbs gives you the ability to connect with your readers in the most effective way.

look	gaze	glare	stare
take	grab	seize	retrieve
like	enjoy	adore	cherish
shine	glisten	glow	radiate
eat	nibble	gobble	munch
run	race	sprint	jog
hold	cradle	grasp	clutch
throw	heave	toss	hurl
cut	hack	split	trim
make	create	construct	build
come	arrive	appear	approach
say	state	remark	speak

Let's Get Specific

Read each of the following descriptions. Notice how the choice of verbs affects your idea of what's happening.

> The puppy *approached* the boy. It *hesitated* before getting onto his lap.

> The puppy *ran* to the boy and *scrambled* onto his lap.

Often, the most precise verb is the verb that is most specific. In the examples above, the words *approached* and *hesitated* communicate a very different image than *ran* and *scrambled*.

Verbs and Connotations

Sometimes you choose between two verbs that are similar in meaning based on the connotation that is connected with each.

What connotation is associated with the verb in each sentence?

> The girl *tattled* about what happened.
> The girl *told* what happened.

The word *tattled* has a negative connotation. The reader gets the feeling that the girl told what happened to get other people in trouble. However, the word *told* is general. It doesn't express much information.

SECTION 4
Vocabulary

Try It!

Replace the verbs to create a more positive image.
The boy glared at his friend as he grabbed his coat.

Vocabulary • Precise Verbs 395

SECTION 5
Grammar, Usage, and Mechanics

Grammar 398

Usage 422

Mechanics 440

You know about rules. When you know and follow the rules of a game, you're better at the game. It's the same with writing. Knowing the rules and following them will make you a better writer.

Grammar

Grammar is about how language is organized. Parts of speech, such as nouns and verbs, are grammar. The names for different parts of a sentence, such as subject and predicate, are grammar. The names for different types of sentences, such as simple, compound, and complex, are grammar. Knowing about grammar helps you understand how to build sentences that make sense to your readers.

SECTION 5

Grammar, Usage, and Mechanics

The rules of grammar tell you about the following concepts:

- Nouns
- Pronouns
- Verbs
- Adjectives and Adverbs
- Prepositions
- Conjunctions and Interjections
- Subjects and Predicates
- Direct Objects and Indirect Objects
- Modifiers—Words and Phrases
- Clauses
- Sentences—Simple, Compound, and Complex
- Problems with Sentence Structure
- Kinds of Sentences

> **EXAMPLE** How would you fix the following run-on sentences?
> - I like the weekend my favorite day is Saturday.
> - The dog was hungry he was lost.
> - Sasha went camping she didn't like the bugs.

Continue reading this section of the Handbook to see more examples and to find out additional information about the rules of grammar.

SECTION 5

Grammar, Usage, and Mechanics

Grammar

Nouns

Nouns name persons, places, things, and ideas. A **common noun** names *any* person, place, thing, or idea. It is *general*. A **proper noun** names a *particular* person, place, or thing. It is *specific*. Notice the two words in the above chart that are capitalized. They are the only proper nouns. Proper nouns are always capitalized. All the rest are common nouns. A common noun isn't capitalized unless it's the first word in a sentence.

	Common Noun	Proper Noun
Person	principal	Ms. Garcia
Place	school	Barkley Elementary
Thing	tour	Statue of Liberty Tour
Idea	war	Civil War

Collective Nouns

A **collective noun** names groups, or collections, of people, animals, or things. Examples of common collective nouns include the following:

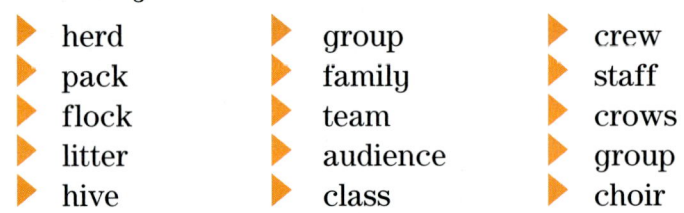

- herd
- pack
- flock
- litter
- hive

- group
- family
- team
- audience
- class

- crew
- staff
- crows
- group
- choir

A collective noun that is the subject of a sentence is usually treated as singular, even though it represents a group of things. So, the verb must take on the singular form.

The audience claps at the end of each scene.

The pack of wolves howls at night.

Singular and Plural Nouns

If a noun names one person, place, thing, or idea, it is a **singular noun.** A noun that names more than one person, place, thing, or idea is a **plural noun.** Most singular nouns become plural by adding **-s**, but note the exceptions below.

Noun Ending	To Form Plural	Example
s, z, ch, sh, x	Add *-es*	fox/foxes
o preceded by a vowel	Add *-s*	radio/radios
o preceded by a consonant	Usually add *-es*	hero/heroes
	Sometimes add *-s*	piano/pianos
y preceded by a vowel	Add *-s*	key/keys
y preceded by a consonant	Usually change *y* to *i* and add *-es*	city/cities
f or *fe*	Usually change *f* to *v* and add *-s* or *-es*	life/lives

Some nouns do not change at all. The singular and plural forms are the same. **Examples:** moose, deer, salmon

Compound nouns that are hyphenated or written as more than one word become plural by adding *s* to the main noun.
Examples: sister-in-law/sisters-in-law, time clock/time clocks

Possessive Nouns

A noun that shows ownership or possession of things or characteristics is a **possessive noun.** Possessive nouns can be singular or plural. Singular possessive nouns are formed by adding *'s*.

Kyle wanted to go to Cameron's house.

Plural possessive nouns are formed by adding *'s* to plural nouns not ending in *s*. Plural nouns already ending in *s* simply add an apostrophe to the end.

The geese's eggs were outside my cousins' tent.

SECTION 5

Grammar, Usage, and Mechanics

Pronouns

A **pronoun** is a word used in place of one or more nouns.

Cody ate a large bowl of strawberries. *He* even asked for seconds.

He is the pronoun that replaces **Cody,** the antecedent.

An **antecedent** is the word referred to or replaced by a pronoun.

Personal Pronouns

Pronouns that refer to people or things are called **personal pronouns.** The three types of personal pronouns—subject pronouns, object pronouns, and possessive pronouns—perform different functions in sentences.

Use a **subject pronoun** as the subject of a sentence and also as the predicate pronoun. *I* would love to go to the laser show. (subject)

It is *I*. (predicate pronoun)

Use an **object pronoun** as a **direct object** or as an **indirect object**.

We remember *him*. (direct object)

The neighbors gave *us* tickets. (indirect object)

***I* hiked to the cliff, and the view gave *me* goose bumps.**

Notice how *I* and *me* are used in this compound sentence. *I* and *me* mean the same thing, but *I* functions as the subject of one clause, and *me* functions as the indirect object of the other clause.

Type	Pronouns	Function
Subject Pronouns	I, you, she, it, we, they	subject or predicate pronoun
Object Pronouns	me, you, her, him, it, us, you, them	direct object, indirect object, object of preposition

Possessive Pronouns

A **possessive pronoun** shows ownership. It can be used alone or before a noun.

She gave me *his* beach towel. Where is *mine*?

These possessive pronouns go before nouns: *my, your, her, his, its, our, your,* and *their*.

Use these alone: *mine, yours, hers, his, its, ours, yours,* and *theirs*.

More Types of Pronouns

A **reflexive pronoun** ends with *-self* or *-selves* and refers back to the subject.

Example: Gabe and Ian made *themselves* co-captains of the soccer team.

An **intensive pronoun** ends with *-self* or *-selves* and emphasizes a noun or pronoun.

Example: Gabe and Ian *themselves* cleaned the field.

An **interrogative pronoun** asks a question.

Example: *Whose* shin guards are these?

A **relative pronoun** introduces a *relative clause*.

Example: The captains organized the team members, *who* were eager to play.

A **demonstrative pronoun** demonstrates by indicating or pointing out something. *This, that, these,* and *those* are demonstrative pronouns.

Example: *That* was an extraordinary shot.

An indefinite pronoun doesn't refer to a specific person, place, thing, or idea.

Example: *Everybody* on the team wants to go to the soccer clinic.

> ### Writing Connection
> Pronouns provide variety and prevent the repetition of nouns.

SECTION 5

Grammar, Usage, and Mechanics

Verbs

A **verb** is a word that expresses action or a state of being.

Action Verbs

An **action verb** expresses a mental or physical action. The words *have, has,* and *had* may be used as action verbs when they tell what the subject is holding or owns. The action of the verbs can be seen or unseen. *I* **understand** *the problem.* **Understand** is a verb in which the action is unseen. *The bottle* **fell** *from the rack.* **Fell** is a verb in which the action is seen.

State-of-Being Verbs

State-of-being verbs do not show action. They express a condition of existence.

Olivia **was** on a vacation.

Forms of *be* are the most commonly used state-of-being verbs. The forms of *be* are *is, am, are, was, were, be, being,* and *been*. *Seem* and *become* are also state-of-being verbs.

Some verbs can function either as an action verb or a state-of being-verb.

remain	appear	look	turn	stay
taste	smell	feel	sound	grow

The dog **smells** the skunk. (action verb)

It **smells** like a skunk. (state-of-being verb)

Linking Verbs

A linking verb does exactly what it says—it links, or connects, the subject to a noun or adjective in the predicate.

▶ Jane **is** an artist.

Helping Verbs

A helping, or auxiliary, verb helps the main verb express an action or make a statement. The most common helping verbs are forms of *be*, *have*, and *do*.

Common Helping Verbs
do, did, does, am, is, are, was, were, be, being, been, have, has, had, may, might, must, can, could, will, would, shall, should

Helping verbs can help show **when** something happens.
- Jane and Emilio **were** painting a mural. (action continuing in the past)
- Jane and Emilio **are** painting a mural. (action continuing in the present)
- Jane and Emilio **will** paint a mural. (action to happen in the future)

Verb Phrases

One or more auxiliary verbs combined with the main verb make a verb phrase.
- We **have been watching** their progress.

Notice that *have been watching*, has two helping verbs.

Active and Passive Voice

The **active voice** of a verb is used when the subject performs the verb's action.
- Emilio **brushed** the dog.

Emilio is the subject performing the verb's action: *brushed*.

The **passive voice** of a verb is used when the subject receives the verb's action.
- The dog **was brushed** by Emilio.

Dog is the subject receiving the action of the verb *was brushed*.

Writing Connection

To keep readers involved, use the active voice in your writing as often as possible.

SECTION 5
Grammar, Usage, and Mechanics

Grammar • Verbs

Adjectives and Adverbs

An **adjective** is a word that describes or modifies a noun or pronoun. Adjectives modify in three ways. They show **what kind, how many,** and **which one.**

- Hurricanes create **rough** seas. (what kind)
- Last year the flooding destroyed **fifteen** houses. (how many)
- **That** hurricane hit harder than most. (which one)

Adjectives usually, but not always, come before the nouns they modify. Notice how these adjectives follow the verb but modify the noun.

- The waves are **strong.** (modifies *waves*)
- The mayor looks **tired.** (modifies *mayor*)

Articles

The, a, and *an* belong to a special group of adjectives called **articles.**

A and *an* are called indefinite articles. They refer to one of a group of people, places, things, or ideas. Use *a* before nouns beginning with a consonant sound. Use *an* before nouns beginning with a vowel sound. Examples: **a** hurricane, **an** overcoat

The is the definite article because it identifies specific people, places, things, or ideas. Examples: **the** storm, **the** houses

Adjectives **Adjectives** such as *this, these, that,* and *those* point out particular nouns.

- **These** moccasins are mine. **That** horse is his.

This, these, that, and *those* are demonstrative pronouns when they take the place of a noun in a sentence.

- **These** are my moccasins. **That** is his horse.

Proper Adjectives

Proper adjectives are adjectives formed from proper nouns. They are almost always capitalized. **Examples:** Chinese lantern, Japanese beetle, English muffin

Hyphenated Adjectives

Adjectives can be created by combining words with hyphens. **Examples:** fresh-picked zucchini, gale-force winds, less-than-friendly lion.

Adverbs

An **adverb** is a word that modifies a verb, an adjective, or another adverb. Adverbs often tell *how, when, where,* or *to what extent* an action is performed.

- The Girl Scouts **carefully** cleaned up the city park. (modifies verb **cleaned**)
- They picked up trash stuck in the **extremely** muddy ground. (modifies adjective **muddy**)
- The troop leader **very** proudly awarded them badges. (modifies adverb **proudly**)
- The girls **happily** accepted their awards. (tells how)
- As a result of the troop's hard work, the park cleanup ended **early.** (tells when)
- The scouts decided to stay **there** for the day. (tells where)

Adverbs often have *-ly* endings: *frequently, calmly, wisely, shyly.* Watch for the few *-ly* words that are adjectives: *lonely, friendly, lively,* and *lovely.* You can tell they are adjectives because they describe nouns and pronouns.

Try It!

Identify the adjectives and adverbs in these sentences.
- The friendly troop leader carefully explained that cleaning the park was the girls' idea.
- The proud parents listened happily as the troop leader spoke warmly about their children.

Writing Connection

Adjectives and adverbs make your writing more powerful. They help the reader to understand your meaning more clearly.

SECTION 5

Grammar, Usage, and Mechanics

Prepositions

A **preposition** is a word that shows the relationship of a noun or pronoun to another word in a sentence. In a sentence, a preposition always has an object. The object of the preposition is the noun or pronoun that follows the preposition.

▶ The actors waited **behind** the curtain.

The preposition is **behind.** It connects the noun *curtain* to the rest of the sentence. *Curtain* is the object of the preposition.

Common Prepositions

aboard	around	by	inside	through
about	at	down	into	to
above	before	during	like	unto
across	behind	except	of	under
after	below	for	off	up
against	beneath	from	on top of	upon
along	beside	in	over	with
among	between	in front of	since	within

Prepositional Phrases

A prepositional phrase consists of the preposition, the object of the preposition, and any words that modify the object.

▶ Akiko climbed **over the boulders.**

Writing Connection

Prepositions help the reader organize characters and events in your writing. They provide order for and show the position of the things you write about.

SECTION 5
Grammar, Usage, and Mechanics

Conjunctions and Interjections

A **conjunction** is a word used to connect words or groups of words.

A **coordinating conjunction** connects independent parts, or clauses, that have equal importance in a sentence. *And, but,* and *or* are coordinating conjunctions.

- Would you like a scavenger hunt **or** a long hike?
- The scavenger hunt sounds like fun, **but** I would like to hike.
- To begin the hunt, walk to the bridge **and** look for a message.

Correlative conjunctions work in pairs to join words and groups of words. *Either-or* and *neither- nor* are correlative conjunctions.

- **Neither** Abby **nor** Lena looked under the log.
- **Either** hunt for small sticks **or** begin digging the fire pit.

A **subordinating conjunction** joins two clauses, or groups of words, in a way that makes one dependent on the other. The clause that a subordinating conjunction introduces is said to be "subordinate," or dependent, because it cannot stand by itself as a complete sentence. The words *after, although, as, because, before, since, until, when,* and *whenever* are subordinating conjunctions.

- The counselors led activities **until** it was time for lunch.
- **After** we set up our tents, the campfire meeting will start.

An **interjection** is a word or group of words that expresses strong emotion. Separated from the rest of the sentence, an interjection is punctuated by a comma or exclamation point.

- **Oops,** I dropped it. **Ha!** I tricked you.

SECTION 5

Grammar, Usage, and Mechanics

Subjects and Predicates

A sentence expresses a complete thought. A sentence has a subject and a predicate.

Subjects

The **subject** tells whom or what the sentence is about. The **simple subject** is the key noun or pronoun that does something or is described.

- A skinny **dog** limped up the driveway.

Some simple subjects are made of more than one word.

- **Mrs. Rodrigo** said she saw a strange dog on her porch.

Some sentences look as if they don't have a subject. That's because the subject is understood.

- **Set the cooler under the trees.**

In the above sentence, the subject *you* is understood.

The **complete subject** is the simple subject plus all of its modifiers.

- **The hot, muggy evening** brought everyone to the pool.
- **The sign near the entrance** was brightly lit.

A **compound subject** is made of two or more simple subjects. The subjects are linked by a conjunction and share the same verb.

- **Masks** and **snorkels** are not allowed at the pool.

Try It!

Locate the compound subject in this sentence. Do you see the two simple subjects? Do you see the complete subject with all of its modifiers?

The YMCA staff and the new lifeguards worked on an activities calendar.

Predicates

The **predicate** is the part of the sentence that describes or tells what the subject does. The **simple predicate** is the verb or verb phrase that expresses an action or a state of being about the subject.

- Dylan **raked** leaves all afternoon.
- He **will rake** leaves tomorrow, too.

The **complete predicate** is the simple predicate plus all the words that modify it or add to its meaning.

- The leaf piles **grew higher than the trampoline.**
- Leaf burning **releases too much pollution into the air.**

A **compound predicate** is made of two or more simple predicates that are joined by a conjunction and have the same subject.

- We **jumped** into the leaf piles and **scattered** the leaves.
- He **raked** the leaves, **piled** them into rows, and **made** a maze.

Inverted Order of Subject and Predicate

The predicate often, but not always, comes after the subject in a sentence. Sometimes the order of the subject and predicate is inverted, or reversed. Questions often begin with part of a verb phrase. Example: Will you find another rake? The subject, *you*, stands in the middle of the verb phrase *will find*.

A sentence may also be written in inverted order to add emphasis to the subject. Example: Across the yard **ran** a squirrel.

The simple predicate *ran* comes before the subject, *squirrel*.

Writing Connection

Understanding subjects and predicates helps us build strong sentences. Strong sentences are the backbone of good writing.

SECTION 5

Grammar, Usage, and Mechanics

Direct and Indirect Objects

Direct Objects

A **direct object** is a noun or pronoun that receives the action of a verb. It answers the question *What?* or *Whom?* and always comes after an action verb.

- We bought **tickets.**
- The Insectarium opened its **doors.**
- The staff welcomed **us.**

A sentence may have more than one direct object.

- We watched the **bees** and **beetles.**

Indirect Objects

An **indirect object** is a noun or pronoun for or to whom something is done. It answers the question *To whom? For whom? To what?* or *For what?*

- The bees gave the **people** quite a show.
- Siri saved **Lena** a place in line.
- The teachers gave the **exhibit** a thumbs-up.

Indirect objects occur only in sentences with direct objects, and they appear *between* an action verb and the direct object.

Try It!

Locate the indirect and direct object in this sentence.
    The museum staff gave the students a tour.

Writing Connection

A direct object and an indirect object show the reader how the action of a verb affects the rest of the words in a sentence.

Modifiers—Words and Phrases

A **phrase** is a group of words. Some phrases are modifiers. A **modifier** describes another word in a sentence.

Prepositional Phrases

A **prepositional phrase** is a group of words that begins with a preposition and ends with a noun or pronoun. Prepositional phrases function as adverbs or adjectives.

- The trail leads **down the mountain.**
  (adverb phrase modifying *leads*)
- A peregrine falcon **with a broken claw** flew overhead.
  (adjective phrase modifying *falcon*)

Participial Phrases

A **participial phrase** includes a participle and other words that complete its meaning. It always functions as an adjective.

- We heard something **shrieking in the woods.**
- The trail leader, **concerned about safety,** went to investigate.
- The noise was made by hungry baby hawks, **waiting in their nest for food.**

Appositives

An **appositive** is a word that renames another word in the same sentence. An **appositive phrase** includes an appositive and the words that modify it.

- The trail leader, **Ben,** told us he likes birds. (appositive)
- The bird book, **a wonderful resource,** is available at most libraries. (appositive phrase)

Writing Connection

Modifiers provide important details for the reader. They make your writing much more interesting.

SECTION 5

Grammar, Usage, and Mechanics

Clauses

A **clause** is a group of words that has a subject and a verb. The two types include independent clauses and dependent clauses.

Independent Clause

An **independent clause** has a subject and a verb and can stand alone as a sentence.

▶ Juan Delgado arrived from Puerto Rico.

More than one independent clause may appear in a sentence. Independent clauses are usually connected by a comma and a conjunction. Sometimes they are connected by a semicolon.

▶ His mother met him at the door, and the rest of his family greeted him warmly.

The two independent clauses can stand as independent thoughts. They are connected by a comma and the conjunction *and*.

▶ We were happy to see Juan; he had been away for a long time.

The two independent clauses are connected by a **semicolon.**

Dependent Clause

A **dependent clause** is a group of words that has a subject and a verb but cannot stand alone as a sentence. A dependent clause always connects to a word or words in the independent clause in a sentence.

▶ Juan, **who went to Puerto Rico,** returned home in July.

The dependent clause, in bold, cannot stand alone as a sentence. The clause is dependent on the independent clause and describes the noun *Juan*.

Adjective Clauses

An **adjective clause** is a dependent clause used as an adjective. It modifies a noun or pronoun.

▶ The meal **that Mrs. Delgado cooked** made everyone smile.

The adjective clause, *that Mrs. Delgado cooked,* tells more about the noun, *meal,* in the main clause. The word that introduces the adjective clause in the example above, *that,* is called a **relative pronoun.** The relative pronouns are ***that, which, who, whom, where,*** and ***whose.***

Adverb Clauses

An **adverb clause** is a dependent clause that is used as an adverb. It modifies the verb.

▶ Juan helped with the chores **as if he had never been away.**

The adverb clause modifies the verb *helped* in the main clause. It tells *how* he helped with the chores. The words *as if,* which introduce the adverb clause in the example above, act as a **subordinating conjunction.** Subordinating conjunctions introduce adverb clauses. Below are some examples of subordinating conjunctions.

after	as though	since	unless	where
although	because	than	until	whereas
as	before	though	when	wherever
as if	if	till	whenever	while

Writing Connection

Independent clauses provide the basic information in a sentence. Relating dependent clauses to independent clauses adds information to simple sentences and helps you avoid short, choppy sentences in your writing.

SECTION 5

Grammar, Usage, and Mechanics

Simple, Compound, and Complex Sentences

Simple Sentences

A **simple sentence** contains only one independent, or main, clause. It contains one subject and one predicate. The single subject may be compound. The single predicate may also be compound.

▶ The breeze blew steadily.

This simple sentence has just one subject (*breeze*) and one predicate (*blew*).

▶ Maya and Alicia walked to the park and flew their kites.

This simple sentence has a compound subject (*Maya, Alicia*) and a compound predicate (*walked, flew*).

▶ One kite dipped and drifted downward.

This simple sentence has a single subject (*kite*) and a compound predicate (*dipped, drifted*).

Compound Sentences

A **compound sentence** consists of two or more simple sentences (also called independent clauses). The sentences are connected by a comma and a conjunction or by a semicolon.

▶ The kite was caught in a current of air, *and* we watched it soar upward.

The conjunction **and** connects the two simple sentences.

▶ Maya changed her kite design; she added two tails.

This compound sentence combines its clauses with a semicolon. Semicolons connect two closely related sentences.

Complex Sentences

A **complex sentence** consists of one simple sentence (independent clause) and one or more dependent clauses. Remember, a dependent clause is a group of words that cannot stand alone as a sentence. The complex sentence below has one dependent clause with the independent clause.

▶ Although the breeze was steady, both kites continued to dive.

Compound-Complex Sentences

A **compound-complex sentence** has two or more independent clauses and at least one dependent clause.

▶ As the storm approached, the wind blew with great force, and Alicia pulled her kite in to safety.

Try It!

Rewrite these sentences so they don't sound choppy. Add, delete, or change words and punctuation to create new sentences out of both the dependent clauses and the independent clauses.

> We arrived at the kite festival. We parked our car. We saw the most amazing kite. It was a Chinese dragon kite. It poked out its tongue. It rolled its eyes. It flew in the air the whole time.

Writing Connection

Compound, complex, and compound-complex sentences help avoid repetition and provide a way to smoothly and accurately connect ideas.

SECTION 5

Grammar, Usage, and Mechanics

Grammar • Simple, Compound, and Complex Sentences

Problems with Sentence Structure

Fragments

A **fragment** does not express a complete thought and should not be written as a sentence.

This sentence fragment lacks a predicate. To form a complete sentence, add a verb.

▶ The canoe leaning against the shed. The canoe leaning against the shed **leaks.**

This fragment is missing a subject. Adding a subject forms a complete sentence.

▶ Wanted to take out a kayak. **Sean and Kate** wanted to take out a kayak.

This fragment is a dependent clause; it cannot stand alone as a sentence. To form a complete sentence, add an independent clause.

▶ When they paddled through the marsh. **They took care** not to disturb wildlife when they paddled through the marsh.

Run-on Sentences

A **run-on sentence** is two or more complete sentences written as though they are one.

▶ Sean saw a giant nest it belonged to a mute swan.

The above run-on sentence is really two sentences. Here are the ways to correct it.

▶ Sean saw a giant nest. It belonged to a mute swan.

▶ Sean saw a giant nest; it belonged to a mute swan.

The following run-on sentence can also be corrected. Insert a period and create two sentences *or* fix it by adding a comma and a conjunction.

▶ The swan grew agitated it couldn't make a sound.
▶ The swan grew agitated. It couldn't make a sound.
▶ The swan grew agitated, **but** it couldn't make a sound.

Rambling Sentences

A **rambling sentence** goes on and on. It connects too many thoughts with the words *and, but,* or *or.*

▶ We came to a patch of mud and had to drag our kayak and our arms hurt, and we became tangled in weeds and it took a while to get to deeper water but we made it. (incorrect)
▶ We came to a patch of mud and had to drag our kayaks. Our arms hurt, and we became tangled in weeds. It took a while to get to deeper water, but we made it. (correct)

Awkward Sentences

An **awkward sentence** is one that is unclear because of its construction. An awkward sentence makes the reader stumble and stop to think about its meaning. The use of *only* in the following sentence can be very confusing to readers.

▶ I only have one kayak.

Does the sentence mean that the only thing the writer owns in the world is one kayak? Does it mean that the writer has lots of boats but just one kayak? Small changes can help make the meaning more clear.

▶ The only thing I have is one kayak. (only thing the writer owns)
▶ I have only one kayak. (lots of boats but just one kayak)

This example below is another awkward sentence with a corrected version:

▶ Incorrect: The kayaks belong to the state park, and they close at 8 P.M.
▶ Correct: The kayaks belong to the state park, which closes at 8 P.M.

Double Subjects

Be careful not to use a pronoun right after the subject of a sentence.

▶ Incorrect: Sean he wants to race kayaks someday.
▶ Correct: Sean wants to race kayaks someday.

SECTION 5

Grammar, Usage, and Mechanics

Using Of When You Mean Have

- Incorrect: We could **of** taken the longer kayak trail.
- Correct: We could **have** taken the longer kayak trail.

Unnecessary Words and Phrases

It is tempting to throw in extra words when we want to emphasize something. Avoid using words and phrases that repeat what has already been written.

- Incorrect: It was the most ultimate rescue ever made.
- Correct: It was the ultimate rescue.
- Incorrect: The state park advertised itself as providing a lot of activities and the state park did provide more activities than any state park we had visited.
- Correct: The state park advertised its range of activities, and it did offer more to do than any park we had visited.

Try It!

Reword these sentences so that they are correct.
The park it didn't have a campground but it had a lodge though which is like a hotel so that's where we stayed. Stayed for two nights. We would of liked to of camped.

Writing Connection

Writing that is redundant or has rambling and awkward sentences is hard to read and understand. Clear, readable writing effectively avoids these traps.

SECTION 5

Grammar, Usage, and Mechanics

Grammar • Problems with Sentence Structure

Kinds of Sentences

There are four kinds of sentences: declarative, interrogative, imperative, and exclamatory.

A **declarative sentence** makes a statement. It always ends with a period.

▶ Meindert DeJong wrote The Wheel on the School.

An **interrogative sentence** asks a question. It ends with a question mark.

▶ Did you enjoy reading the book?

An **imperative sentence** gives a command or makes a request. Imperative sentences usually end with a period, but sometimes imperative sentences end with an exclamation point. The subject *you* is usually understood.

▶ Please read the first four chapters by tomorrow. Begin now!

An **exclamatory sentence** expresses a strong feeling. It ends with an exclamation point.

▶ I couldn't believe the teacher let his students put a wagon wheel on the school roof!

Try It!

What kind of sentence is this?
   Sit down with me and tell me all about it.

Writing Connection

Use different kinds of sentences to add variety and interest to your writing.

SECTION 5

Grammar, Usage, and Mechanics

Usage

Usage is about how we use language when we speak and write. For example, the rules of usage tell you when to use *was* and when to use *were*. They tell you when to use *broke* and when to use *broken*. They tell you when to use *smaller* and when to use *smallest*. Learning and using the rules of usage will make it easier for people to understand what you say and what you write.

SECTION 5

Grammar, Usage, and Mechanics

The rules of usage tell you about the following concepts:

- Verb Tenses
- Subject-Verb Agreement
- Using Pronouns
- Comparative and Superlative Adjectives
- Comparative and Superlative Adverbs
- Contractions
- Transition Words
- Double Negatives
- Misused Words

Continue reading this section of the Handbook to find out more information about usage rules.

SECTION 5

Grammar, Usage, and Mechanics

Verb Tenses

The form, or **tense,** of a verb tells when something happened. In English a verb form indicates the past (sailed), and another form indicates the present (sail). Unlike other languages, there is no special form of verbs to indicate the future.

A **present-tense verb** shows action that is happening now or on a regular basis.

- Jade **runs** to the net for the winning shot. (what is happening now)
- Selena often **runs** to the net. (a regular action)

A **past-tense verb** shows action that has already happened.

- Jade **won** the first three games. (what already happened)

A **future-tense verb** shows action that will happen. Use the helping verb *shall* or *will* with the main verb to show what will happen in the future.

- I **will attend** the tennis tournament. (what will happen)

The **present-perfect tense** shows an action completed in the present or one that began in the past and is continuing in the present. Use the helping verb *has* or *have* before the main verb to form the present-perfect tense.

- Jade **has studied** for the test. (a completed action)
- Selena **has played** tennis for four years. (a continuing action)

The **past-perfect tense** shows an action that began and ended in the past. Use the helping verb *had* with the main verb for the past-perfect tense.

- We **had cleared** the puddles off the court.

The **future-perfect tense** shows an action that will begin and end in the future, usually before another future event begins. Use the auxiliary verbs *will have* or *shall have* before the main verb.

- By the end of the day, the players **will have practiced** for five hours.

Forming Tenses of Regular and Irregular Verbs

Regular verbs add *-ed* to the present-tense verb to form the past tense or (with a helping verb) one of the perfect tenses.

Present Tense	Past Tense	Past-Perfect Tense
I **watch** tennis.	I **watched** tennis.	I had **watched** tennis.

Irregular verbs do not add *-ed.* Instead, they change their form.

The forms of some common irregular verbs are listed below. There are many others.

Present Tense	Past Tense	Past-Perfect Tense
I **take** lessons.	I **took** lessons.	I **had taken** lessons.
begin	began	had begun
drink	drank	had drunk
ring	rang	had rung
sing	sang	had sung
sink	sank	had sunk
swim	swam	had swum

Try It!

What verb tenses will make these sentences correct?
- We practiced with our tennis coach tomorrow.
- She joins us for an hour yesterday.

Writing Connection

Keep the verb tenses consistent in your writing so your readers know when the events happened.

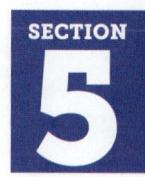

SECTION 5

Grammar, Usage, and Mechanics

Subject-Verb Agreement

A subject and a verb must agree in number. The present-tense verb form used is determined by whether the subject of a sentence is singular or plural. The verb form for regular **present-tense verbs** usually ends in *s* or *es*.

Singular Subject and Verb	Plural Subject and Verb
A **pioneer searches** for a new way of life.	**Pioneers search** for a new way of life.
He **swings** a rope.	They **swing** ropes.

Agreement with Irregular Verbs

Irregular verbs, such as *be, have,* and *do,* take different forms in order to agree with the subject.

- I **am** a cowboy. He **is** a cowboy. They **are** cowboys.
- She **has** many books. We **have** many books.
- It **does** sound interesting. They **do** listen.

Agreement with Compound Subjects

A **compound subject** is made of two or more simple subjects that use the same verb. Two or more subjects connected by **and** use the form of the verb that agrees with a plural subject.

- Songs **and** stories **spark** Bill's imagination.

Compound subjects joined by **or** or by **nor** use the verb form that agrees with the subject closest to the verb.

- A coyote or **wolves creep** into the hen houses.

Agreement with Collective Nouns

A **collective noun** names groups, or collections, of people, animals, or things. **Examples:** class, family, herd. A collective noun that is the subject of a sentence is usually treated as singular, even though it represents a group of things. So, the verb must also take on the singular form.

- The family eats dinner at 6:00.
- The herd of cows grazes on the grass.

SECTION 5

Grammar, Usage, and Mechanics

426 Usage • Subject-Verb Agreement

Agreement with Indefinite Pronouns

When an **indefinite pronoun** is the subject of a sentence, the verb must agree with the indefinite pronoun in number. Below is a chart showing singular and plural indefinite pronouns.

Singular		Plural
another	much	both
anyone	neither	few
anything	no one	many
each	nothing	others
either	one	several
everybody	somebody	
everything	something	

- Everybody leaves the stadium at the end. *Everybody* is a singular indefinite pronoun. The verb must agree with a singular subject.
- A few leave early. *Few* is a plural indefinite pronoun. The verb must agree with a plural subject.

Try It!

Choose the correct verb in the sentence below.
    Everybody (is, are) seeking autographs.

Writing Connection

Taking the time to find and use the correct verb form, even with tricky indefinite pronouns, results in good, consistent writing.

SECTION 5

Grammar, Usage, and Mechanics

Using Pronouns

Pronoun/Antecedent Agreement

The words or word referred to by a pronoun is called the **antecedent.** *Antecedent* means "going before."

▶ **Dad and Liana went to the mall. They love to shop.**

Dad and Liana are the antecedent of *They.*

A pronoun must agree with its antecedent in **person** and **number.**

▶ **Dad likes to shop more than anyone in his family.**

The pronoun *his* and its antecedent *Dad* are both singular.

▶ **Liana spends her entire allowance every week.**

The pronoun *her* and its antecedent *Liana* are both singular.

▶ **The Changs do most of their shopping in department stores.**

The pronoun *their* and its antecedent *Changs* are both plural.

▶ **If there is a new gadget out, it will surely tempt them.**

The pronoun *it* and its antecedent *gadget* are both singular.

Agreement with Indefinite Pronouns

Pronouns such as *another, anybody, each, either, everyone, one, someone, something, much, no one,* and *nothing,* which do not refer to a particular person, place, or thing, are singular indefinite pronouns.

When the antecedent is a singular indefinite pronoun, use a singular personal pronoun.

▶ **One of the girls lost her money.**

The pronoun *her* and its antecedent *One* are both singular.

▶ **Each of the stores had a sale sign in its window.**

The pronoun *its* and its antecedent *Each* are both singular.

When the antecedent is a plural indefinite pronoun, use a plural personal pronoun. Plural indefinite pronouns include *both*, *few*, *many*, *others*, and *several*.

▸ **Several of the fifth graders spent their money on trading cards.**

The pronoun *their* and its antecedent *Several* are both plural.

The indefinite pronouns *all*, *any*, *enough*, *most*, *none*, and *some* can be singular or plural.

▸ **Will any of the boys eat his lunch in the food court?**

The pronoun *his* and its antecedent *any* are both singular.

▸ **Some of the boys ate their lunch in the food court.**

The pronoun *their* and its antecedent *Some* are both plural.

Agreement with Demonstrative Pronouns

The demonstrative pronouns *this*, *that*, *these*, and *those* point out something. They must agree with their antecedent. *This* and *that* are singular. *These* and *those* are plural.

▸ **These are the books I need.**

The demonstrative pronoun *these* agrees with the plural noun *books*.

▸ **That is my favorite book.**

The demonstrative pronoun *that* agrees with the singular noun *book*.

Try It!

Complete the following sentence using the correct pronoun.

Many of the girls brought _____ CDs to the party.

Writing Connection

Pronouns save time and space. They improve the flow of writing by helping you avoid repeating words.

SECTION 5

Grammar, Usage, and Mechanics

Comparative and Superlative Adjectives

The **comparative** form of an adjective compares one person or thing with another. The **superlative** form of an adjective compares one person or thing with several others.

For most adjectives with one syllable and some with two syllables, add **-er** to form the comparative and **-est** to form the superlative.

▶ The sun is higher than it was an hour ago.

▶ Today is the hottest day of the week.

Adjectives with two or more syllables form the comparative by using *more* before the adjective. Form the superlative by using *most* before the adjective.

▶ Today's climb was more difficult than yesterday's climb.

▶ Tomorrow's climb will be the most difficult of all.

Irregular Comparative and Superlative Adjectives

Some adjectives do not follow a specific pattern. It helps to remember their forms.

▶ That was a bad mistake. His mistake was worse. Mine was the worst of all.

Base Form	Comparative	Superlative
good	better	best
bad	worse	worst
many	more	most
little	less	least

Try It!

Complete the sentence below using the superlative form of an adjective.

He ran the _____ of all the athletes.

SECTION 5

Grammar, Usage, and Mechanics

Usage • Comparative and Superlative Adjectives

Comparative and Superlative Adverbs

The **comparative** form of an adverb compares one action with another. The **superlative** form of an adverb compares one action with several others.

For most adverbs with one syllable and some with two syllables, add *-er* to form the comparative and *-est* to form the superlative. Use an adverb to modify a verb, an adjective, or another adverb.

> I arrived earlier for practice than most of the players.

> Kyle was the earliest player to arrive at the field.

Adverbs with two or more syllables form the comparative by using *more* before the adverb. Form the superlative by using *most* before the adverb.

> Kyle runs the bases more quickly than I do.

> Nate runs the bases most quickly.

Irregular Comparative and Superlative Adverbs

Some adverbs do not follow a specific pattern. It helps to remember their forms.

> Kyle usually plays better than everyone else.

> Jose played best in the last game.

Take care not to use the adjectives *good* and *bad* as adverbs. Use the words *well* and *badly* as adverbs and *good* and *bad* only as adjectives.

> Our team played *well*. (adverb)

> It was a *good* game. (adjective)

> The other team did not play *badly*. (adverb)

> They made a *bad* play at the end. (adjective)

Base Form	Comparative	Superlative
well	better	best
badly	worse	worst
little	less	least

Usage • Comparative and Superlative Adverbs

Contractions

A **contraction** is a word that is usually formed by combining two words and replacing one or more letters with an apostrophe. Some contractions use the word *is*.

▶ Sam is going to the competition. Sam's going to the competition.

Many common contractions are formed with the word *not*.

▶ I do not want to go. I don't want to go.

Contractions help writing and speaking sound natural and less choppy.

Common Contractions

are not	aren't	have not	haven't
did not	didn't	was not	wasn't
has not	hasn't	would not	wouldn't
should not	shouldn't	could not	couldn't
will not	won't	does not	doesn't
cannot	can't	is not	isn't
do not	don't	were not	weren't
I am	I'm	they are	they're
I have	I've	you are	you're
I will	I'll	you would	you'd
he is	he's	we will	we'll
she is	she's	we have	we've
they will	they'll	it is; it has	it's

Try It!

Write this sentence with contractions.

I could not go to the competition with Sam because I was not allowed.

SECTION 5

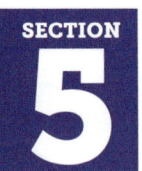

Grammar, Usage, and Mechanics

Transition Words

When you have many different ideas to communicate to your readers, it's important to help them follow along. You can do this by using **transition words,** which connect ideas in a piece of writing. Transition words help your readers move smoothly from one idea to the next. They also make your writing clearer and more accurate.

Different kinds of transition words are used for different purposes. For example, transition words can signal a time or place, a comparison or contrast, or a summary.

Transition Words to Indicate Time

about	then	soon
after	until	later
at	meanwhile	finally
before	today	then
during	tomorrow	as soon as
first	tonight	now
second	yesterday	when
third	next	

EXAMPLE Read the paragraph and identify the transition words.

> This evening I used a page from my journal to write a fantasy story. This morning when Mr. Frazier gave us the assignment, I didn't have any ideas for a fantasy story. Then I remembered something I had written yesterday about talking turtles and was able to use my journal entry for the story.

SECTION 5

Grammar, Usage, and Mechanics

Transition Words to Show Location

above	by	on
across	down	on top of
against	in	outside
along	in back of	over
among	in front of	through
around	inside	throughout
behind	into	to the left
below	near	to the right
beneath	nearby	under
beside	next to	underneath
between	off	

EXAMPLE Read the paragraph below and identify the transition words.

We saw a boat tied to a dock on the other side of the river. Across the river were three men running toward the boat. They untied the boat, jumped inside, and rowed to the dock right near us. Then they began searching for something underneath the dock.

Location words may be used for school reports and for other nonfiction writing. The following paragraph shows how location words can help with the detailed descriptions required for an observation report.

> **EXAMPLE**
>
> I placed an ice cube **in** a bowl of water. I sprinkled salt **on top of** the ice cube, then I rested the **center** of a piece of string on the ice cube for 45 seconds. When I lifted the string **above** the water, the ice cube stuck to it.

Transition Words to Show Contrast

Use transition words to contrast things that are different. When you want to show readers how one or more things are different, transition words help signal a contrast.

although	however	still
but	on the other hand	yet
even though	otherwise	

> **EXAMPLE**
>
> Rocks that look like icicles that hang from the ceiling of a cave are called stalactites. Formed when water drips minerals from a cave's ceiling, they taper to thin, fragile points. Stalagmites, **on the other hand,** are formed on the floor of a cave. **Unlike** stalactites, they have broad bases that taper to thick, rounded domes.

Do you see how the transition words *on the other hand* and *unlike* signal the reader that the information that is about to follow will tell how stalagmites are different from stalactites?

SECTION 5

Grammar, Usage, and Mechanics

Usage • Transition Words   435

Transition Words to Show Comparison

Sometimes you will need to show how two or more things are the same. Cue the reader with words that emphasize similarities.

also	in the same way	like	both
too	just as	similarly	likewise

EXAMPLE

Some caves have waterfalls that flow from underground streams. Most caves have formations called flowstones that look **like** waterfalls but are actually limestone. **Like** waterfalls, they too are formed by water. Flowstones appear **just as** an actual waterfall might appear if it were frozen.

Transition Words for Summarizing

as a result	last	lastly	in conclusion
finally	in summary	therefore	

These words alert readers to the points of a summary or a conclusion. Like most transition words, they help writers communicate effectively by providing organization and transitions.

EXAMPLE

Bats that sleep in caves during the day have been known to flee when they are disturbed. People who are afraid of bats sometimes swat at and injure them. Bats are usually harmless and can be very helpful by eating pesky insects. **In conclusion**, when you are doing activities near bats, take care not to disturb these creatures.

Double Negatives

Use a **negative word** to express the idea of *no* or *not*.

That team **never** wins any games.

Nobody attends their competitions.

> **Negative Words**
>
> no   never   nobody   none   no one   nothing   nowhere   hardly

A **double negative** occurs when *two* negative words are used to express a single idea when *one* negative word should do the job. Many contractions use the negative word *not*. As a result, double negatives sometimes find their way into our speech and writing. Watch for the contraction trap, however, to avoid double negatives.

Incorrect:	Sam didn't do nothing wrong while winning his match.
Correct:	Sam didn't do anything wrong while winning his match.
Correct:	Sam did nothing wrong while winning his match.
Incorrect:	He doesn't know nothing about karate.
Correct:	He doesn't know anything about karate.
Correct:	He knows nothing about karate.
Incorrect:	We don't have no lesson today.
Correct:	We don't have a lesson today.
Correct:	We have no lesson today.

Try It!

Fix these sentences.
- We don't have no place for our lesson.
- Our instructor doesn't see nothing wrong with practicing tomorrow.

SECTION 5

Grammar, Usage, and Mechanics

Misused Words

This lesson will help you choose between words that are often misused.

To, Too, Two

To suggests direction.

Go to the kitchen.

Too shows degree or means "also."

Make sure the gravy isn't too thin.

Check the roast, too.

Two is the number before *three*.

Add two tablespoons of flour to the gravy.

Sit and Set

Sit is what you do when you place yourself on a chair. Sit does not take a direct object. These are the verb forms of *sit*: **sit, sitting, sat.**

Will you please sit here? No! I've been sitting all day.

Set involves putting something somewhere. Set usually has a direct object. These are the verb forms of *set*: **set, setting.**

I set my helmet on the counter. He was setting up the goal.

Rise and Raise

Rise means "to move upward." It does not take a direct object. These are the verb forms of *rise*: **rise, rose, rising, risen.**

Blue smoke will rise from the fire. The bread dough is rising.

Raise means "to cause something to move upward or to grow." *Raise* normally has a direct object. These are the verb forms of *raise*: **raise, raising, raised.**

Jeb will raise corn this year. The runner raised the torch.

More Misused and Confusing Words

▶ **can, may** If you have the ability, you *can*. If you have permission, you *may*. **I can leave the building whenever I'm ready. You may join me if you like.**

▶ **its, it's** To make *it* possessive, use *its*. To form the contraction of *it is* or *it has*, use *it's* with an apostrophe. **Our dog has its fur shaved in the summer. It's funny when you see her for the first time.**

▶ **many, much** Use *many* for things that can be counted. Use *much* for things that cannot be counted. **I have too many apples for one pie. The apples I have won't make much applesauce.**

▶ **which, who** *Which* refers only to things. *Who* refers only to people. **Use the small bottle, which is almost empty. After you wash the dishes, hand them to Carmen, who will dry them.**

▶ **then, than** Use *then* as an adverb to suggest another time. Use *than* as a conjunction to make a comparison. **The chili was spicy enough then. This chili is spicier than last week's.**

▶ **lay, lie** Use *lay* when you mean "to put or place." **Just lay the books on the table.** Use *lie* when you mean "to rest or recline." **I think I will lie down.**

Try It!

Review the commonly misused words that were covered in this lesson. Choose the words that cause you the most problems, then use them correctly in sentences.

Writing Connection

To prevent misunderstanding, take the time to spell the word you mean. Look it up, if you must.

SECTION 5

Grammar, Usage, and Mechanics

Mechanics

The rules of mechanics are very important in writing. Imagine a paragraph with no capital letters at the beginnings of sentences and no punctuation at the ends of sentences. How confusing would that be? Of course, there is a lot more to mechanics than capitalizing the first word of a sentence and using end marks. The following lessons will give you what you need to know to understand and use the rules of mechanics to improve your writing.

The rules of mechanics tell you about the following concepts:
- Abbreviations
- Commas
- Colons and Semicolons
- Quotation Marks, Underlining, and Apostrophes
- Parentheses, Hyphens, Dashes, and Ellipses
- Capitalization
- Formatting
- Using Electronic Technology

Try It!

Can you find the mistakes in the sentences below?
- Barb and joe are going to the zoo on monday.
- My family got a new dog?
- My dad bought apples bananas and oranges at the store.

Continue reading this section of the Handbook to find out more information about the rules of mechanics.

Abbreviations

An **abbreviation** is a shortened form of a word. Most abbreviations use periods and are capitalized.

If an abbreviation occurs at the end of a sentence, use only one period.

▶ **Ms. Kurz asked us to meet at 5 A.M.**

Use periods for abbreviated titles used before a person's name.

▶ **Dr. Strauss   Mrs. Jagdish   Mr. Foreman**

Use periods for abbreviations that follow a person's name.

▶ **Martin Luther King Jr.   Jill Theophano, M.D.**

Use periods when using initials for a person's first and/or middle name.

▶ **Ursula K. LeGuin   H. G. Wells**

Use periods for these time and date abbreviations.

▶ **12:15 A.M.   7:34 P.M.   1100 B.C.   A.D. 1066**

Abbreviations for Specific Uses

The following abbreviated words may be used for charts, envelopes, maps, and scientific writing. Most other times, these words should be spelled out.

Days and Months

Thurs., Fri., Sat., Sept., Oct., Nov.

Use the longer form in your writing. **Example:** Mon. should be written as Monday.

Streets and Roads

(printed on maps): St., Ave., Blvd., Rd., Ct., Ln.

Spell these out in your writing. **Example:** Mulberry St. should be written as Mulberry Street.

U.S. Units of Measure

Notice that an abbreviation may be different from the actual word.

oz. (ounce), *lb.* (pound), *in.* (inch), *ft.* (foot), *yd.* (yard), *tsp.* (teaspoon), *tbsp.* (tablespoon)

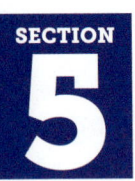

Abbreviations That Do Not Use Periods

Acronyms

An **acronym** is a word created from the first letters or syllables of other words. Acronyms are abbreviations, but they do not require periods. Acronyms are usually capitalized.

SCUBA (self-contained underwater breathing apparatus)

NASA (National Aeronautics and Space Administration)

AWOL (absent without leave)

Initialisms

An **initialism** is formed from the first letters of the words it represents. Pronounce each letter of an initialism when speaking; when writing, do not use periods.

ATM (automatic teller machine)

UFO (unidentified flying object)

SUV (sport utility vehicle)

Postal Abbreviations

These two-letter state abbreviations used by the U.S. Postal Service save space on envelopes. Avoid them elsewhere in writing.

CA (California)   **DE (Delaware)**

ID (Idaho)   **SC (South Carolina)**

Metric Units of Measure

Metric system abbreviations do not use periods.

cm (centimeter)   **L (liter)**   **m (meter)**

Other Units of Measure

C (Celsius)   **F (Fahrenheit)**   **mph (miles per hour)**

Writing Connection

Abbreviations can help us write things such as telephone messages more quickly. Use abbreviations only if readers will easily understand the abbreviation.

SECTION 5

Grammar, Usage, and Mechanics

Commas

Commas are punctuation marks that help organize thoughts and items. They show the reader where to pause and what thoughts go together.

Commas in a Series

Use a comma to separate three or more items in a series. A series of three or more groups of words also uses a comma after each group.

- Please grab the leash, collar, and treats. (series of words)
- Was it a toy poodle, miniature poodle, or standard poodle? (series of phrases)

Commas also separate the items in a series of three or more predicates.

- The dogs stepped out of their crates, sniffed the ground, and began to play.

Commas After Introductory Phrases or Clauses

Use a comma after a long introductory phrase or clause. A short introductory phrase or clause does not need a comma.

- When you become really good at handling dogs, I will let you show them. (long introductory clause)
- Until we arrived at the dog show, we had no idea what the schedule was. (long introductory phrase)
- At 12:00 the show began. (short introductory phrase) When it started we had a schedule. (short introductory clause)

Commas in Compound Sentences

Compound sentences contain two or more independent clauses. Use a comma and a connecting word, such as *and*, *but*, or *or*, to join the independent clauses.

- The Irish terrier wanted to play catch, and the beagle wanted to chase him.
- I would really like to see the Weimaraners, but the Saint Bernards are showing next.

Do **not** use commas to separate the compound subjects or compound predicates of simple sentences.

▶ Jed brushed his dog from head to tail and walked it outside near the barn. (compound predicate)

Commas and Interjections

Use a comma to set off an interjection not followed by an exclamation point.

▶ Oh, well, I came to the dog show mostly for fun.

Commas with Appositives

Use two commas to set off an appositive, a word or phrase placed next to a word to provide extra information.

▶ Roger's dog, a German Shepherd, is my favorite.

Commas with Direct Address

Direct address is a name or phrase used in speaking directly to a person. Use one or two commas to set off a noun of direct address (the person being spoken to) from the rest of the sentence.

▶ Kara, which is your favorite breed?
▶ Actually, Mariah, I really like mixed breeds.

Commas Used to Separate Adjectives

Use commas to separate two or more adjectives that have equal importance in modifying the same noun.

▶ The sleek, fast greyhound easily outran the basset hound.

Do not use a comma between adjectives when the adjective closer to the noun functions as a part of it.

▶ She is an experienced dog trainer.

Commas with Interrupters

Use commas to set off interrupters, words or phrases that interrupt the central idea of a sentence.

▶ English Setters, on the other hand, require lots of exercise.
▶ They will be quite happy, however, in a large yard.

SECTION 5

Grammar, Usage, and Mechanics

Commas with Introductory Words

Use a comma to set off the introductory words *yes*, *no*, and *well*.

▶ No, I have never seen that type of dog.

▶ Well, would you like to see it?

▶ Yes, I would.

Commas in Dialogue

Use one comma to set off a direct quotation when the speaker is named at the beginning or end of a quotation. Use two commas, one on either side of the speaker tag, in the middle of a quotation.

▶ Jasmine asked, "When will we get to see the greyhounds?"

▶ "They will be in the show area," he answered, "when the whippets are finished."

▶ "That will be about thirty minutes from now," he added.

Commas with Parts of a Letter

Use a comma after a friendly letter's greeting and after the closing of all letters.

▶ Dear Mrs. Woodhouse,

▶ Sincerely,

Commas with Dates

Use a comma between the day and year of a complete date. Do not use a comma when you write only the month and year.

▶ Champion Master Briar was born April 12, 1996.

▶ He won the best-of-breed award in August 1999.

Commas with Tag Questions

A tag question is a short question added to the end of a positive or negative statement. The statement and the tag are always separated by a comma.

▶ Bella reads a lot of books, doesn't she?

▶ You're coming to the party, aren't you?

▶ He's not French, is he?

Commas in Large Numbers

Use commas in numbers with four digits or more, except for years.

▶ Barbara Woodhouse trained more than 17,000 dogs and their owners.

▶ Mr. Singer left an inheritance of $50,000 to his dog in 2015.

Commas in Addresses

Use a comma after a street address when it is followed by the name of a city. Use a comma to set off the name of a state or country when it follows the name of a city. Do not use a comma between a state and a ZIP code.

▶ Regal Rustin prefers to live with his owners in Tiverton, England.

▶ Write to Ruff and Ready at 236 Lonesome Highway, Cut Bank, MT 59736

Try It!

Add commas to these sentences.
- The teacher Mrs. Liu handed me my certificate.
- Madonna my best friend said "Good job Violet."
- Yes I saw Jesse yesterday.
- Matthew got a new car didn't he?
- I'll bring cheese fruit and salad for the picnic.
- After we count all the votes Ms. Ryan will announce the winner.

Writing Connection

Commas help organize writing into ideas so readers know when to separate thoughts or items and when to pause.

SECTION 5

Grammar, Usage, and Mechanics

Colons and Semicolons

Introduce a List with a Colon

To introduce a list with a colon, use the words *the following* or *as follows* at some point in the sentence before the colon and list.

▶ The things you will need for the sleepover are as follows: a toothbrush, pajamas, a sleeping bag, and a change of clothes.

Colons After Salutations

Use a colon after a business letter salutation.

▶ **Dear Ms. Pulaski:**

Colons Between Hours and Minutes

Use a colon to separate the hour and the minutes of a precise time.

▶ Drop your daughter off at 6:15 P.M. and pick her up at 9:30 A.M. tomorrow.

Semicolons

A **semicolon** is a punctuation mark used to join the independent, or main, clauses in a sentence and to help separate clauses joined by some adverbs.

Use a semicolon to connect independent clauses not joined by *and, but, or,* or *nor*.

▶ Everyone finally fell asleep; some of the girls snored.

Try It!

Add a colon and a semicolon to these clauses.
The alarm clock went off at 8 15 I realized I had missed the play.

Writing Connection

Colons and semicolons save space and help organize writing. They are not used often.

Quotation Marks, Underlining, and Apostrophes

Quotation Marks

Use **quotation marks** to enclose the exact words of a speaker. Periods and commas should be inside closing quotation marks. Question marks and exclamation points should be inside the quotation marks if they are part of the quotation.

- Dana said, "Let me show you my telescope."
- "May I look through it?" asked Tiana.
- "Look at the moon!" she said excitedly.

Quotation Marks for Titles

Use quotation marks for the titles of poems, songs, and short stories.

- "Wander-Thirst" (poem)
- "Vergil, the Dog" (short story)
- "Yankee Doodle" (song)

Underlining and Italics

Use underlining or italics for book titles.

- <u>Julie of the Wolves</u>
- *Charlotte's Web*

Apostrophe

To show **possession,** add an apostrophe and *s* to the end of singular indefinite pronouns and most singular nouns.

- Someone's constellation chart
- Saturn's rings

Possessive pronouns do not have apostrophes.

- its size
- whose notebook
- The telescope is hers.

In **contractions,** apostrophes take the place of missing letters.

- *It's* is formed from *it is* or *it has.*
- *I'm* is formed from *I am.*

Parentheses, Hyphens, Dashes, and Ellipses

Parentheses

Parentheses are punctuation marks used to enclose information that either adds to or helps explain other words in a sentence.

- The introduction (page 6) tells where some lynx live (North America).

Hyphens

Use a hyphen for some compound nouns.

- good-bye
- teeter-totter
- sister-in-law

Use a hyphen when creating a compound modifier, usually an adjective formed from two words written in front of a noun.

- second-place finish
- orange-red sun
- New York-style pizza

Use hyphens for numbers and fractions that are written out.

- ninety-nine pins
- forty-six eggs
- one-fourth

Dashes

Use a **dash** to show an interruption in speech or a sudden change of thought.

- Pumas—people rarely see them—live in these mountains.

Ellipses

Ellipses consist of what look like three periods, each one with a space before and after it. Use ellipses to show a pause in speech.

- It's interesting . . . Does it climb trees?

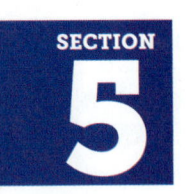

Capitalization

When you **capitalize,** you make the first letter of a word a capital letter. Letters that are not capitalized are called *lowercase*.

Capitalize the first word of every sentence.
- The bicycle race takes place tomorrow.

Capitalize the first word in a direct quotation.
- Mom shouted, "Don't forget your water bottle and your helmet!"

Capitalize proper nouns and proper adjectives.
- **Proper Nouns:** Brazil, Texas, Yankee Stadium
- **Proper Adjectives:** Brazil nuts, Texas resident, Yankee fan

Capitalize the pronoun *I*.
- Once I start one of her books, I can't put it down.

Capitalize initials **that stand for part of a person's name.**
- *J. R. R. Tolkien*
- *L. Frank Baum*

Capitalize abbreviations and acronyms.
- We had dinner at 6:30 P.M.
- The SWAT team surrounded the building.

Titles

Capitalize people's titles.
- Houston Baker Jr.
- Wendy Falb, Ph.D.
- Dr. Alexis Mazza
- Governor Hannah Fernandez

Do not capitalize titles used as common nouns or those following names.
- Joan Cohen, a doctor of pediatrics, is running for councilwoman.

Capitalize titles used in place of names.
- Will you change your vote, Senator?

Capitalize words used in place of names.
- Will Grandpa ask Sergi's grandmother to go?

Notice that *grandpa* used as a name is capitalized. *Sergi's grandmother* describes a person; it is not capitalized.

SECTION 5

Grammar, Usage, and Mechanics

Geographical and Historical Terms

Capitalize the names of historic periods.

> **Stone Age**
> **Great Depression**
> **Harlem Renaissance**
> **Victorian period**

Capitalize the names of historic events.

> **Holocaust**
> **Pearl Harbor Day**
> **American Revolution**
> **Battle of Bunker Hill**

Capitalize geographic place names. These include bodies of water, mountains, and other features that have been named.

> **Great Salt Lake**   **Everglades**
> **Snake River**   **Chesapeake Bay**
> **Atlantic Ocean**   **Mt. Hood**
> **Blue Ridge Mountains**   **Death Valley**

Capitalize the regions of a country.

> **Snow Belt**   **New England**
> **Pacific Northwest**   **Mid-Atlantic**

Capitalize direction words used for a specific place.

> **the South of France**
> **the North Pole**
> **the East**
> **the West**

Use lowercase for general direction words.

> **eastern shore**
> **northwest current**
> **south side of the mountain**

SECTION 5

Grammar, Usage, and Mechanics

452   **Mechanics** • Capitalization

Capitalize the names of holidays and special events.

Labor Day **Fourth of July**
Olympics **World Series**

Capitalize the names of months and days.

May **September**
Tuesday **Saturday**

Capitalize the names of countries, cities, states, and counties.

Portugal **Seattle**
Kentucky **Orange County**

Capitalize titles of businesses, institutions, and organizations.

Salvation Army
Cook County Hospital
Westminster College

Capitalize brand names.

Crazy Crunch cereal
Super Spin yo-yos
Speedy sneakers

Capitalize the titles of books, movies, magazines, and newspapers.

Harriet the Spy (book)
Spider Magazine (magazine)
Chicago Tribune (newspaper)

Capitalize the titles of musical compositions and works of art.

The Magic Flute (opera)
Starry Night (painting)
The Thinker (statue)

SECTION 5

Grammar, Usage, and Mechanics

Mechanics • Capitalization

Capitalize the names of important documents and awards.

Magna Carta

Nobel Peace Prize

Declaration of Independence

Bill of Rights

Capitalize the names of important structures.

Vietnam Memorial

Pentagon

Golden Gate Bridge

Lincoln Tunnel

St. Louis Arch

Capitalize religions, nationalities, and languages.

Religions	Nationalities	Languages
Judaism	Polish	Mandarin
Islam	Colombian	English
Hinduism	Senegalese	Russian
Christianity	Norwegian	Spanish
Buddhism	Malaysian	Japanese

Capitalize only those school subjects that refer to a language.

English	**Spanish**
German	**French**

Use lowercase letters for most school subjects.

math	**science**
social studies	**reading**

SECTION 5

Grammar, Usage, and Mechanics

454 Mechanics • Capitalization

Capitalize greetings and closings in letters. Use a capital letter to begin the greeting or salutation and also the first and last name of the person to whom you are writing. The first letter of every word in the salutation of a business letter should be capitalized.

Dear Ms. Valente,   **To Whom It May Concern:**

Dear Sir: **Sincerely,**

Capitalize the parts of a topic outline. Use capital Roman numerals and capital letters to label main topics and subtopics. Use lowercase letters for the subdivisions of the subtopics. The first word of each heading, subheading, and subdivision should also be capitalized.

I. Swimming for fun
    A. Provides exercise
        1. Effects on whole body
            a. Low impact on joints and muscles
            b. Works wide range of muscles
        2. Heart benefits
            a. Strengthens the heart
            b. Increases red blood cell production
    B. Provides relaxation
        1. Soothing effects of water
        2. Stress-relieving effects of the exercise

Try It!

Add the correct capitalization to this sentence.
we were driving over the golden gate bridge when i realized that i had left my math book, spanish homework, and ranger magazine at uncle charlie's house.

Writing Connection

When you capitalize correctly in your writing, you alert your readers when sentences begin and when you are being specific.

SECTION 5

Grammar, Usage, and Mechanics

Formatting

Flip through this book, looking for text that catches your eye. Did you notice bulleted lists? Boldfaced or colorful headings? Different kinds of letter styles? All of these things are kinds of formatting. **Formatting** is the way in which the words appear and are arranged on the page. You can use a word-processing program to electronically format your own writing.

Boldface, Italics, and Underlining

Words that are in **boldface,** or bold, are darker and thicker than the surrounding text. For example, the word "**Formatting**" in the previous paragraph is in boldface. In this case, the word was made bold because it is being defined. But perhaps the most common use for boldface is to make a word stand out from the others, such as in headings of text sections, charts, and so on.

In most word-processing programs, you can make a word bold by simply double clicking on the word to highlight it, and then clicking on the B in the toolbar at the top of the page. You may also be able to turn on the bold function by pressing the control button and the letter B on the keyboard before you type in the word that is to be bolded. Then you type the word, and then press Ctrl+B again to turn off the bold function.

Words that are in *italics* are slanted to the right, as in the word *formatting*. In this case, the word is italicized because it is being called out as a word. Italics are commonly used for other things as well. For example, the titles of books and magazines should be in italics in electronic text. You can italicize words using the same steps as those for boldfacing words, by clicking the I instead of B on the toolbar.

Another way to make words stand out is to underline them. You can use underlining for the headings of columns or sections, for example, or in place of italics. You can underline words using the same steps as for boldfacing and italicizing, by clicking the U on the toolbar instead.

Font

The **font** is the style of type that you use for your letters. Here are several examples of fonts: Times New Roman, Helvetica, Papyrus, Jester. The kind of font depends on what you are writing. For example, for a report for school, you should use a common font that is easy to read and that is not distracting. Times New Roman is an example of this. You might use another, more "fun" font for letters you write to friends, or if you are making a flyer or poster on the computer.

To choose a font, as well as the size of the letters you want to use, click "Format" on the toolbar at the top of the screen, and then click "font." A list of fonts will appear, and you can see what they look like by clicking them. Simply click the font you would like to use, and under "Size," the size of font you would like as well. You can also choose to make your words a variety of different colors by clicking "font color," and clicking a color.

Bulleted and Numbered Lists

Bulleted and numbered lists are just that: lists that have bullets— large dots—or numbers before each list item. To create a bulleted or numbered list, click "Format," and then "Bullets and Numbering," or a similar heading, such as "Bulleted and Numbered Lists." If you want to create a bulleted list, then click the "Bulleted" or similarly labeled tab. You can then choose from a variety of styles of bulleted lists. Do the same to create numbered lists, this time clicking "Numbered," and then choosing a style.

Lists are most often used in nonfiction writing to draw attention to and explain certain related items or steps. For example, in a report about healthy eating, you might use a bulleted list for the different food groups, and list examples of food for each food group. You might use a numbered list if you are writing directions.

Lists often help readers to better understand facts because they show relationships between things. Lists also help to break up big blocks of writing on the page, which makes the text more visually appealing to readers.

The Tab Key

Use the Tab key to indent your paragraphs, instead of just spacing over a few characters. This way, your paragraphs will always be indented the same length.

Using Electronic Technology

Creating and Revising Text

Create your own computer file, write your ideas down, and print your document so that others may read it—you can do all of these things using only your fingertips!

Opening a New File

Before you can begin to write, you must first open a new file. You can do this one of two ways:

1. Click the **New** button on the toolbar; or,
2. Click the **File** button on the menu bar, and then click on the **New** button.

Saving and Closing a File

You have just opened a new file, so now you can begin typing the text. When you are finished writing, you should save your file and then close it:

1. Click the **File** button and click **Save As.**
2. In the **File Name** box, write the name that you want your file
to have. It should be the subject or topic of your writing. Try to keep the name short.
3. Click on the **Save** button.
4. To close your file, click the **File** button, and then drop down and click on the **Close** button. Click **Yes** when it asks you if you would like to save the changes you made. Your file is now closed.
5. If you would like to open your existing file, just click the **File Open** button, find the file name on the list of files, and double-click your file. Now you can begin adding text or revising your document!

Deleting, Cutting, and Pasting

Part of the writing process is revising and editing what we have written. Using a computer to write a document makes revising and editing easier.

Suppose you have reviewed your document, and you decide that a word, phrase, or even paragraph is not needed. You want to take it out, or **delete** it. Simply select the text that you want to delete using the mouse, and then press **Delete** on your keyboard.

But what if you want to move a piece of text from one place to another?

1. Select the text that you want to move.
2. Click the "Cut" button in the toolbar. (It often is shown as a pair of scissors.)
3. Use the mouse to move the cursor to the place where you want to insert the text you just cut.
4. Click the "Paste" button.
5. Once you have cut and pasted, make sure the text that you pasted fits where you put it, and that you included all of the text that you wanted to move. Then go back to the place you cut the text from to make sure the remaining text still makes sense.

Printing Your Document

So now you have revised, edited, and proofread your document. You want to print your document. The quick way to print your document is to simply click the "Print" button on the toolbar. It usually is a picture of a printer. Your document will begin to print automatically.

However, if you want to print more than one copy, or only certain pages of your document, then click **File,** and then **Print.**

Under "Page Range," you can choose which pages you would like to print by inputting the page numbers. Use commas after each page number. You can even print just a part of a page. In this case, you would first select the part you want to print, and then click the button next to "Selection."

If you want to print more than one copy, then type in the number of copies you would like in the appropriate box.

Finally, click the "okay" button, and your file will begin to print.

SECTION 5

Grammar, Usage, and Mechanics

Retrieving and Reviewing Information

What kinds of resources do you use when you are looking for information on a certain subject? You most likely have used printed resources, such as reference and other books, and magazines. You can also use electronic technology to find and evaluate a wealth of information.

Search Engines

One of the most popular ways to find information electronically is to use a search engine. A **search engine** is a program you use to find Web sites on the Internet that have information about the subject you are researching. Follow these steps to use an Internet search engine to help you find and review information:

Decide on Key Words

Key words are usually the most important words or phrases of the topic you are looking for. These might be the same words that you would use when looking for your topic in an encyclopedia, or the index of a book. But instead of looking up the words in the back of a book, you type in these words in the search engine box.

Be Precise For example, suppose that you want to find information about what causes earthquakes. You would type in the words "Causes of Earthquakes." To make sure you get results that include only "Causes of Earthquakes," with the three words appearing directly next to each other in this order, put quotation marks around the phrase.

When you have typed in a key word or phrase you are satisfied with, click the "Search" or "Go" button.

Scan the Results

Once you press the search button, the search engine will list Web sites that include the key words you entered. In each Web site listed, the key words will be in bold. There is usually a short description of what is included on the site. Study the listings to find information that relates to the topic you are interested in.

You might find that the search engine lists few, if any websites that are related to the topic you are interested in. Or, there may be way too many to choose from. This means that the key words you chose were either too specific or too general. For example, "earthquakes" would be too general if you are more interested in the causes of earthquakes than in specific earthquakes or the effects of earthquakes. Change your key word or key words and conduct other searches until you find websites listings that you can use. For example, if you are interested in the causes of earthquakes, you might search "causes of earthquakes," "what are earthquakes?" or "what causes earthquakes?"

When you find a listing that seems to cover the topic you are interested in, simply click the underlined words of the website to launch the website.

Online Databases

You can also use online databases to find information electronically. Databases are large collections of information. They may include information about specific topics, such as animals or American history. Or, they may be dictionaries or encyclopedias that you can use online. You can use many databases through your local library. In many cases, you find information within the database by entering a key word or phrase, as you do for search engines.

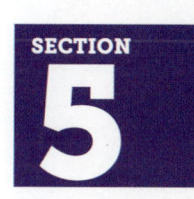

Glossary

A

abbreviation the shortening of a word, such as St. for Street. Most abbreviations are followed by a period.

abstract nouns words that name ideas, qualities, and feelings

acronym the short form of several words, usually as in the name of an organization, such as NASA for National Aeronautics and Space Administration

active voice when the subject performs the verb's action adjective clause a dependent clause that modifies a noun or pronoun in the main clause of a sentence

adverb clause a dependent clause that modifies the verb in the main clause of a sentence

alliteration the repetition of the consonant sounds at the beginning of words

analogy a comparison of two words based on how the two words are related

antecedent a word referred to or replaced by a pronoun

appositive a word or group of words that rename another word in the same sentence

appositive phrase includes an appositive and the words that modify it

assonance the repetition of the sounds of vowels in words

auxiliary verb a helping verb that helps the main verb show action or express a state of being

B

bibliography a list of research materials used and referred to in the preparation of an article or report

biography a written account of a person's life

C

callout in a news story or magazine article, a quotation or interesting portion of a sentence printed in large, bold type in the middle of a column

caption a sentence or phrase written under a picture or illustration that tells more about the picture

cause-and-effect chart a type of graphic organizer that shows the cause and possible effect or effects of that event

character analysis looking closely at a character in a piece of writing to learn as much as you can about that character

chronological order an organizational pattern that tracks events in time order

cinquain a poem that has five lines and follows a special pattern

clause a group of words that has a subject and a verb

closed compound word a compound word that has no space between the words, such as *popcorn*

collecting grid a type of graphic organizer used to record information gathered from many different sources

collective noun a noun that names a group, or collection, of people, animals, or things, such as *family*, *audience*, and *herd*

comparative form the form of an adjective or adverb that compares two of something

complex sentence a type of sentence that is made of an independent clause and one or more dependent clauses

compound predicate two or more simple predicates joined by a conjunction that share the same subject

compound sentence two or more simple sentences joined by a conjunction

compound subject two or more simple subjects connected by a conjunction that share the same verb

compound-complex sentence a sentence that has two or more independent clauses and at least one dependent clause

concrete nouns words that name things you can see, touch, hear, smell, or taste

connotation the feeling a word creates in the reader, or a word's suggested meaning

context clue words or sentences that surround an unknown word that give the reader clues about the meaning of the unknown word

conventions the mechanics of writing that include spelling, punctuation, grammar, capitalization, and usage

coordinating conjunction a word used to connect compound parts of a sentence, such as *and*, *but*, and *or*

correlative conjunction words that work in pairs to join words and groups of words, such as *either . . . or* and *neither . . . nor*

couplet a type of poetry that has two lines that rhyme

D

declarative sentence a sentence that makes a statement and ends with a period

definite article the article *the* that identifies specific people, places, things, or ideas

demonstrative pronoun points out something. *This*, *that*, *these*, and *those*, are demonstrative pronouns when they replace a noun.

dependent clause part of a sentence containing a subject and a verb that cannot stand alone as a sentence

dialogue journal a type of journal in which two people write back and forth about a subject as if they were having a conversation

diamante a diamond-shaped, seven-line poem that has specific information in each line and an exact number of words

direct object a noun or pronoun that receives the action of the verb

drafting the second stage, or phase, in the writing process, in which the writer starts writing

E

editing/proofreading the fourth stage, or phase, in the writing process, in which the writer makes corrections in spelling, grammar, usage, capitalization, and punctuation

expository writing a form of writing used for giving information or explaining something, such as textbooks

F

fantasy a story that has characters, places, or events that could not exist in the real world

figurative language words or groups of words that stand for more than their literal meaning, such as similes and metaphors

fragment a group of words that does not express a complete thought and is missing a subject, a predicate, or both

free verse a type of poetry that doesn't follow any specific form and usually does not rhyme

H

haiku a three-line poem about nature that has a specific number of syllables for each line

heading the part of a letter that includes the address of the writer and the date the letter was written

helping verb a verb that helps the main verb

historical fiction a story that takes place in an actual time and place in the past. The story gives lots of accurate details about the period in which the events take place.

homographs words that are spelled the same but have different meanings and origins

homophones two or more words that sound the same but have different meanings and spellings

hyperbole an extreme exaggeration often used for humorous effect

I

idiom a word or group of words that cannot be understood by knowing only the literal meaning, such as *being in the dog house*

imperative sentence a sentence that gives a command or makes a request and ends with a period or exclamation point

indefinite article the articles *a* and *an* that refer to a general group of people, places, things, or ideas

indefinite pronoun a pronoun that does not refer to a specific person, place, thing, or idea, such as *everyone* or *something*

independent clause a group of words that has a subject and a predicate and can stand alone as a sentence

indirect object a noun or pronoun for whom or to whom something is done

informative paragraph a paragraph that gives or explains information

informative report a report that gives information about facts, ideas, or events using nonfiction sources

informative writing a type of writing based on facts, such as giving a summary, giving directions to a location, explaining a process, or writing a report

initialism formed from the first letters of the words it represents, such as *ATM* (Automatic Teller Machine)

intensive pronoun a pronoun that ends with *-self* or *-selves* and is used to draw special attention to a noun or pronoun already mentioned

interjection a word or group of words that shows strong feeling

internal rhyme words that rhyme in the middle of lines of poetry

interrogative pronoun a pronoun that asks a question, such as *whose*

interrogative sentence a type of sentence that asks a question and ends with a question mark

interrupter a word or phrase that interrupts the central idea of a sentence

irregular plural nouns nouns that do not follow the rule for most plural nouns, such as *child* and *children*

irregular verb a verb that does not follow the rule for adding *-ed* to form the past tense

L

lead the first sentence or paragraph of a piece of writing, meant to capture the reader's interest

learning log where you write about something you are studying, such as a science experiment.

linking verb a state-of-being verb that links the subject of the sentence with a word in the predicate

lyric a type of poem that expresses strong personal emotions, often using details of the five senses

M

memo (memorandum) a short message that communicates something to a person or group of people with whom you are working

metaphor a figure of speech that compares two unlike things without using the words *like* or *as*

N

narrative writing a form of writing that tells a story or gives an account of an event

nonrhyming poetry poetry in which the words at the ends of the lines do not rhyme

O

object of the preposition the noun or pronoun that follows the preposition in a prepositional phrase

object pronoun a pronoun used as a direct object, object of the preposition, or indirect object, such as *him* or *us*

onomatopoeia a word that imitates the sound made by or connected with the thing to which you refer, such as the *pitter-patter* of rain

open compound word a compound word that has a space between the two smaller words, such as *rain forest*

opinion the way you think or feel about something

opinion writing a type of writing in which the writer gives his or her opinion about a topic

order of importance a way of organizing information by putting ideas from least important to most important

outline a type of graphic organizer used to show main topics and subtopics. An outline uses Roman numerals, capital letters, Arabic numerals, and lowercase letters to label these ideas.

P

participial phrase includes a participle and other words that complete its meaning and always functions as an adjective

passive voice when the subject receives the verb's action

GLOSSARY

pattern poetry poetry in which the lines use the pattern or format of another poem or song to create a new poem

personal narrative a piece of writing that is a story about something that happened in the writer's life

personification a figure of speech in which an object or idea is given human qualities

persuasive essay an essay that is written to change the thinking, feelings, or actions of the readers about a specific issue or to get the reader to recognize the writer's point of view

persuasive writing a type of writing in which the writer tries to change the way the readers think or feel about a topic, inspire action, or get the reader to recognize the writer's point of view

phrase a group of words that does not have a subject and predicate

plot analysis the process of identifying the problem, conflict, climax, and conclusion of the plot

point of view the viewpoint from which a story is written, either as the first person telling the story as it happens to them or third person as an observer of the story

portfolio a type of folder or notebook in which a writer keeps his/her pieces of writing

possessive noun shows who owns something

possessive pronoun a pronoun that shows who owns something

predicate the part of a sentence that tells what the subject is or does

predicate noun a noun in the predicate that tells about the subject. It is linked to the subject by a linking verb.

prefix one or more letters added to the beginning of a root or base word that changes the word's meaning

preposition a word that shows position or direction

prepositional phrase a phrase that begins with a preposition and ends with a noun or pronoun

presentation how your writing looks in its final form

prewriting the first stage, or phase, of the writing process, in which the writer thinks, brainstorms, and makes a list or web to write down thoughts he/she wants to include in the piece of writing

proofreading marks a set of commonly agreed upon marks that are used to show where corrections are needed in a piece of writing

proper adjective an adjective made from a proper noun that always starts with a capital letter

proper noun a noun that names a specific person, place, thing, or idea and always starts with a capital letter

prose all types of writing that are not considered poetry

publishing the final stage, or phase, of the writing process, in which the writer makes a final and correct copy of the piece of writing and then shares it with the selected audience

purpose the reason for writing something, usually to inform, to explain, to entertain, or to persuade

Q

quatrain a four-line poem or a stanza of a longer poem that expresses one thought and has a variety of rhyming patterns

quotation the exact words a person speaks

R

reflective paragraph a paragraph that ends a piece of writing and causes the reader to reflect on or think about what has been written

reflexive pronoun a pronoun that ends with *-self* or *-selves* and refers to the subject of the sentence

relative pronoun a pronoun that introduces a word group called a dependent clause that modifies a noun or pronoun used in the main part of the sentence

research report a report that gives information about real facts, ideas, or events

revising the third stage, or phase, of the writing process in which the writer improves the writing by adding, deleting, consolidating, rearranging, and/or clarifying material

rhythm the beat or pattern in a song or poem

run-on sentence two or more sentences incorrectly written as one sentence

S

salutation the greeting of a letter

sentence fluency a quality of writing in which the sentences flow smoothly

signal words words that tell the order in which things happen in a process, such as first, next, and last, also called transition words

signature the part of a letter in which the writer signs his/her name

simile a figure of speech that compares two or more things that are not alike by using the word like or as

simple sentence has one subject and one predicate

singular noun a word that names one person, place, thing, or idea

source a place where one seeks information when doing research, such as encyclopedias, dictionaries, books, almanacs, atlases, videos, magazines, newspapers, personal interviews, and the Internet

state-of-being verb a verb that does not show action but shows a condition or state of being

story map a type of graphic organizer that is used to outline the events of a story

subject the part of a sentence that tells who or what the sentence is about

subject-verb agreement when the verb agrees with the subject of the sentence. They both must be singular or plural.

subordinate clause another name for dependent clauses that are introduced by a subordinating conjunction

subordinating conjunction a word that introduces a dependent clause

subtopic a subdivision of the main topic of a piece of writing

suffix one or more letters added to the end of a root or base word that changes the word's meaning

superlative form the form of an adjective or adverb that compares three or more of something

supporting sentences the sentences in a paragraph that tell more about the paragraph's main idea

T

TIDE graphic organizer a type of graphic organizer that organizes the important details and facts for informative writing

topics-and-subtopics chart a type of graphic organizer that lists topics and subtopics in an outline form

topic sentence states the paragraph's main idea. Topic sentences are often used in informative, opinion, and persuasive writing.

TREE graphic organizer a type of graphic organizer that organizes the reasons and explanations for opinion and persuasive writing

triplet a type of poetry that has three lines of rhyming words

V

Venn diagram a type of graphic organizer used to compare and contrast two items

verb phrase a main verb plus one or more helping verbs

verb tense the time of the verb, such as present, past, and future

voice the trait that makes a piece of writing your very own

W

word choice the words a writer uses to have the maximum effect on the reader

writing process a process used to develop writing. The stages, or phases, of the writing process are prewriting, drafting, revising, editing/proofreading, and publishing.

Index

The index is a list of words and page numbers. It lists the different things that are in the Handbook. The words are in alphabetical order. You look in the list for the word you want to find. Then you look at the page number of the Handbook where it can be found. The index is a good tool. Learn to use it. It can save you a lot of time.

A

abbreviations, 442–443
abstract nouns, 400
acronyms, 443
academic language, 329
academic vocabulary, 390–391
action verb, 404
active voice, 405
ad copy, 228
adding, 38–39
addresses, 447
addressing an envelope, 78
adjective clause, 415
adjectives, 191, 272, 392–393, 406, 430, 445
adverb clause, 415
adverbs, 272, 392–393, 407, 431
advertisement, 228–229
analysis, 108–133
analogies, 372
antecedent, 402, 428
antonym, 370, 372
apostrophe, 401, 432, 449
appositive, 279, 413, 445
appositive phrase, 279, 413
articles, 406
audience, 19–20, 31, 50, 51, 101, 183, 227, 229, 235, 239, 330–331, 333, 335–336, 339, 340–341
autobiography, 148–153
auxiliary verb, 405
awkward sentences, 419–420

B

bibliography, 99–101
biography, 142–147
body (letter), 70–71, 73, 74, 76–77, 79
brainstorm, 18
business letter, 58–65, 74–79. See also,
    letter of complaint, 58–59, 75–77
    letter of concern, 75, 77
    letter of request, 75, 77

C

capitalization, 451–455
captions, 54
cast of characters, 179
cause and effect, 36, 300, 320, 388
cause-and-effect chart, 320
chain-of-events organizer, 149, 153
character, 27, 85, 108–115, 118, 136, 154, 158, 160–161, 164–165, 172–173, 176, 178–179, 185, 187, 294, 325
character analysis, 108–115
characterization, 111
chart, 26, 320–321
chronological order, 142, 146, 147, 149, 152–153
cinquain, 247
clarifying, 38, 42
clarity, 10
clauses, 414–415, 444
climax, 123–127, 137, 140, 295
closed compound word, 368
closing (letter), 70–71, 73, 74, 76, 79, 446
closing paragraph, 236, 324–325

closing sentence, 282, 285
collecting grid, 321
collecting information, 25
collective noun, 400, 426
colon, 79, 448
combining sentences, 272–274, 276–277
comma, 73, 272, 274, 279, 281, 354, 409, 414, 416, 444–447
common nouns, 400
comparative form, 430–431
compare, 212–223, 298–299, 330–331, 430–431
compare/contrast, 212–223, 298–299, 318, 388
complete predicate, 411
complete subject, 410
complex sentence, 274, 417
compound predicate, 411, 416
compound sentence, 274, 416, 444
compound subject, 272, 410, 416, 426
compound words, 368
compound-complex sentence, 417
computer, 49, 53–54, 72, 80
conclusion, 152, 198–199, 236, 324
concrete nouns, 400
conferencing, 45
conflict, 27, 110, 117, 123–127, 137, 140–141, 172, 177–178, 185, 295
conjunctions, 272, 274, 281, 409, 414, 416, 418
connotation, 374–375, 393, 395
consolidating, 38, 41
context clues, 388–389
contractions, 432, 437, 449
contrast, 212–223, 299, 433, 435
conventions, 14, 73, 79, 101, 147, 153, 165, 177, 195, 199, 205, 211, 223, 233, 239, 346–355. See also,
    conventions in dialogue, 354–355
    editing, 348–351
    end marks, 352–353
coordinating conjunctions, 409
correlative conjunctions, 409
couplet, 243

D

dash, 450
dates, 446
deadline, 21
decimal points, 352
declarative sentence, 270, 352, 421
definite article, 406
definition, 388
deleting, 38, 40
demonstrative adjective, 406
demonstrative pronoun, 403, 406
dependent clause, 274, 414
describing an event, 206–211
descriptions, 190–195, 311
descriptive paragraphs, 190, 287
descriptive writing, 188–223, 286–287, 344. See also,
    comparing and contrasting, 212–223
    describing an event, 206–211
    descriptions, 190–195, 311
    magazine articles, 200–205
    observation report, 196–197
details, 10, 39
diagram, 84
dialogue, 111, 140, 178–179, 185, 187, 323, 354–355, 446
dialogue journal, 82
diamante, 246
direct address, 445
direct object, 402, 412
direct quotes, 451
double negative, 437
double subjects, 419
draft, 19, 32–33
drafting, 19, 32–37, 58–59, 73, 79, 91, 101, 147, 153, 165, 177, 187, 195, 199, 239

E

editing, 19, 46–49, 62–63, 73, 79, 91, 101, 147, 153, 165, 177, 187, 195, 199, 239, 348–351
editing checklist, 48, 351
effective beginnings, 322–323
effective endings, 322–325
electronic technology, 458–461
ellipsis, 450
e-mail, 72
end marks, 352–353
entertain, 9, 337–338
evaluating growth, 364–365
evidence, 284–285
exaggeration, 332–333
examples, 228, 284–285, 340
exclamation point, 271, 353–354, 409, 421
expanding sentences, 278–279
expert opinion, 226, 228, 235
explain, 9, 288, 298, 311, 337–338
explaining a scientific process, 196–199
expository paragraph, 288
expository writing, 86–133, 288, 298–303. See also,
    problem-and-solution essay, 102–107
    research report, 92–101
    responding to literature, 108–133, 260–261
    summary, 88–91, 258–259

F

facts, 228, 284–285, 323, 338, 340
fantasy, 172–177
fiction, 136–141, 160, 172–173
fictional narrative, 136–141
figurative language, 129–130, 330–333. See also,
    exaggeration, 332–333
    hyperbole, 332
    idiom, 333
    metaphor, 191, 331, 333
    personification, 331, 333
    simile, 191, 330, 333
figures of speech, 330–333
first-person point of view, 137, 297
focus, 10, 23
formatting, 456–457
forms of writing, see
    descriptive writing, 188–223, 286–287
    expository writing, 288, 298–303
    informative writing, 86–133
    narrative writing, 134–187, 286
    opinion writing, 224–239
    personal writing, 68–85
    persuasive writing, 230–239, 289, 340–343
    poetry, 240–251
fragment, 280, 418
friendly letter, 70–73
future perfect tense, 425
future tense, 424

G

grammar, 398–421. See also,
    adjectives, 272, 392–393, 406, 430, 445
    adverbs, 272, 392–393, 407, 431
    clauses, 414–415, 444
    collective nouns, 400, 426
    conjunctions, 272, 274, 281, 409, 414, 416, 418
    direct object, 402, 412
    indirect object, 402, 412
    interjections, 353, 409, 445
    kinds of sentences, 270–271, 421
    nouns, 400–401
    phrases, 273, 277, 413, 444
    predicate, 270, 275, 280, 410, 411
    prepositions, 408
    pronouns, 402–403, 428–429
    sentence problems, 418–420
    sentences, 416–417
    subject, 270, 280, 410
    verbs, 278, 394–395, 404–405
graphic organizer, see
    cause-and-effect chart, 321
    chain-of-events organizer, 149, 153
    story map, 27–28, 165, 177, 317
    TIDE organizer, 96, 319
    time line, 143, 146–147, 318
    topics-and-subtopics chart, 319
    topic webs, 22, 56, 316
    TREE organizer, 226, 227, 236, 320
    Venn diagram, 215, 219, 318
Greek roots, 382–383
greeting, 446, 455

H

heading, 58, 70–71, 73, 74, 76, 79
helping verb, 404–405
historical fiction, 160–165
homograph, 378–379
homophone, 376–377
hyperbole, 332
hyphen, 368, 407, 450
hyphenated adjectives, 407
hyphenated compound word, 368

I

ideas, 10, 44, 165, 177, 187, 292–305
idiom, 333
imagery, 130
imperative sentence, 271, 352, 421
indefinite articles, 406
indefinite pronoun, 403, 427–429
indent, 34
independent clause, 274, 414, 448
indirect object, 402, 412
inform, 298, 337
informative writing, 29, 86–133. See also,
    problem-and-solution essay, 102–107
    research report, 92–101
    responding to literature, 108–133, 260–261
    summary, 88–91, 258–259
initialism, 443
inside address, 58, 74, 76, 79
intensive pronoun, 403
interjections, 353, 409, 445
interrogative pronoun, 403
interrogative sentence, 271, 352, 421
interrupters, 445
interview, 142, 234
introductory words, 446
inverted order, 411
irregular plural nouns, 401
irregular verbs, 426

J

journal entry, 80–81
journals, 80–85

K

key words, 94, 460
kinds of sentences, 270–271, 421

L

Latin roots, 382–383
learning log, 83–84
letter of complaint, 58–59, 75–77
letter of concern, 75, 77
letter of request, 75, 77
letters, see
    business letters, 58–65, 74–79
    friendly letters, 70–73
    letters over the web, 72
    letter to the editor, 75
linking verb, 404
lists, 18, 448
literary criticism, 128–133
literature response journal, 85
location words, 36–37, 194–195, 311, 434–435
lyric, 245

M

magazine article, 200–205
main idea, 91, 282, 284–285
mechanics, 440–455. See also,
    capitalization, 451–455
    punctuation marks, 19, 270–271, 352–355, 416–418, 421, 442–450
metaphor, 191, 331, 333
misused words, 438–439
modifier, 413
mood, 116
multiple-meaning words, 380–381
multimedia sources, 358–359

N

narrative paragraph, 286
narrative writing, 134, 136–187, 286. See also,
    autobiography, 148–153
    biography, 142–147
    fantasy, 172–177
    fictional narrative, 136–141
    historical fiction, 160–165
    play, 178–187
    science fiction, 166–171
    tall tales, 154–159
    timed writing: narrative, 262–263
narrator, 137, 185, 297
negative word, 437

INDEX

nonrhyming poetry, 246–249
note cards, 95
notes, 34, 101, 199
nouns, 278, 400–401
numbers, 447, 450

O

object of the preposition, 408
object pronouns, 402
observation, 196–199
observation report, 196–199
open compound word, 368
opening paragraph, 236, 322
opinion paragraph, 225–229
opinion writing, 224–239. See also,
    opinion paragraph, 225–229
    persuasive writing, 230–239, 289, 340–343
oral presentations, 360–363
order of importance, 301, 310, 343
order words, 36, 309, 433
ordering information, 308–311. See also,
    compare, 298–299, 330–331, 430–431, 433, 436
    contrast, 298–299, 433, 435
    location words, 36–37, 194–195, 434–435
    order of importance, 301, 343
    order words, 36, 309
    time words, 36–37, 303, 308, 433
    transition words, 14, 35–37, 146–147, 152–153, 301, 303, 308–311, 433–436
organization, 11, 27, 44, 73, 79, 91, 101, 147, 153, 177, 187, 195, 199, 239, 306–325
organization of details, 191–195
outlines, 312–315, 352, 455

P

page design, 52, 54
paragraphs, 34–35, 37, 282–289
paragraphs, types of, 286–289
parentheses, 450
participial phrase, 278, 413
passive voice, 405
past perfect tense, 424
past tense, 424
paste-up, 53
pattern poetry, 250–251
peer conferencing, 45
perfect tense, 424
period, 352, 442–443
personal pronouns, 402
personal writing, 68–85. See also,
    business letter, 58–65, 74–79
    dialogue journal, 82
    e-mail, 72
    friendly letters, 70–73
    journals, 80–85
    learning log, 83–84
    literature response journal, 85
personification, 331, 333
persuade, 289, 337–338
persuasive essay, 234–239
persuasive letter, 58–65, 230–233
persuasive paragraph, 289
persuasive writing, 230–239, 289, 340–343. See also,
    persuasive essay, 234–239
    persuasive letter, 230–233
    persuasive paragraph, 289
    timed writing: persuasive writing, 264–265
phrases, 273, 277, 413, 444
play, 178–187
plot, 122–127, 137, 160–161, 164–165, 172–173, 176–178, 185, 187, 294–295
plot analysis, 122–127
plural nouns, 401
poetry, 240–251. See also,
    nonrhyming poetry, 246–249
    pattern poetry, 250–251
    rhyming poetry, 242–245
point of view, 137, 164, 294, 297
possession, 449
possessive nouns, 401
possessive pronouns, 402–403
postal abbreviations, 443
precise verbs, 394–395
predicate, 270, 275, 280, 410–411
predicate pronoun, 402
prefix, 384–385
prepositional phrase, 278, 408
prepositions, 408
present perfect tense, 424
present tense, 424

presentation, 15, 50, 52, 73, 79, 91, 101, 147, 153, 165, 177, 187, 195, 199, 239, 356–365
prewriting, 18, 20, 26, 31, 56–59, 73, 79, 91, 147, 153, 165, 177, 187, 195, 199, 239
problem and solution, 102–107, 302
process, 196, 303
pronoun/antecedent agreement, 428
pronouns, 402–403, 428–429
proofreading, 46–49, 348–349
proofreading marks, 47, 62–63, 348–349
proper adjectives, 406
proper nouns, 400
prose, 242
public service ad, 229
publishing, 19, 50–55, 64–65, 73, 79, 91, 101, 147, 153, 165, 177, 187, 195, 199, 239
punctuation marks, 19, 270–271, 352–355. See also,
- apostrophe, 401, 432, 449
- colon, 448
- comma, 272, 274, 279, 281, 354, 409, 414, 416, 444–447
- dash, 450
- ellipsis, 450
- exclamation point, 271, 353–354, 409, 421
- hyphen, 368, 407, 450
- parentheses, 450
- period, 270–271, 352, 442–443
- question mark, 271, 352, 354
- quotation marks, 354, 449
- semicolon, 414, 416, 448
- underlining, 449

purpose, 20–21, 44, 337, 339, 341. See also,
- entertain, 338
- explain, 288, 298, 311, 337
- inform, 9, 337
- persuade, 9, 289, 338

Q

quatrain, 244
question mark, 271, 354, 421
questions and answers, 301, 342, 362
quick write, 256–257
quotation, 449
quotation marks, 354, 449

R

rambling sentence, 281, 419
rearranging, 38, 43
reasons, 340, 343
reflection, 324–325
reflexive pronouns, 403
relative pronoun, 274, 403, 415
repetition, 345
research, 234, 321
research report, 92–101
resolution, 27, 136–137, 141, 164, 178, 295
revising, 19, 38–45, 60–61, 73, 79, 91, 101, 147, 153, 165, 177, 187, 195, 199, 239
revising checklist, 44
rhyme, 242–245, 248, 250
rhyming poetry, 242–245
rhythm, 14, 242
run-on sentence, 280–281, 418

S

salutation, 58, 70–71, 73, 74, 76, 79, 446, 448, 455
scene (in plays), 178, 187
science fiction, 166–171
semicolon, 414, 448
sensory details, 190–191, 195, 206–207, 209–211, 215, 221, 223, 344
sentence expansion, 278–279
sentence fluency, 14, 44, 73, 91, 268–291
sentence length, 291
sentences, 270–275, 276–279, 280–281, 291, 389, 416, 421
setting, 27, 116–121, 136, 160, 164, 172–173, 176, 178, 185, 187, 294, 296
setting analysis, 116–121
signal words, 14, 36–37. See also,
transition words, 14, 35–37, 146–147, 152–153, 301, 303, 308–311, 433–436
signature, 70–71, 73, 76, 79
simile, 191, 330, 333
simple predicate, 411
simple sentence, 416
singular noun, 401
skimming tips, 94
sound of language, 345. See also,
- alliteration, 345
- assonance, 345
- onomatopoeia, 345
- rhythm, 14, 242

INDEX 477

sources, 93, 99–100, 142, 234
speaker tags, 354–355
spelling, 19, 46, 348–351
stage directions, 179, 185–187
state-of-being verb, 404
story map, 27–28, 165, 177, 317
story writing, 136–141, 294–297, 325. See also,
    character, 27, 136, 160–161, 164–165, 172–173, 176–179, 185, 187, 294, 325
    dialogue, 179, 185, 187, 325, 354, 355, 446
    plot, 137, 160–161, 164–165, 172–173, 176–178, 185, 187, 294–295
    point of view, 137, 164, 294, 297
    setting, 27, 136, 160, 164, 165, 172–173, 176, 178, 185, 187, 294, 296
subject, 270, 280, 410
subject pronouns, 402–403
subject-verb agreement, 426–427
subordinate clause, 414
subordinating conjunction, 274, 409, 415
subtopic, 29–31, 35, 319
suffix, 386–387
summary, 84, 88–91, 433, 436
superlative form, 430–431
supporting details, 91, 101
supporting sentence, 34–35, 282, 285
symbolism, 131
synonyms, 290, 371–372, 374

T

tall tales, 154–159
theme, 110, 113–114
thesaurus, 328
third-person point of view, 137, 297
TIDE organizer, 96, 319
timed writing, 252–265
time line, 143, 146–147, 318
time words, 36–37, 303, 308, 433
titles, 449, 451
topic, 22–24, 92, 234, 283
topic (choosing), 20, 23, 29–31, 44, 56
topic sentence, 34–35, 94, 101, 282, 285
topic web, 22, 56
topics-and-subtopics chart, 319

traits of good writing, see
    conventions, 14, 73, 79, 91, 101, 147, 153, 165, 177, 187, 195, 199, 239, 346–355
    ideas, 10, 44, 147, 153, 165, 177, 187, 292–305
    organization, 11, 27, 44, 73, 79, 91, 101, 147, 187, 195, 199, 239, 306–325
    presentation, 15, 50, 52, 73, 79, 91, 101, 147, 165, 177, 187, 195, 199, 356–365
    sentence fluency, 14, 44, 73, 91, 268–291
    voice, 12, 44, 73, 79, 91, 153, 239, 334–345
transition words, 14, 35–37, 146–147, 152–153, 301, 303, 308–311, 433–436
TREE organizer, 226, 227, 236, 320

U

underlining, 449
units of measure, 442–443
usage, 422–439. See also,
    comparative/superlative form, 430–431
    contractions, 432, 437, 449
    double negatives, 437
    misused words, 438–439
    pronoun/antecedent agreement, 428
    subject-verb agreement, 426–427
    transition words, 14, 35–37, 146–147, 152–153, 301, 303, 308–311, 433–436,
    verb tenses, 424–425

V

variety in writing, 14, 44, 276–279, 290–291
Venn diagram, 215, 219, 318
verb phrases, 405
verb tenses, 424–425
verbs, 394–395, 404–405
visualization, 344
vocabulary, 366–395. See also,
    academic vocabulary, 390–391
    analogies, 372
    antonyms, 370, 372
    compound words, 368, 450
    connotation, 374–375, 393, 395
    context clues, 388–389
    Greek and Latin roots, 382–383
    homographs, 378–379
    homophones, 376–377
    multiple-meaning words, 380–381
    prefixes, 384–385
    suffixes, 386–387
    synonyms, 290, 371–374
vocabulary strategy, 326–333
voice, 12, 44, 73, 79, 91, 153, 239, 334–345

W

web, 18, 22, 56, 316
word choice, 13, 44, 165, 187, 195, 199, 326–333
word origins, 382–383
word web, 84
words to avoid, 393
working title, 27
writing process, 16–65. See also
    drafting, 19, 32–37, 58–59, 73, 79, 91, 101, 147, 153, 165, 177, 187, 195, 199, 239
    editing/proofreading, 19, 46–49, 62–63, 73, 79, 91, 101, 147, 153, 165, 177, 187, 195, 199, 239, 348–351
    prewriting, 18–31, 56–59, 73, 79, 91, 101, 147, 153, 165, 177, 187, 195, 199, 239
    publishing, 19, 50–55, 64–65, 73, 79, 91, 101, 147, 153, 165, 177, 187, 195, 199, 239
    revising, 19, 38–45, 62, 73, 79, 91, 101, 147, 153, 165, 177, 187, 195, 199, 239

Photo Credits:

15 McGraw-Hill Education; **27** JGI/Tom Grill/Blend Images/Getty Images; **29** Hill Street Studios/Blend Images LLC; **32** Blend Images - Tanya Constantine/Brand X Pictures/Getty Images; **50** ©Hero Images/Corbis; **68** Don Mason/Blend Images LLC; **86** Mark Edward Atkinson/Blend Images/Getty Images; **88** McGraw-Hill Education; **95** Blend Images - Tanya Constantine/Brand X Pictures/Getty Images; **118** Don Mason/Blend Images LLC; **132** Monkey Business Images/Shutterstock.com; **134** Blend Images - Tanya Constantine/Brand X Pictures/Getty Images; **186** ©Hero Images/Corbis; **188** JGI/Tom Grill/Blend Images/Getty Images; **213** Mark Edward Atkinson/Blend Images/Getty Images; **224** McGraw-Hill Education; **240** Monkey Business Images/Shutterstock.com; **247** Blend Images - Tanya Constantine/Brand X Pictures/Getty Images; **253** ©Hero Images/Corbis; **268** Don Mason/Blend Images LLC; **285** Don Mason/Blend Images LLC; **292** Monkey Business Images/Shutterstock.com; **306** JGI/Tom Grill/Blend Images/Getty Images; **326** Mark Edward Atkinson/Blend Images/Getty Images; **334** McGraw-Hill Education; **347** Don Mason/Blend Images LLC; **356** ©Hero Images/Corbis; **369** JGI/Tom Grill/Blend Images/Getty Images; **398** Hill Street Studios/Blend Images LLC; **422** Monkey Business Images/Shutterstock.com; **440** Mark Edward Atkinson/Blend Images/Getty Images.